Arctic Odyssey

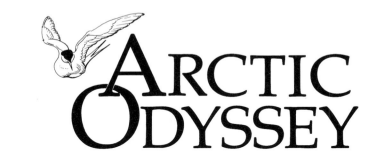

ARCTIC ODYSSEY

TRAVELLING ARCTIC EUROPE

Richard Sale & Tony Oliver

The Crowood Press

First published in 1991 by
The Crowood Press Ltd
Gipsy Lane
Swindon
Wiltshire SN2 6DQ

British Library Cataloguing in Publication Data

Sale, Richard 1946–
  Arctic Odyssey.
  1. Europe. Arctic. Description & travel
  I. Title   II. Oliver, Tony
  914.8

  ISBN 1 85223 329 X

Credits

All colour and black and white photographs by Richard Sale and Tony
Oliver; maps also prepared by the authors.
The photograph on the half title page shows the polar bear we met at
Agardh Bay, Spitsbergen, Svalbard.
The frontispiece is 'Dog sledging into the Arctic night'.
The section opening for Iceland is ''Jökulsárlón'.
The section opening for Scandinavia is 'Evening sledging at Devdisvatn'.
The section opening for Greenland is 'Icebergs on the horizon of Disko
Bay, West Greenland'.
The section opening for Svalbard is 'Gustav Adolf Land from across
Wahlenbergforden'.
The end page is 'Iceberg and pack ice at Nordaustland, Svalbard'.

Typeset by Chippendale Type Ltd., Otley, West Yorkshire
Printed in England by Richard Clay Ltd.

# Contents

Introduction

The hotel in Oslo was grim. The man behind the desk eyed us suspiciously, heavy rucsacs on tired shoulders, pinched faces from the frozen air. He pushed a book towards me, and raised an eyebrow as I signed my name. I wondered if this might have been from surprise over the fact that I could write, but it was just one of a fair catalogue of mannerisms he had to offer. He took a wrist-rupturing key from a rack and shuffled around to our side of the desk. We followed him in silence up a flight of stairs to a corridor too dark for eyes to pick out its furthest point.

'That's the bathroom,' he said, vaguely indicating a door to the right behind which, we were to discover, an array of ancient pipework gurgled and glugged.

He opened our room. It was long enough to need semaphore to signal from one end to the other, dark enough so you would never have seen the flags, and so narrow we had to squeeze past

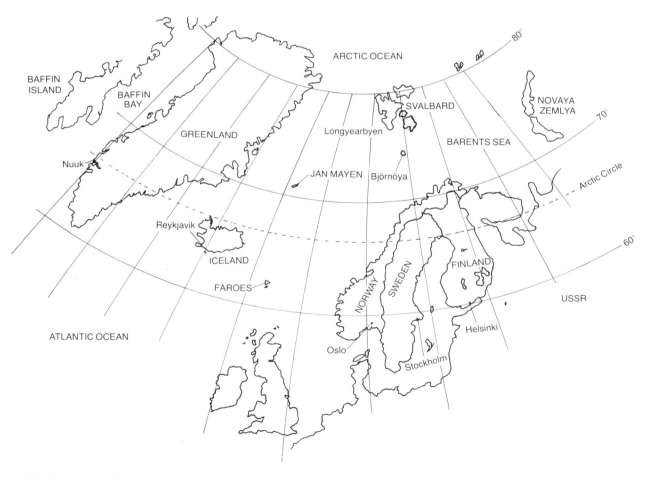

The European Arctic.

7

the single bed by the door to reach the open land before the next one. It had just one redeeming feature. It was cheap.

Nathan moodily poked the bed, hiked down to the window and stared out at the night, then came back and sat on a seat in no-man's land. 'OK?' I asked. A dumb question really. He gave me a thin smile and shrugged. It was not what he had in mind.

Nathan had just turned teenager and we were in North Wales for his birthday. Being a lazy lad, much given to the idea of rising late when given half a chance, he had delayed his arrival in the world until 1 January. It had been only by a few hours, but that was enough to ensure that birthdays would always fall on public holidays and the correct number of hours could therefore be spent languishing.

We had languished yesterday. Today we were in the Ogwen valley, in indifferent weather, wondering what to do. A big peak was out of the question; it was a little too late, a little too wet and miserable. It was a day for fingering duvets in Capel Curig or Betws, but Nathan, though difficult to start on cold mornings, was active once moving and would find that too dull. We parked downhill from the cottage and ambled over to the top of the falls. I started climbing down, without too much in mind, and Nahan followed. We went down a hundred feet, perhaps a bit more. We moved in closer to the stream and, attracted by something (though now I have no idea what) I went to the stream edge. I ducked under a large rock and stepped forward. Planting a booted foot securely on a rock in the stream, I stood up. It is difficult to know what of the next few seconds I remember, or have pieced together, or have been told by Nathan. I think I heard a loud, but muffled thump. I do remember fighting to stay balanced on the rock and not

The Polar Cathedral and Storskarfjell from Tromsø

managing it, and I do remember that when the world came back into focus I could not see out of my left eye.

Nathan had watched while I went under the rock, had been surprised when I vigorously stood up and had stood transfixed as I gently pitched forwards off the rock. Within seconds the blood from the gash that once been the left side of my head had poured all over the side of my face and filled up my left eye; so that was why I could not see. He started to pour cold water over me, in part to staunch the blood, in part to revive me. He got me out of the stream and a bit further back from the drop to our right. He sat me down. The wound bled enough to turn the semi-still pool in front of us red, but the cold water eventually stopped it. Nathan helped me to my feet and very cautiously picked a way up through the boulders and small crags towards the road. He led on the easy bits, followed and pushed on the worse sections. We reached the road. Nathan took my keys, brought the first aid kit from the car, and broke open some antiseptic wipes to attend to the cut. Only when he had to stare straight into it did he flinch; it was not, his face said, a pretty sight. He offered to drive the car, but I was not convinced that was a good idea. He offered to stop someone, but I was feeling a bit better. My head didn't hurt at all, although it did feel a bit light. It was my neck that hurt.

I drove to the hospital in Bangor with Nathan watching the road intently and hanging on to the handbrake. When they tried to take me away he explained, politely, that he was staying with me. They shaved off my hair and sewed up my head. They stuck needles in me and wheeled me in and out of X-ray rooms peering inside for evidence of the impacted fracture they were sure I had. And through it all he stayed. He was not saying much, but he was being there.

We agreed, after it was over – after the stitches (a large number) had been removed – that he had shown he was good enough now to go on a big trip.

He had stood in the queue at Heathrow, a very new Condor on his back, eyeing others who were obviously preparing to go to warmer places than we were. He was a mountaineer. The big boots, the gaudy anorak, the heavy rucsac. This was definitely the way to live.

But not, he might now have added, if it meant staying in crumby hotels in places like Oslo.

Nathan Sale above Tromsdalen.

I had needed to break our journey north in the capital to see someone in the tourist board's head office. We could not do the trip in and out of the town in time to catch the last plane that evening, so we were condemned to this place and an early flight. We dumped our kit and went out to find somewhere to eat.

Oslo is very much a capital city. Go to the right places and there will be a big railway station or a billboard full of flickering neon lights. It is pleasant in the port area, impressive near the castle, interesting at Bygdøy where the Viking ships are displayed on part of the large and excellent museum complex. It is also, as with other capitals, impersonal, lonely and vaguely hostile. There was the same combination that I had seen before:

brightly-lit streets and squares where people collected in groups that seemed threatening because you were not part of them, and between these bright areas black, empty alleys full of odd forebodings.

Our search for something to eat led us up these darkly menacing alleys. It was freezing – literally – so after a not-too-exhaustive search we settled for a place that was warm and, as it turned out, very good. Nathan cheered up a touch when he had eaten his way through half the menu, and was even able to smile at the prospect of spending the night in our corridor-like room. Sleep came to the distant noise of a ship's siren, blown once, but echoing, a long way off.

Breakfast was forgettable, but it didn't matter by then. Nathan had not been on enough flights to be anything but excited, and he was going north of the Arctic Circle for the first time. We took off on time, but we had unknowingly booked on to the milk run. We stopped at Trondheim and Bodø, and then at Bardufoss. On every leg they gave us a cheese roll and several cups of coffee, and by the time we took off for the third time we were wearing a rut in the carpet down the aisle to the tail-end gents.

The weather worsened the further north we went, and by the time we crossed the Circle it was snowing. Nathan peered through the thick flakes at the wagon that serviced the plane at every stop. It was always the same shape and size, built, it seemed, solely for the transportation of cheese rolls. On its side, in Gothic letters, was written 'Dog Bladder' – a strange name. What did they put in the coffee that made it such a diuretic? A day or two later we were enlightened – *Dagbladdet* is the name of the daily paper.

We took off on the last leg for Tromsø. The snow was falling thickly and poured past the window in blizzard proportions as the plane hurled itself into the Arctic night. Nathan was awestruck with the audacity of it all, but when he turned to tell me how impressed he was I was asleep. Nothing his old man did in the rest of the trip came close to commanding such respect as falling asleep during that take-off. He saw it as indicating the travel weariness of the great adventurer. In reality I was bored to distraction by the journey.

As we approached Tromsø the snow grew thicker and Nathan asked, as casually as he could manage, whether they would clear the runway. No, I told him, we'll land on the ice. He gave me a

pityingly look. We taxied in close to the runway and were all pushed down the exit ladder to make a sprint for the terminal building; no automatic concertinaed walkways here. We started out into the snow and stepped on to the ice-covered apron; that soon took the look off Nathan's face. I was grateful when the rucsacs appeared on the carousel; Troms7 was a full jacket cooler than Oslo had been.

Next day saw us in Trømsdalen. Nathan had not been prepared for the bus trip into and out of the town and the long walk through the snow to a campsite either. But he had performed well. The day dawned grey and cold, but the snow had stopped. At this time of year, mid-Autumn, the snow has usually not arrived in Tromsø and it is possible for you to have the hills to yourself in Tromsdalen or, better, in Lyngen, but this year there was already a metre of the stuff down at sea level. During the days that followed our plans to backpack up into the hills had to be curtailed because of the weather, but to compensate there was the pleasure of watching Nathan explore the Arctic. He edged down some unsafe planking in the harbour to poke his hand into the ocean and recoiled with the cold of it. He peered into its depths amazed at the clarity. He tried making snowballs as he had in Britain only to find that in these low temperatures he was left with a handful of flour-like snow that simply blew away when he threw it. He looked for the Pole Star on nights so intensely black that you almost had to touch your limbs to make sure they were still there. He was staggered that he had to look almost straight up to find it.

We climbed Storskarfjell on a long and hard day that started before the sun came up and finished long after it had gone down. It was memorable for the endless grind in one gully where the snow was waist-deep and we had to swim upwards, and for the point where we emerged on to the easterly ridge with views to Lyngen, and a wind that had bared the slopes and put our teeth on edge. The plateau we crossed before the final pyramid was hostile, the snow wind-beaten to a hard, glittering crust that squeaked at the approach of our boots and then gave a satisfying crunch as we went through it. We put on crampons for a steep section, Nathan all excitement at this new level of experience and commitment. Then it was over, and with the end came that sense of anti-climax because tops are never as perfect as they should be, nor the last few steps as brilliantly conceived or executed. The view is never as good as it ought to be. And you still have to go down.

Down was reversing the route until a bold decision to descend through trees was taken, a decision that in retrospect seemed debatable. The maddening way-finding kept us interested, which did postpone the onset of real tiredness. The way was down this slope, then crash through those low pine branches, then round the top of that steep bit, then over there – I think.

The coffee back at our base was good, the meal cooked from the sleeping bag the better for being so. Tomorrow was another day.

We did our best in weather that got worse the longer we stayed. One day's effort failed in a blizzard that was so thick route-finding became impossible. We stopped and built a makeshift shelter to get away, as best we could, from snow that filtered its way through every opening to produce melt water that trickled coldly over us. I made tea, my ungloved hand sticking to the Trangia when I tried to move it from its snowdrift. The blizzard was worse now, and what little light made its way between the flakes was failing. In a brief lull we moved quickly down to the river and followed it back down the valley.

On our last afternoon we went back to Tromsø to see a man about a dog. To be precise to see a man about a good number of sledge dogs. That night we stayed in the town as our flight was too early the next day to get to the airport from the good country to the south. We treated ourselves to a reindeer steak, then went for a last walk over the bridge towards the Polar Cathedral. The sky was clearer than it had been for a week, and massive, but hardly elegant, Storskarfjell stood out like a white tent. Nathan kicked snow off the bridge, watching it explode in orange light as it swept past the navigation lights on the bridge supports. Tromsø was huddled and silent below and he took a long time over his last look.

11

ICELAND

In the strictest sense of the word Iceland is not an 'Arctic' country; the Circle nicks only the northern tip of the isle of Grimsey and so leaves the main island in a sub-Arctic no man's land. The pilot of a plane Tony and I shared with a bunch of drunks *en route* to Akureyri once told a very poor story. No one in Iceland ever wanted to cross the Circle he said, except for one man, the vicar of Grimsey. The Circle went through the middle of his bed, he told us, so he had a reason for crossing it every night. But it was, as I said, a poor story and I won't trouble you with it.

Iceland has about forty per cent of the land area of the UK, but a population of only 250,000. The great majority live in Reykjavik or a couple of towns close to it, and that leaves the country wonderfully bare, especially in the centre – what remains of the population is concentrated on the coast, where the chief occupations of fishing and farming are best practised. The centre is vast and uninhabited. It is also difficult for access. The Icelandic road system is remarkable, with a continuous coastal road and numerous side roads, even if the majority are gravel rather than tarmac. Each isolated farm has electricity, a newish car or two and is full of gadgets and gizmos. The economics of the country are a disaster.

Iceland was discovered in the tenth century by Viking seafarers from the Scandinavian mainland. The discoverer – reputedly Ingolfur Arnarson after whom a fine peak near Þingvellir and Ingólfshöfði is named – called the country 'Iceland' because of the ice he found there; this created the first half-truth about the islands of the north. Iceland is actually very green. The next country to be discovered, Greenland, is actually very icy. Even today the

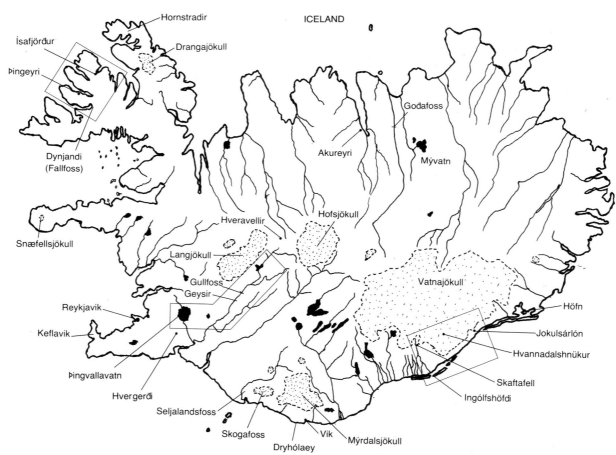

Iceland.

14

Viking influence is deep-seated, especially in naming, where the old Norse method of patronymics is used. A child's surname is the father's first name with *son* (for a boy) or *dóttir* (for a girl) added. Our friend Pétur Björnsson (Pétur, son of Björn) has a lovely blonde daughter Marta, who speaks no English and talked to me all night when we were last there in a glorious mixture of Icelandic and sign language. Her name is Marta Pétursdóttir. In a family of four, with a boy and a girl, there will be four different surnames.

The Icelanders have a fine attitude towards their country. The majority of the population – which has one of the world's longest average life expectancies – are active in one or more outdoor activities, with walking and horse riding especially popular. (Riding is a fine way of seeing the interior of the country, and the high-stepping Icelandic horses are tireless over the difficult terrain.) This love for their land is refreshing – they consistently enthuse about their country rather than being swift to bad-mouth it – and it is also reflected in their desire to protect large areas from exploitation.

It is easy to assume that with so limited a population and tourists numbering a fraction of those who head for the sun, protection of the countryside is straightforward. Still, there are some areas that are 'better' than others, and these need special care. Iceland has, therefore, a surprisingly large number of National Parks and nature reserves with regulations that must be observed by all visitors. Each of these parks has its own appeal; Skaftafell and Mývatn are favourites, while Þingvellir is historically important. The lesser-known areas are also very good – Herdubreid, around the very dangerous mountain of the same name and the Askja volcanic area; Hornstrandir at the extreme north-west tip, beyond Drangajökull, an area of superb walking and bird cliffs; and Jökulsárgljúfur, to the east of Akureyri.

All air travel to Iceland is through Keflavik airport, about fifty kilometres from Reykjavik, a beautiful modern terminal, and one of very few where duty free is available on arrival. Once in the country there is a good system of internal flights and buses.

Summer – NW Iceland

Keflavik is one of the best air terminals in the world, an old plane hanging above the excellent facilities. The journey to Reykjavik is not so good, and, although it is along a very reasonable road, it can be a bit daunting for the newcomer. First you go past an array of AWACS planes, wondering whether you are actually allowed to see such things. In the UK it is easy to form the impression that if you tried to get a closer look at something like this someone in a uniform would break both of your legs. Beyond the planes you have the sea to the left, and to the right the surface of the moon, an endless lava field with sharp brown rocks and occasional patches of greenery. Desolation. If you have a weak stomach you may wonder why you bothered to come at all.

I sat at the front of the coach, next to the driver. He had a punk haircut and used his right knee to drive down the middle of the road. His right hand caressed the gear stick while his left hand constantly fiddled with the knobs on the radio cassette, ensuring that the coach was flooded with a continuous stream of heavy metal. Just as you were getting to like a track he would tune it out. Periodically, a vehicle would come the other way, its lights flashing furiously. The punk would turn to me with a conspiratorial grin – hey, man, it's you and me against the world, eh? – then shift the bus across with his knee. The furious lights would flash past and we would move into the middle again.

The coach dropped me at the Lofleiðir, a palatial hotel. The closest I will ever come to staying there is when I pass through it to reach the stop for the buses into town. My next flight is from Reykjavik airport. Many a visitor has been embarrassed by the fact that Reykjavik airport is different from Keflavik. I can see the town airport from where I am, indeed I can touch its tarmac with a digit thrust through the chain-link fence – all that separates it from the Lofleiðir – but to get from here to there is not so easy, and involves taking a bus into town and back out again or taking a taxi. You could

walk of course. By fence climbing and tarmac crossing it is 400 metres to the terminal building; by the allowed route round it is five miles. I take a taxi since my next flight leaves in an hour. The taxi driver speaks no English and I spend a fraught moment or two wondering whether he has understood that I don't want to go to Keflavik, but after the shorter tour of Reykjavik we arrive. I now discover that he speaks English numbers, as the bill is near perfectly pronounced. For all that he has no words he then asks in the most eloquent and elegant way for a tip. It is a really virtuoso performance – can I put the tip down on my tax form as 'entertainment'? – and I am reminded of R2D2, the smaller robot in the *Star Wars* films. Although he only chirped, peedled and burped, he had the best lines in the film.

The next flight is northward, to Ísafjördur, a rough ride, with the uplift over the highlands and the sea throwing the little plane about. Across the aisle from me a young boy is telling his mother that he doesn't like it. My Icelandic only runs to 'coffee, please,' but I can tell the essence of his story from the colour of his face. His mother is less than willing to be involved, ignoring him in favour of the in-flight mag – an in-depth article on drainage ditch construction in the Middle East is far more interesting to her than her child's welfare. At length the little lad grabs her sleeve and becomes insistent, and she is only just in time with the sick bag. Pity, I thought after the performance, it might have done her good if he'd missed. At journey's end she folded over the top of the bag and thoughtfully replaced it behind the netting on the back of the seat in front. All in all I was glad she did not live next door to me.

The landing was one of the more memorable moments of my life. The plane flew up the fjord, which seemed so narrow that the mountains were on both wing tips at the same time. Having reached the end it went up on one wing, round through 180° in the space of fifty metres, and plummetted out of the sky on to the tarmac. It was an interesting airport, the first one I had visited where, in order to get the planes to land and take off, they have to go and shift the seals off the runway. The town of Ísafjörður is on the far side of the fjord, a long way from the town, and reached by a bus ride past the first fish-drying frame you will see in this part of the island. But I was not going for a bus ride, I was looking for the gents.

Travelling with Nathan, my son, when he was young, we occasionally stopped at motorway service areas. In the gents of these there would sometimes be those urinals – you know the ones, shaped like a maiden's hand – with one positioned for kids ten centimetres up the wall and not sixty centimetres up like the rest. Nathan hated them because they implied that he was terribly little and when you *are* terribly little you don't want the world to keep pointing it out to you at every opportunity. He was really pleased when he graduated to the bigger ones. At this airport the pottery was the same, but it was placed so high up the wall that I was on tiptoe and firing upwards. I know that having a seventy-eight-centimetre leg makes me shorter than average, but *Jesus*. I beat a heavy retreat: what I did not want to do was find out what the locals were like. Men who could use these things comfortably would have to be three metres tall, and when they came I really didn't want to be there.

From Ísafjörður the best way to explore Iceland's north-west is to jump on one of Ernir Air's mail planes. Ernir has the contract to deliver the post and fly planes out every morning. You get on and fly to somewhere that takes your fancy, the airline being quite willing to take the odd traveller with his rucsac. Once off you walk over the mountains to the next town, and over again to another. As soon as you have had enough you wait until the plane arrives, going on to newer ground or back for a return flight to the bright lights of Reykjavik. It is an elegant way to travel, much better than waiting for the buses which, at this time of year, seem to come every other Tuesday.

Later, at Reykjavik, I was chatting to somebody, telling them about the Ernir flights. Ah yes, they said, the man in charge up there is a legend for landing his plane in appalling conditions and absolutely ridiculous places. Stories abound of his having landed on a handkerchief in blizzards in order to take people to hospital or to bring in desperately needed supplies. I mentioned that the man I had spoken to had an old check suit and a limp. That was almost certainly him, I was told.

Footprints on Hattersdallfjall, north-west Iceland.

Did he get the limp in a flying accident on one of his stupendous runs, I asked. Oh, no, they said, he fell off the roof when retiling it.

When I arrived in Þingeyri I was expecting this, the second-biggest town in the area, to be a place worth seeing. It had a church and a garage which sold Mars bars. It had a handful of houses and that was Þingeyri. Unimpressed, I went down to the edge of the fjord to find somewhere to camp. Nearby the sea terns and eider ducks were nesting, the ducks beautifully camouflaged, sitting tight as long as they could, then moving quickly to reveal eggs of a gorgeous sage green looking so warm in their nest of breast feathers that it made me long for the comforts of my sleeping bag. The eggs were not pure poetry though, and many of

Meðadalur, north-west Iceland.

them had lines and streaks of yellow duck shit across their smooth surfaces.

I pitched the tent back from the sea, close to a river. The view from my chosen balcony was superb. Meðadalur is wide and flanked by peaks that are proudly pointed. The last of the winter snow was melting off the steep slopes, but the flatter areas and the passes still seemed to be well covered. I decided to go for a walk westward along the side of the fjord.

So far it has been calm, but now the wind is picking up and white-topped grey waves move across the fjord. The road goes through a small hamlet where there is a pond, a few square metres of tired water with a few pieces of rusty iron breaking its surface. The land beside the pond looks tired too, the grass burnt by the frosts and ice of winter, the bare earth looking cold and wind-thrashed. Two horses in a nearby field come

towards me, curious about this thing in brightly coloured clothes. Clearly there is little traffic on this road. Further on two men on horses say 'hello' to me and one of them, hearing my English reply, stops to talk. He asks where I am going. I tell him Dynjandi – the local name for the waterfall that most visitors to Iceland would recognise as Fjall-foss – and he thinks a little. It is possible, he tells me, that the pass over the mountain to the falls will be open now, but he is not sure. Certainly it was not open two days ago. The weather this winter has been very harsh with a lot of snow and wind. In view of the fact that I am walking this is somewhat academic, but it gives us a point of contact. I ask if they know anything about the snowy owl. When I arrived in the airport I had seen the local paper which reported the sighting of one near Ísafjörður. Yes, the man has heard about it. It was sighted near Bolungarvík, the other side of Ísafjörður from here, but, who knows? These birds fly far. I ask if they are frequent visitors. Oh no. If they were that common they would not be on page one of the paper. He laughs. It is a fair point.

We talk a little more, about the eider ducks and the weather, then the two men ride off. They would look incongruous, like far-flung gouchos, were it not for their high-stepping Icelandic ponies. They keep to the road and ride with amazingly straight backs. I watch as they disappear down the road, then turn and walk through the hamlet which seems completely free of people. Beyond, the road becomes pot-holed – it was only gravel at its best – as it continues to a headland where it is blocked by a rock fall. I go up on to the headland where there are huge cliffs shot with crevices and water streams down the walls from melting snow. The whole place is a shambles of falling rock, soft shaly rock, slaty rock; everything has been split apart by erosion. It is an interesting place to stand and watch rocks falling; all the time I am there I hear them crashing down. I am stopped by an unstable-looking scree slope. When I walk on it the whole thing starts to move and I am soon covered in the grey dust I am stirring up; it fills my nostrils and triggers a memory that links the smell with rock climbing. I recall a day when I was new to the sport and I recall too the smell when lightning struck the limestone cliff on which I was climbing. Whether it is the memory of ancient insecurities, or the real threat of new ones I do not know, but I decide to go back. Discretion would appear to be 'the better part'; about fifty to sixty metres down from me on the right are some very steep – probably vertical – cliffs falling the last thirteen to seventeen metres into the sea and I have no desire to ride an avalanche down.

Back at the tent it is getting late, so I set up the Trangia and cook myself a meal. It feels cold: I had hoped for spring but what I am finding is winter. I eat the meal inside the tent to get away from the wind, and even there I need an extra jacket. The wind drops slightly as I am making myself another cup of tea and I like the idea of going out to watch the sun go down. I take a camera and sit on the edge of the water. A vee of geese goes over, one goose honking at the setting sun. It is one in the morning before the sun finally disappears and I am left with twilight rather than lowlight. I edge back to the tent. I feel lonely, desperately lonely, and it's not just being alone that is doing it. It is many

things – the lethargy of the travel, and all that space. In one direction only a little earthy bank separates me from the edge of the ocean, while in the other the valley goes back for miles and miles. It goes back for *ever*. Once I catch a glimpse of the light of a car or maybe a tractor a long way up the valley, and this seems to make my isolation even more profound. Most of the time this isolation is what I seek, but today I just feel lonely. I make hot chocolate so that I can sleep more easily and as I sip it I am suddenly overcome with weariness. I crawl into my sleeping bag and curl up in a tight ball.

When I wake the air is full of the sound of curlews. It would be nice to see gyrfalcon and sea eagle, king eider and divers, but it is the sound of the curlew that is the call of the wild. All the blues have gone away.

The morning is grey and windy, but I can see all the way up the valley. I breakfast quickly, drinking several cups of tea, knowing that in this wind I need to avoid dehydration on the grind over the pass. It takes a long time to reach Dynjandi, but the weather improves as the day wears on, leaving me with wonderful views across the Arnarfjörður, its far peaks wreathed in clouds. As the sun dips low the clouds bounce refracted red light off their bases. It hurries across the sea towards me, in the way that only light can, making the water turn brown and pink, making its wave ends sparkle and flash. At the water's edge snipe rise and trill, while on the valley side there are wheatears and redwings. A quick search reveals one female redwing on a nest in the short scrubby beech-like bushes on the leeward side of a stream cutting.

Dynjandi is almost frozen at its sides, the light brilliantly reflected from the rivulets of snow and ice. I sit near the fjord's edge and wonder whether to continue south towards Latrabjarg or whether to return north towards Drangajökull. In the end the decision is made by the snowy owl. I know it is unlikely that I will see it, but just the thought that I might is enough.

Next morning over breakfast I decide to go back into Þingeyri to catch a plane back to Ísafjöður in the hope that I can get a boat or bus from there. This means retracing my steps for a mile or so, but the country is wild and beautiful, full of new things to see. I start up the hill towards Dýrafjörður but before I reach the top I am treated to some Icelandic weather. In this country they say that if you don't like the weather all you have to do is

Eider duck nest, Dýrafjödur, north-west Iceland.

Red-necked phalarope, near Höfn.   *Harlequin duck, Mývatn.*

wait five minutes and it will get better. By the same token, if it is good you only have to wait five minutes and it will get worse. A storm arrives from the west, the snow falling so thickly in a few minutes that I fear I will lose my way. The temperature rises with the cloud cover, and the snow underfoot becomes wet and soft, making progress difficult and tiring. I move to my left, knowing that there is a road there somewhere – it is always best to avoid roads, but it is even better to be able to see where you are. The storm is terrible now, the snow thicker, the visibility worse. I fall into the occasional thigh-deep drift and expend a great deal of effort in escaping. Life is becoming bleak.

Eventually I reach the road and follow it to its top, surprised by how close I was to the summit of the pass. At the top, just off to the left, is a hut, placed there, I assume, to help struggling people like me. I gratefully go in. There are candles and a gas cylinder. It is a place to be warm, a place to be dry, a place to hang up my jacket and to pull faces at the storm outside. I assemble my Trangia and cook food, avoiding the almost overwhelming temptation to use the gas cylinder. Some day, someone will be in greater need than me. The hut seems the ideal place to stay the night if the storm holds, but I am not sure if I am allowed to: it is full of instructions which are all written in Icelandic.

Next morning dawns bright and clear; the storm has blown itself out in the night. Icelandic weather is really buggering me about, I decide, and conditions are now near perfect except for the metre of soft snow that lies over everything in sight. I make it down to Þingeyri in time to hear the good news that the plane has gone. No matter. A local man offers to ferry me across the fjord and I am soon on the way to Holt. There is no real news there of the owl, but someone suggests that I try the hills above Núpur where there has been much activity lately. 'Activity' seems to be one car – all I see as I meander my way through the hills above the lonely hamlet of Núpur. Beyond it is the biggest fish-drying frame I have so far seen, with overflow fish hung on a wire fence alongside. Some of these have fallen off and are blowing around, suffering, it would appear, from a tragic case of neglect. I put one or two out of their misery by introducing them to a cup of coffee and my insides, not necessarily in that order. It is like eating cardboard, and tastes about as good.

In the hills that side a long valley on the way to Sæbol there is another emergency hut. I contemplate a hut-to-hut tour of north-west Iceland. Outside

Fish drying, Flateyri, north-west Iceland.

this one there is a lone snow bunting pecking mournfully at a muddy patch of shingle that is all that shows through the snow. The bunting is the only bird I see all day. By nightfall I am fed up with the search and determined to leave tomorrow for at least one day on Drangajökull.

Starting early, I traverse the long ridge of hills that separates me from Ísafjörður, arriving late in the afternoon. The road from the town that goes east towards Drangajökull has collapsed and no buses or lorries can get through. I try for a boat. *Fraganes*, a good way of getting to the more remote spots – it makes an eleven-hour round trip regularly, several times each week – has gone, and no one is going my way. I stay local for a night, then climb the ridge above the far side of the fjord, making for Hestöfjordur and a view of the big glacier. Snow conditions are perfect, and so is the view to Drangajökull. On Hestfjördur a diver – probably Great Northern – sculls away across the water as I approach. It is not enough to make me forget that the owl remains elsewhere.

The Tourist Round

The bus that goes east from Reykjavik can be used to visit the better-known and most important sites. But before you go that way – real joy lies at the end of each bus trip to the east – it is compulsory, or so you might think, to visit Þingvellir. The site has a special significance for Icelanders, whose independence has been compromised on several occasions over the years. In World War II there were Allied landings here. The Icelanders protested, not because they supported the cause of Facisim or German expansion – given the choice they would doubtless have stood with the Norwegians, fellow Vikings – but because they were not asked to choose. The Allies arrived one day by boat and threatened dire consequences if their wishes did not rapidly become the law of the land.

Today there is a US air base at Keflavik. Indeed, until recently the flight that took you to Iceland landed at the base itself rather than on 'real' Icelandic soil. Go any day to the Blue Lagoon, a

Site of the world's oldest parliament, Þingvellir.

curious place of billowing steam clouds and science-fiction B-movie film-set machinery, and the place will be filled with Americans, all of them covered in sulphur when they emerge. The Icelandic attitude to the new usurpers is ambivalent. 'Not sure that I want the Americans, fairly certain I want their dollars.'

To a people with such a tenuous hold on real freedom – one puff at the fish export market from the US would blow Iceland away – roots are important. Therefore Þingvellir is important. It is the site of the oldest parliament in the world. Iceland was a democracy while white Americans were still Poles or Irish, still several dozens of generations from crossing the Atlantic. (Isn't it even the case that it was an Icelandic Viking who discovered America? And isn't it also true that he kept fairly quiet about it?) Þingvellir is a curious place. What the tourists come to see is a raised dais of grass hemmed in by a retaining wall. Behind, a stiff Icelandic flag waves in the breeze. As a thrilling spectacle it has little to offer, but as a powerful totem it is almost unique in its place in European and western culture.

To reach the dais from the windswept coach park the tourists file down a narrow gorge before negotiating a series of ladders and bridges. Few of those disgorged from the solitary coach on the day that we were there noticed the gorge, yet it is spectacular in a way that the dais is not; a volcanic fissure and a geological feature of startling proportions and beauty. If you follow it along from the historical site it leads you to a perfect waterfall, and then to a point where flat grass lies between the vertical gorge sides. The walls here can be negotiated for a view of the Icelandic interior – stunning wildness and extent.

We travelled east on a fine, clear morning, heading towards Gullfoss, the golden waterfall. The first Arctic fox I had ever seen watched me as I arrived at Gullfoss late at night, then turned and headed off with its huge tail laid out behind it. The waterfall takes your breath away when first you see it. Its vast volume of water pours into a huge cleft in the earth that is thirty-three metres deep and in some places only thirty-three metres wide; a long, parallel-sided cleft that becomes a gorge or even a canyon. The river that makes the falls runs down towards us, hitting the cleft at right-angles. First there is a series of rapids where beautiful mists of water hang above white horses that gallop

Gullfoss – a detail of the centre of the falls.

over rocks, then the water disappears into the cleft. The spray from the falls is so dense that you cannot peer into it and you must rely on logic to believe that it is the same water that makes the river that snakes along the gorge a few hundred metres away. In the spray perpetual rainbows are fixed in position as though their unseen feet were nailed to the base of the cleft.

Tony and I were alone at Gullfoss. Alone, and exhilarated by the noise, the spray and the view – and also by the fact that we were not ankle-deep in wrinkled cans and other crap, or being persuaded to buy Gullfossburgers by bright neon signs. Nothing was there to compete with this wonder of the natural world.

We camped upriver from the falls, stalling the leap into the chasm of some of the water by boiling it on the Trangia and making it into Earl Grey tea. I did not sleep well that night: it had been a great day and the call of the wild kept me nervous and excited. Tony, most unusually, was already up and hard at work with his camera when I emerged to sniff the morning air. The sky was a beautiful blue, the sun in just the right position for the rainbows to come out of the cleft in exactly the right position photographically. I made tea for him as he worked, watching a vee of geese heading for the interior as the kettle boiled. For three hours we worked and drank, worked and ate, worked and packed. And in all of that time we had Gullfoss to ourselves.

Geysir is more what the tourist from Western Europe – or America – is used to, with its hotel and constructed pathways. Yet for all it is more visitor-orientated it really is very low-key. The hotel is elegant and modern, but it does not have a bolted-on section where you can buy spoons with 'Present from Geysir' written on them. There is a garage/café where souvenirs of a kind can be bought, but only a very good marketing man could

Gullfoss in winter.

Gullfoss in summer.

come up with something stunning from a spot where most of the time nothing is happening.

The constructed path is to help keep visitors off the basalt pavements which are delicate and fragile, taking aeons to create and seconds to destroy. Follow it – it is an Orange Brick Road, which proves how close you can come to a real advertising coup without quite getting it right: I wonder if the café serves 6-Up – and it will lead you to the Great Geysir. This is the daddy of all geysirs, the one that gave its name to the (now better-known) hot-water spouts elsewhere in the world. Sadly, it no longer spouts, or if it does it has a frequency measured in years. Interest lies with its small brother, *Strokkur*. This does erupt, but not to a defined time schedule. Stand close and you can watch the hot water of last time's spray pouring back into the spout hole. The whole area, a thicker, stronger basalt pavement, is funnel-shaped and the water pours back into the central hole that has been emptied to a depth of three or more metres. I am not precise on depth because there is no great temptation to hang over the hole and peer down.

When the water has almost filled the hole, to perhaps a foot or so below the top, there is an audible pause in the proceedings. The water level drops and then, *woosh*, up it all comes, first rising like a column – at this stage it looks like a vaguely blue shaggy ink cap toadstool – then blasting itself apart in a flourish of steam. Stand close enough to see the column form and you will probably be pelted with near-boiling water.

Other than *Strokkur* the Geysir site is a little disappointing. There are bubbling pools and mud that goes *gloop*, but there is nothing to compare with Krísuvík or Hveragerdi. Krísuvík is south and slightly west of Reykjavik, reached by a road across a beautiful lava field and through valleys that are almost civilized, or by a fine walk that takes these valleys and continues along a ridge above the bird-filled lake of Kleífarvatn. The Krísuvík pools are not signed, either on the road or when you get there. If you do not know they are there, or if you do not know where they are, you will miss them. The site offers only one clue – a continuously blowing steam hole that in the right weather is visible from the road. You will be alone when you arrive, almost certainly. Duck boards will take you past a hot waterfall towards the blow hole. Pass on the windward side if you don't want a hot bath, and you will reach an area of incredible beauty. Sulphur and soil have combined to produce colours of Van Goghian purity. Things go *hiss* and *glug*. At one point a whole area steams gently so that the visitor can view the sun through a vapoury haze.

By contrast, Hveragerdi – 'Hurdy Gurdy Land' to Tony and I, as the real pronunciation is a jaw-breaker – is an upper-class thermal area. Genteel pools of startling transparency lie quietly amid small, measured, tidy heaps of yellow and orange soils. Mud pools wait until you are looking the other way before plopping discreetly. I felt that if I looked back early the mud pool would blush and say 'pardon'. A pipeline meanders among the springs, collecting steam for distribution to rows of neat houses. Iceland's horticultural college is here, the steam heating its greenhouses. The tourist literature speaks of banana trees, but the singular of the noun 'tree' would be better employed. It is certainly not a good idea to arrive hoping to fill a basket, or even a hand (unless you know an employee) with greenhouse fruit.

Beyond Geysir there is lazy travelling. In Selfoss the assistant in the chemist's tries to sell us surgical spirit when we ask for meths and there is a pantomime while Tony explains to her, in best sign language, that what he wants is spirit for a Trangia. Watching him perform is like watching charades. Two words. The whole thing. You want to pour it? No, no. You want to rub it on your buttocks? No. Sounds like . . . I am reminded of the time when we were leaving Italy after a while in the Dolomites and spent all our Italian cash in the last café making a phone call, only to find that the café owner was adding a surcharge to the bill. She wanted another 35p (about two hundred million lire) and was insistent. One lad with us, a genuine Cockney, finished up by explaining to this (probably normally) mild-mannered Italian who spoke no English at all that we couldn't pay because we were 'borassic'. I remember thinking that use of rhyming slang was going to help clear matters up in no time.

The assistant fetched a man from the back – please can I see the male assistant to explain what I want? – who nodded gravely. *Raudspirit*, he said.

Seljalandsfoss is a ponytail of a waterfall throwing itself clear of the rim of its cliff to look like a 1950s American college girl shaking her head. For just that reason Seljalandsfoss is best viewed from the side, unlike most other waterfalls. Skógafoss is a sixty-seven metre monster, so wide and so tall,

Skógafoss.

and so much falling in a single sweep that clouds of spray are produced. Tony sends me forward into the spray. It will make a lovely picture he yells at me above the crashing noise. I go forward, reluctantly. Periodically I pause and look back. Each time he waves me forward. It is, he assures me when I get back, a really good shot. I am delighted for him. I am also wet through.

Beyond the big waterfall is a desert of black sand, then lava fields, the black and red-brown lumps dotted with a whitish lichen, then another lava field where the lichenous moss is bright green. The moss looks soft and springy, like the moss of the UK, but is hard and rough and dry like tinder.

We camped in the official site at Skaftafell. The

thought of doing so appalled us, but there are regulations. We are aware that those who follow us may be judged by our behaviour, and exploration of wilderness areas brings responsibilities as well as pleasures. As we erected the tent Tony became wistful again. Many years ago Tony came to Iceland as a raw teenage cyclist. While I came to the Arctic when I realized that climbing, my first love, was losing its appeal, Tony was born to the area, loving it, one might believe, even before he saw his first photograph of it. His trip here was a homecoming, and there were times when I could see in his eyes that he was reliving his first memories.

That first trip was a bold move. The Cod War

Strokkur erupting, Geysir.

was at its height, and an Englishman in Iceland was less than popular. To get over the problem he sometimes insisted that he was Welsh, claiming that the Welsh disliked the English as much as the Icelanders. It doesn't sound like much of a cover story to me, and I prefer the idea that the locals thought Tony was just an eccentric who should not be allowed near sharp objects. At the time of his trip he was such a novelty that he was featured in several Reykjavik newspapers, and treated with great hospitality wherever he went. He even managed to bring a touch of real culture to the island, having arrived with tea (leaves *not* bags) and a teapot. He told me the story again as we sat in the campsite in Skaftafell. Then he told me about his climb up Iceland's highest mountain.

——— ◆ ———

My first view of Hvannadalshnúkur was from the plane as I flew into Höfn from Reykjavik. In those days the final link in the Iceland circle road had not been made and I needed a plane, bound for Fagurhólsmýri, to reach the National Park. I arrived at Skaftafell to find several groups of campers, all wild-eyed outdoor types, I suppose not unlike me. It was nice to be with others; I had just had three weeks on my tod with company only in Reykjavik campsite. The only other official

Strokkur, Geysir.

site I used was in Ísafjörður but in the first week of June, at minus five degrees, I had been alone.

The other campers were good company and we all had a good laugh. 'Would you like to join us on a walk?' they asked. The casual conversation turned to panic on my part. 'We're going up Hvannadalshnúkur . . . ' I had never been on a glacier before. Could I make it? It was nearly 2,200 metres and from sea level. Ben Nevis was a long drag; Snowdon is less than half the height and there you cheat by starting at 300 metres. And, unlike cycling, there is no freewheeling downhill. Was I fit enough? Would my cycling shoes grip on the ice? So many questions flashed through my mind. What am I to do? But, yes, I was fit – I had, after all, cycled 22,500 kilometres last year and had walked the Pennine Way the year before. Anyway, what the hell? This was the chance of a lifetime. Before I could think any more my mouth had decided. I was going.

That afternoon I went to the café at Fagurhólsmýri and bought a pair of Tuf workman boots. They didn't have my size but they would be OK. They would have to be OK. I was going to make it.

The others had paid a lot of money to go on this guided trip. Their package included walks around the Skaftafell area and, should the weather allow,

Hot water pool, Hveragerði.

Descending from the summit of Hvannadalshúkur.

a climb of Hvannadalshnúkur. After five days' walking they were obviously all fit and experienced. They were a group of twelve, mainly Icelandic, but with two Norwegians and a Canadian, and now joined by an English cyclist who pretended, when convenient, to be Welsh.

The intended route was up the south-west side of the Öræfajökull, the glacier being climbed during the night, although in June the sun only barely dips below the northern horizon at midnight. Even so, I was assured, the sun being low and behind the mountains would allow a firm crust to develop on top of the snow; there is nothing worse than deep, soft, wet snow. We left the campsite at ten in the evening, the party reduced because a few thought they wouldn't make it, in a bus rescued from a St Trinians film set. Although Iceland had changed some years before to driving on the right, the bus – which was well past its sell-by date – was right-hand drive; the first bit of England I had seen for three weeks. Thankfully we left it behind at Sandfell, a small isolated ruin about half-way down the road to Hof. Our guide was there to meet us, his silver hair outshone only by the enormity of his rucsac containing about twenty-five flags on long poles. Were we marking out a soccer pitch? I had never been walking with flags before. This was more power for the cause – these people use tea bags and drive on the wrong side of the road, they hang fish on clothes lines and then eat them dry.

The climb to the snowline was not pleasant, and I was haunted by memories of the boredom of Ben Nevis's path, even though here there was no path. Neither was there Wendy, a girl in my form (it had been a school trip) who had legs that never quit, long legs, the type rampant fell men dream of. She made the ascent of Nevis a pleasure, but now I was grown up and Wendyless. I had also become a cyclist. I remembered again why I preferred my bike: when you are shattered you can get off and walk. Here I was shattered and there was no alternative.

Rocks splintered by centuries of cyclic thaws crumbled under my boots. Our way was up to one of the few glacier tongues that wasn't too steep and broken up by crevasses. 'If we climb high on the rock we can then drop to flatter ice.' How I longed for this, inspired by the word 'flatter.' I hate steep, relentless climbs, especially at two in the morning in low cloud.

Two young lads from Hafnarfjöður, a small fishing village near Reykjavik, were going like loonies. I decided to keep a low profile, after all I was a guest. And I hadn't paid. Anyway, I could go no faster, being the slow-starter, long-distance plodder type. Helgi, the guide, laughed at them. 'You watch them tire,' he said to me, 'those youngsters can't pace themselves. It is a long, long way.' Well thank you Helgi for those words of encouragement. And why was he confiding this dire information to me? Couldn't he see I was knackered?

The ice eventually came, small snow fields at first leading to the vastness of the great glacier. Pleasure was dawning and so was the sun. The snow, hard snow, was easy to walk on. The slopes were gentle and convex like the outer optic of a huge fish-eye lens. The sun rose magnificently over one of these slopes, warm hues glistening off the windswept, spiky blue ice. Being anchor man, the one at the back of the rope, and because we were walking directly into the sun, I delighted in the shadows of those in front. The light danced about, we were above the thin cloud line and suddenly my pains had gone. Oh, how I love the light. Am I all there? Why am I moved by such simple things?

The obvious was now explained. Helgi dumped the flags and revealed all – he had some farming to do and was going back! Was this guy real? A guide that didn't. He insisted it was simple – go in that direction and plant the flags at regular intervals. If the wind blows and snow fills your footprints the safe way between the crevasses will be lost. The flags they tell you where to go, you see? OK? He left, and we were left confused.

The morning sun compensated for our loss by offering inspiration. The Icelanders had seen precious little sun that summer and peeling noses were instant and plentiful. Handkerchiefs held in place by the nose clips of sunglasses alleviated some of the worst effects but the speed of burning was staggering. For me it was paradise; I was already brown.

Glacier walking is a piece of cake; well this bit was, with rolling hills of dazzling serenity. Crevasses were walked around or jumped over, and those of any size were given respectful avoidance. Wow, I was enjoying this. It was not comparable to cycling, in fact it was so different that comparison was a nonsense. The youngsters were also enthusiastic, but tiring, their antics and extreme youth catching up on them. To help I now had three rucsacs on my back. I am not really a hero, they were only small daysacks, but my fitness surprised me. Mars bars, a rip-off at three times the UK price, taken at regular intervals, got us there.

The final peak stands quite proud of the regular ice and we pondered the way up. Large caves guarded by huge icicles, some fifteen feet tall, sheltered us from the wind as we ate lunch and did some more pondering. Without an ice axe and with only borrowed instep crampons my climbing ability was somewhat limited, and this was not the place to take risks. But who could get this far and not just push it a little bit? So, still roped from the crevasse fields, we gingerly crawled to the top. The clouds that were with us on the climb had gone, opening the way to spectacular views, views helped by the air being free of dust and haze.

There were views to the sea, views west towards Reykjavik, in fact views in every direction, as long as it was down. I was on top of the world.

———— ◆ ————

The Selfoss chemist's *raudspirit* was awful. It spat a worrisome mixture of steam and flame out periodically and covered the bottom of the pans with black ooze, a treacly goo that got itself on to my pile jacket and put me in good humour for an hour or so. I washed the jacket. Overnight there was a frost and it went hard and crinkly.

Tony offered to make breakfast, an event so rare that there was a chance parliament would reconvene at Þingvellir. He manufactured a concoction of such awesome vileness that it defies, even now, reasonable description. It bore a marked resemblance to something that had already been eaten once before. I made an excuse and settled for tea and muesli.

Tony went back to his past trip again, this time concentrating on the visual aspects of an air stewardess. The memory was triggered by talk of a young woman I had met on one trip who showed me Dyrhólaey and the sea pinnacles of Reynisdrangar near Vik. She was at pains to tell me – several times – that her male friends were divided into two groups. There were 'friends', with a small 'f', people, like me, whose company was interesting and pleasant but who were just casual acquaintances. Then there were 'Friends' with a big 'F' who were lovers. I had been greatly amused, although I think I should not have been. Tony was equally amused at the story, and wondered

whether there was a third group, too, of 'FRIENDS' with a big 'F', big 'R', big 'I' and big 'ENDS'.

Our trip had been timed to coincide with nesting, although the birds were confused by the late spring and many had not yet started to build. Nevertheless, on such a good day we decided to visit Ingólfshöfði. We gratefully accepted a lift to the nearby village of Fagúrholsmýri. Tony assured me that there was a supermarket in the village, which seemed unlikely in a place that had less than ten houses, but turned out to be almost true – the garage sold bits and pieces. As he said (and not for the first time), you can't beat a bit of local knowledge. We had a coffee, bought some reinforcements, deciding to leave the *skyr* that we had both become addicted to until later, turned south and headed for the sea.

Ingólfshöfði is an island about six or seven kilometres off-shore, but separated from the mainland by a saltwater lagoon rather than by open sea. Between us and the lagoon a number of rivers made their way seaward. As we crossed ground that became increasingly boggy, the vegetation increasingly salt-spattered and sparse, Tony began to enthuse on the likelihood of our seeing geese and red-necked phalaropes. I was more interested in how we were going to reach the sea, and in how we were going to cross it. The reaching was straightforward enough: at the first river we took off our boots, rolled up our trousers to mid-thigh and, dividing about thirty kilograms of photographic and emergency equipment between us, waded across. It was icy-cold, and soon numbed both feet and legs into submission. By the time we had crossed two more we had decided to stop drying our feet and re-booting after each one, and set off across the bogs in bare feet.

We saw no phalaropes, but did find, quite by chance, the nest of a pink-footed goose. The goose was sitting on eggs and flew off as we approached. That worried us as there were several great skuas working the sky above the bog, and we spent some time waiting for the goose to return before setting off again. The sea lagoon turned out to vary in depth from a few inches to a couple of feet. Beneath the water the sand was, not surprisingly, the sinking, knackering type. Mid-way, after a long, hard time, we stopped for a rest – at least, as much of a rest as you can get standing in knee-deep water unable to put down your rucsac. Ultimately we escaped the cold, sticky grasp of sand

En route *to Ingólfshöfði.*

Puffin, Ingólfshöfði.

Ptarmigan, Mývatn.

and sea, only to be faced by three miles of sand on its own. The sand was not golden-brown and sun-kissed. This being Iceland it was black, jet-black weathered lava, and was kissed only by a light breeze coming off the glacier. As it is occasionally covered by the sea this sand is not compact so that at times we could walk fairly comfortably, but at other times we sank in unexpectedly, which broke up our rhythm and made us tired and frustrated. Finally, after a desert journey of Lawrencian proportions – or so it seemed – we reached the base of Ingólfshöfði.

The island, in truth little more than a detached headland, is about seventy metres high, and progress on to it is by way of one of many gullies filled with sand. This sand was dry, but climbing a 70-metre high-angled sand dune is not easy. In fact it is downright unfriendly and I was very pleased to be at the top. Pleased, that is, until I discovered that I had forgotten to bring the tea bags – the subsequent 'Well, why didn't you bring them

then's, 'Why is it always my fault's reminded me of the Quentin Crisp line that marriage was impossible for him because he could not have tolerated an endless succession of mornings when the first words he heard were, 'And another thing' – and that there were no birds. I lug the kitchen sink and assorted extras – but no tea bags, Tony points out – to this island to look at birds and what do I find? And so on.

We crossed to the seaward, as opposed to the lagoonward side, where there are 70-metre cliffs. Interestingly, it was not, as is usual, the noise that told us we were approaching a large nesting cliff, but an almost overpowering smell of *guano*. The cliff on Ingólfshöfði is the only sea cliff for miles. There are several inland cliffs, but these are too far from the sea for auks and gulls, and so the whole, and large, sea bird population of this part of Iceland is concentrated on to this one cliff. The result is that every ledge, from those that would take a small tent to those that a modern rock

The black sand beach, Ingólfshöfði.

climber would blanch to see, is packed with birds. To add to this confusion the steep-angled grass above is riddled with puffin burrows; later in our stay we found that attempts to move tripods closer to the edge put us in real danger of disappearing downwards, compete with the odd half-acre of apparently stable cliff top.

The sun came out and it grew warm on this sheltered side of the island. We had been led to expect all the guillemots, but there were no black guillemots either on the ledges or in the sea. There were commons, some of them bridled, and there were also Brünnich's. There were plenty of kitti-wakes, but on closer inspection some of them turned out to be Icelandic gulls. We saw no razor-bills, which was a surprise, and the few little auks we saw were all out on the water, but the puffins made up for the loss. Never before have I seen puffins that are *so* red, *so* yellow, *so* black. In the high-angled sun the feet of some reflected the light so that their breasts appeared red too.

We put Tony's tripod close to the cliff edge, wishing that we had a rope when each of us fell into unexpected crevasses in the cliff-top grass. I retreated to leave the master to it and lay happily in the sun. It really was difficult to believe that we could be so far north. Surely this must be the UK – kittiwakes, puffins and guillemots. And that small bird there must be a . . . snow bunting. It was a pair, in fact, doing a little late courting, and then, just to push the point home, a great skua floated into sight.

Tony finished his work and we set off back towards the sea. I went a little ahead, drawn towards a huge black sand dune on the island's top. The dune offered the definitive photograph of Iceland, its top an absolutely flawless surface of jet-black lava sand and, behind it, Vatnajökull, even bigger, and glowing white and pink in the evening sun. So taken was I with this vision of perfect Iceland that I did not realise that I had walked into a skua colony, not, that is, until one fearless great skua hit me. Whatever he hit me with, feet or wings, it hurt and almost knocked me off balance. For as long as it took me to get out of range, several birds used me for bombing practice, coming so close on occasions that ducking was a necessity rather than a flamboyant gesture. Tony enjoyed it all hugely.

After that there was just the gully to descend, the sinking sand to cross, the sea to wade and the bog to hop. As we hopped we saw grey phalaropes,

inquisitive little birds seemingly unbothered by our presence, happily showing themselves now that there was insufficient light to film them.

After a night during which vengeful wind pushed rain through flysheet and tent, spraying our sleep-ing bags, we were joined by Ann and John, friends of Tony. Their chief interest was in walking rather than in birds, so we compromised with a day that started near Svartifoss, a waterfall that tumbles between black basalt columns. Beyond, the ground became awkwardly mixed. At first there was semi-cultivated land covered with tufted grass. The rusting remains of an old piece of farm machinery were evidence of some Icelander break-ing his back to extract a living from the land. And, it would seem, failing. There is an area where the micro-ecology changes rapidly, so that almost with every pace there is new vegetation clinging pre-cariously to the spare soil. Then there is that saturated semi-peat that is often underfoot in the island, especially on the middle ground. Here, though, even the higher ground was wet, so that the difficulty of making progress barely relented until we reached the snow.

There had been no real objective, except a vague idea that if conditions were good Hvannadal-shnúkur might as well be climbed. But we were barely half-way before clouds crept down the high peaks to threaten us with rain or sleet. The temper-ature rose a little and the snow became impossible; at every step we had to haul our legs out of deep holes. We stopped. From here Skeiđarársandur, an unusual feature when seen from ground level, becomes even more extraordinary. There are square miles of shifting, sinking sand where the normally clean-cut edge between sea and land has become blurred. In the opposite direction, above us and to the left, was a high serac-edged glacial wall with, far below it, a run-out – a broad, lethargic river the colour of putty.

We retreated, crossing a ridge of the mountain to reach a glacial tongue of Öræfaejökull. From far above the glacier looked like modern art, a canvas of grey-white curiously etched with black lines that appeared random at first sight, but in which a symmetry could at length be discerned. We used the tongue in its lower reaches, where it licked land close to the edge of the Skaftafell site. For our latest companions this was a new experience, but the glacier was benign and they were confident, unhurried walkers who found pleasure rather than fear on the ice. Getting off was a pain, but not because of the crevasses or steep, unstable cliffs. Here the problem was the muck. All glaciers are dirty where they end, with that sticky paste of ground-up rock. But this was dreadful, threatening to cover everything and to get inside it too. We were pleased to reach the river and the ground beyond. On the way to the camp we passed a boulder where Tony and I competed for rock climbing idiot of the evening. Tony jumped from high up, landed heavily and pulled a face.

In the years we have been going to the Arctic (at least one summer and one winter trip now for as long as I can remember), we have acquired odd niggles. Each of us carries an unreliable ankle for instance, and Tony had just given his a jolt.

He eased it back to the site. When morning came he was in pain and not best pleased. An easy day was called for, using the new car – what luxury! – to visit the northern hemisphere's largest great skua colony. I tried to cheer him up with memories of the last time his ankle was hurting, when we slept in a sheep herder's cave – lined with graffiti that was centuries old – on the way from Landmannalaugar to the coast near Vik. The country in the south had been really weird, with mushrooms of crumbling lava and wide flat rivers to cross, and it had rained for days, which had added to the general air of unreality as these features kept emerging from the mist. He did not respond.

The skua colony turned out to be impressive, with few eggs but a host of great and Arctic skuas all intent on protecting their chosen nest site at all costs. Such dedication was admirable, as was the aerial ability of the birds, which wheeled and dived, pulled up over our heads, wheeled and dived again. Tony limped along with his tripod sticking two feet out of the top of his rucsac to protect his head. We left the birds in peace, moving on to a river and lake site that offered Tony better angles for his camera. He was finding walking a chore so we left him, following the river inland towards its glacial snout source. We searched for kilometres – it seemed – to find a crossing point, eventually reaching a lake and being forced to cross at a place that was nowhere near as good as a dozen we had passed and dismissed as unsuitable. The glacier beyond was dirty and torturous, but we trekked down it to reach a sandspill outfall. The river we had crossed was to our left and was not, as we first thought, melt water from the spout; that formed a river to our right. We trekked across the wet sand towards Tony on the far bank ahead of us.

By the time we reached Tony it was obvious we would never find a crossing point. He was hugely amused by it, the more so as we paced up and down in exasperation. Finally, sensing that we were on a loser and not keen on the mile-long trek back to the crossing point, I took off boots and socks and walked into the fast-flowing stream.

I had expected it to be cold but it surprised me with a suddenness that wrenched my breath away. The river bottom was ridged sand, a difficult and unkind footing, that combined with the cold and the rush to make me want to go fast while forcing me to go slow. I teetered across, on the edge of tipping up, a tightrope walk between panic and despair. Tony caught it all on film.

Jökulsárlón is a beautiful place. Close to the sea Breiðamerkurjökull, a broad flat snout of Vatnajökull, dies into this lake, the melt water exiting along a wide, fast channel into the sea. On the southern side there is a tern colony, and the birds hover above our heads like noisy butterflies while we pad carefully between groups of their precious eggs. In the lake seals surface and stare. The glacier ends in a cliff that calves small icebergs that head seaward, grind to a halt when they hit the sand base of the river and dissolve in tears at the indignity of it all. By Svalbard or Greenland standards the bergs are small, but they are nice enough in their setting, the stranded ones, sculpted by wind, sun, and rain, are brilliant blue on their shadowed sides.

Along at the river's mouth, at the standing wave formed where the incoming sea and outgoing melt water meet, a flock of terns hover and dive like gnats in the summer air. Each surfaces from its dive with what looks like a sand eel. Among the cloud of terns a solitary Arctic skua spins and wheels, selecting an individual bird and pursuing it to try to persuade it – bully it – to drop its catch. The tern is swift, turning tightly among the flock to avoid the pirate. The skua is astonishingly agile for so big a bird, but cannot keep up among the throng and gives up. Four or five times as I watch the skua tries and each time it fails. It would surely take less effort to catch a fish itself.

Back at the campsite beside the iceberg lake Ann and John have made tea (much to Tony's disgust, since he is mainly a coffee man). Earl Grey never seemed such a decent chap, and we laze back to enjoy his brew. It is foul. After a few moments we realize why. The tidal reach of the sea fills the lake so that at all times the water is brackish. There is a resigned look from Ann and Tony, but John and I (the more English pair?) take ice axes and haul a small berg ashore, beating lumps off it for the tea. The Trangia looks good with ice clumps poking out of its kettle. And the tea tastes even better.

Next day I am taken to Höfn to catch a plane back to Reykjavik, leaving the others to continue to Mývatn and the north. On the way red-necked phalaropes at last show themselves, tame, almost friendly birds that come towards the camera. They are nothing like the divers we have tried to photograph and largely failed to capture because of their timidity. Tony surprises an oncoming motorist by assuming a position that leaves his legs on the gravel road but takes the rest of him down among the lake-side vegetation. It is an amazing sight, the more so for being a waste of time. On our side of

the road, where the water is within a metre of the gravel edge, the phalaropes have come within spitting distance for a better look.

Höfn is a straggling village – aren't they all? – with a row of brightly-coloured ships in the harbour and a fine memorial out on a headland. Of the town itself I remember only two things. One was a small café that sold pizza and chips for less than the small fortune we expected, and served by a girl friendlier than we could have hoped for. The second thing was . . . I can't remember the second thing.

The plane lifted off but the weather did not and I was denied a view of Vatnajökull and the central plateau. Below and behind Ann, John and Tony moved east and north. Tony takes up the journey.

———— ◆ ————

I remember the desert crossing, vividly. The dust storms made my new bike very dirty. Now, many

The surface of Skaftafellsjökull from Kristinartíndar.

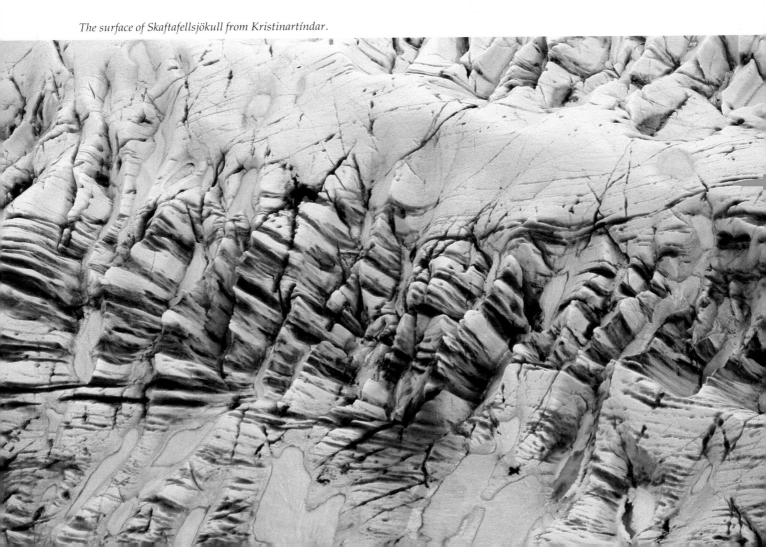

Lava formations, Mývatn.

years later, I am in the luxury of a hire car. Luxury? I think not in truth. It is very tedious, although it does minimize the more boring distances, allowing detailed exploration, by boot, of the areas of greater interest. Having been forced out of the eastern fjords in endless rainswept misery we headed for Mývatn, Goðafoss and Akureyri, three attractions in the north of Iceland. The route to Dettifoss, the greatest waterfall in Europe (fifty metres high and enormous in volume) was still closed, and perhaps will not open this year due to the extraordinarily long and hard winter. True four-wheel drive vehicles or those with time for a 30-kilometre trek could have probably made it, but we, having neither time nor lockable differentials, carried on across the edge of Mývatnsöræfi, a huge featureless desert of lava and ash fields. A desperate place.

Civilization is once again reached, the steam jets from prolific geothermal activities like flagpoles bending in the wind. This is the area of Mývatn famous in the guidebooks for everything except the bleeding obvious – the stench. Námafjall is a yellow mountain, offering (to those of no nose) stupendous views of the whole Mývatn area.

But first we make a stop at the east foot of the hills, a highly active area of slimy, bubbling sulphur pits. There are memories you never forget – and they are revolting memories – and here they come again. On my solo bike trip I spent two nights and a day in the Reykjahlið campsite thunderbox after a visit here. My insides were coming out. This time I got out of the car and felt my stomach heave again. Reflex action? John accused me of wimpish behaviour, so we did the tourist bit around the pits. Blurps and blops emit gases, and the smell is devastating. *I'm* the wimp?

Sulphur pits, Mývatn.

Where are *you* going John? 'I'm just going,' he said, his face the colour of the ground – yellow. Some poor Dutch guy was being ordered by his woman to stand right in the steamy fumes for a photo. Jesus, love is . . . having to stand in a sulphur plume? Not bloody likely. It was time to leave. I couldn't take any more.

Ahead the round-Iceland ring road (sorry, rubble trail) leads to a newish geothermal power station called Krafla, generating steam from subterranean heat. This area is active. One impressive crater, Viti – the name means hell – some 300 metres in diameter, was formed on 17 May 1724 as part of a five-year eruption. The area last saw eruptions in 1975 and 1984: perhaps it's time to go. Access to Viti is through the power

station grounds and on to the road's end, although with the late spring the road was just another snow field. The power station was unlike any I had previously seen. There was the same turbine house, but there were also huge plastic multi-coloured geodesic domes covering steam taps, pipes leaking noxious gas and a general weirdness.

Mývatn is over the hill, past more vile-smelling industrial delights. Some hero has at last heard our cry and painted a blue sky. It had been a long time since we last saw one of those, so we bought ice cream, sat in the sun and wrote postcards at the Reykjahlid shop. Life can be good on the tourist trail.

Close by are the famous Dimmuborgir, Grjótagjá

and Stóragjá underground hot springs. On my last visit I swam in the Grjótagjá pools – a true delight for someone so young and so unused to mixed nude dipping. Geothermal activities have so increased in recent years that these baths are now closed; they are too hot, too dangerous. Even access is not encouraged, and the tracks leading to the caverns are also closed. Instead we did the trail just south of Reykjahlið, climbing a lava mound overlooking the great lake. The warmth was stupendous, the east and north of Iceland enjoying some amazing summer temperatures, over 20°C and climbing.

Mývatn itself is famous for its peculiar lava formations and its birds. Only a very disinterested idiot could miss, and be unimpressed by, either.

John and Ann (although Ann to a lesser extent) were close contenders as they actively tried to get a tan. I went to do some work, attempting to photograph some ducks and mergansers that were sheltering from the sun. They steadfastly refused to come anywhere near close enough. But I am long on stamina and waited for a red-breasted merganser aimlessly doing nothing under the cliff on which lay the dozing duo. Patiently, even more so than usual, I wished it out of the shade. A 60th at full bore is a bit dicey with a 500mm lens hand held in a stagnant bog. Come out in the open you, you . . . delightful, beautiful . . . that's it.

'DO YOU WANT SOME TEA, TONE?' The shout terrified the bird as well as me, and I captured whitish streaks just discernible on an

Bubbling mud pit, Mývatn.

Goðafoss.

otherwise blank Kodachrome. I was soaked from lying in manky bog-like horrids, stalking some half-witted bird around lava lagoons, and John asked if I want tea. Of course I bloody well did. It was a delicious, if small, compensation.

The south-west outflow of Mývatn was more successful. Harlequin ducks were enjoying the rapids and sun, toing and froing, preening and looking most elegant, and I was enjoying myself, crawling commando-style at the water's edge, despite the odd passer-by's curious gaze. Strange people, tourists.

Despite my luck with the Harlequin ducks the Barrow's goldeneyes declined to come close enough and I had still not got a good shot when, with reluctance, we left Mývatn. It was sad to go, but Goðafoss was waiting to be photographed in the evening sun. I thought the land beside the 'Fall of the Gods' would make a good campsite, and it did. I spent a long time photographing the falls, taken with their grace. They are not particularly high, but very elegant and their remote location makes a visit a must. The falls were in good fettle for the shots, with a lot of spring melt water and plenty of ptarmigan (for us, 'chainsaws', because of their call). They were in unusual plumage. In the mating season the male usually has a striking red-orange eyebrow, but these were still nearly all white although it was already June.

We ate well and watched yet another super sunset, a pastime any northern traveller will soon develop, the acute angle of the sun giving hours of once-off enjoyment. At times like these, while I am watching a midnight sunset or sunrise, I shed a tear for those poor campers putting up with long hours of dark in the Himalayas or the like. But then, we are all different.

A quick bit of mental maths told me that 4.30am was the ideal time for photographs; then the sun would fill the natural arc of Goðafoss with light, a low, warm-coloured morning delight. My schoolboy physics reminded me that the sun would be well below the magic 42°, the limit of its elevation that will create – from the waterfall's mist – a single refraction rainbow. It should be very good.

It probably was, but we didn't get up; we aren't completely stupid.

———— ◆ ————

Akureyri is the capital of North Iceland with a population of about 14,000, with, amongst other attractions, three memorial museums and Listigar-ðurinn, a public park and botanical garden with various types of trees and over 400 Icelandic plants. My immediate interest is the pool. Every town in Iceland has a swimming pool, usually geothermally heated and part of social normality. Swimming in open-air hot bathwater in view of ice-topped peaks is different, wonderfully different – cleansing, relaxing and just good. At the edge there are usually secondary pools where hot water, up to 45°C in some cases, will drain you away, assuming you can even get into the water. I close my eyes and forget the world. Tomorrow it is on to Reykjavik and another trip will be over. Tomorrow.

Just after midnight on 23 January 1973 a 2 kilometre-long fissure opened to the east of Heimaey, the town on the island of the same name, the largest of Vestmannaeyjar (the Westmann Islands) off Iceland's southern edge. From the fissure poured lava, blood-red lava glowing like the fires of hell in the night. Most, but not all, of the islanders retreated to the mainland, returning five months later to discover that their island had grown by over a square mile and that nearly half the town had been destroyed. The statistics of the eruption are outstanding. Over one and a half million cubic metres of ash were swept out of what remained of the town. The new land comprised 240 million cubic metres of lava which had spewed out at 1,100°C (2,012°F) and was cooled by dowsing with six million tons of sea water in an effort to halt its relentless drive.

There are two volcanoes today, Eldfell having been created by the 1973 eruption and joining Helgafell to create a twin pair of cones to the south-east of the new town. Helgafell is a disappointment. From afar it looks like the classical volcanic cone and it is with a mounting sense of excitement that I climb the last section of loose lava gravel and sharp, welded lava rock. A snow bunting twitters away to my left, laughing – as it turns out – at what is about to happen next, when I find that the volcanic dish is shallow and filled with grass and wind-blown rubbish. The view, however, is spectacular, taking in most of the fifteen islands of the Westmann archipelago. An incongruous panorama dial names the islands, except Surtsey. The eye is inevitably drawn to this huge Dundee cake, the world's newest land, born after a four-year gestation that started in 1963.

Northward, the edges of Eldfell are startlingly coloured with the browns, reds and oranges of burnt rock. The warmth of the sub-lava magna can still be felt through the feet. Dig down – use a stick, not your hand – for a foot or so and drop in a piece of paper. It chars, turns black and crinkles. Smoke wisps up and then it explodes in flames. I wish, silently, that I had my Trangia. Oh, to boil a kettle on red-hot rock.

The walk back to the town through the new lava fields is strange. Weird shapes abound, here a Red Indian profile, there a church steeple. The journey through the lava forest ends at the town, a fish-smelling old port, seedy and in need of a coat of paint, yet vibrant and friendly. Beyond, the huge sea cliffs of the northern edge of Heimaey form a sharp ridge that offers an airy walk. In spring those cliffs are alive with auks and gulls, and my favourite bird, the gannet.

On a sea of evening light Páll Helgason steers his boat towards the sun, poking it between stacks and through arches, sometimes into gaps that leave me thinking I can touch the rock walls on either side. Here and there the ropes of egg and bird collectors flap against the cliffs. Páll tells me that no one catches puffin any more, not since the government tried to tax the hunt. But every eating house in town has puffin on the menu, I say, where do they come from? Who knows? he asks with a grin.

As we head back towards Heimaey I watch the last of the light tinkering with the wave-tops. I have seen photographs of orca, both still and movie, close-up and underwater, but nothing prepares me for the sight of a real one that scythes out of the water 100 metres or so away from the boat. There is a triangular fin and the arch of a back. It is a lazy movement but in an instant it is gone. In that instant the power and grace of the animal is evident. It is an awesome sight. Páll tells me he once had his boat in the centre of a leaping school of orca. In Norway, I tell him, the orca is called *spekkhogger*, flesh ripper. He smiles.

That night we eat puffin, just to be sociable. It is dark red with the crumbling consistency of pig's liver. I expect it to taste mildly fishy or, perhaps, mildly gamey. It is neither. It is vile.

# Winter

From an early age Hafþor Ferdinandson has been in love with 4WD vehicles. He bought one as soon as his bank balance could survive the impact of bringing all that fancy engineering from Japan to Iceland and immediately set about modifying it to suit his own very special requirements. Soon, he became the first man to drive on an Icelandic glacier. Today he has also become the first man to drive across Langjökull, and the first to drive across Drangajökull. His newest toy, a Toyota Land Cruiser with Gumbo Monster Mudder tyres so big that oxygen is required when you reach your seat, has CB, a radio telephone, an anenometer and a Loran radar set fixed in to transmitters on Greenland, Iceland and Norway. It can accurately tell him where he is to the nearest ten metres or so.

Hafþor is a big man, nearly two metres tall and

Hafþor's truck.

Upskiing in the Þingvellir National Park.

weighing over 100 kilograms. He is immensely strong, but also shyly gentle and has great sense of humour. He decided to put up with Tony and I in order to support our attempt to cross the interior plateau in winter, using ski parachutes to help our progress.

So we sat in the swimming pool in Reykjavik knowing that outside we had all the food, all the clothing, the skis, the chutes. Everything. But we also had the attendant holding the door for us as we came out of the changing room because the wind was threatening to tear it off its hinges, as well as relentlessly trying to move the deep end up to the shallow end. In the Icelandic centre the weather was worse, with snow drifting to over seven metres, and temperatures down around −20°C (−4°F) to act as a good prelude to wind-chill calculations. Our pool was the middle of three small heated tubs and had a jet spray to it, a powerful jacuzzi that relaxed our minds as well as our bodies. We talked and gradually came to a decision that was quite contrary to the one we had held when we hauled ourselves out of our clothes a half-hour before. Then it had all been defeat and misery. Now it was still defeat – well, you have to be realistic – but cheerfulness. We would give it a go. What was the worst that could happen? Failure? If you travel in the Arctic you must never expect to succeed every time. Worse? No chance, not with Hafþor's truck.

The journey had been impressively straightforward to date. We were intending to reach Hveravellir, now about thirty kilometres away, to be dropped there and to get out. We had stopped in Geysir for diesel and here it was, only three in the morning and we were half-way from the end of the road. Progress was occasionally slow but the big driver was coaxing the big wheels gently over and through the snow. Tony and I shared the navigation seat, and right now I was in the back, warm, comfortable and dozing gently.

I was brought rudely back to the real world by Tony's tripod coming off the top of the pile of clatch (odds and ends) piled up above the seat and hitting me on the head as the truck lurched to a halt, diving itself into a drift of deep snow. Hafþor eased us forward again. Yawn, settle down again. But not this time. This time there was no relief. Hafþor tried hard, but eventually admitted defeat and asked us if we would walk a little.

Five minutes later Tony and I were trudging

through deep snow, wishing we had spared the time to search out the snow shoes and wondering whether there had ever been a previous occasion in Iceland when the approach of a car had been heralded by walkers. All we needed was a red flag to warn the locals that we might be about to frighten the horses.

We walked for a mile or so, easily outpacing the vehicle which was soon just a pair of yellow lights back down the valley. We stopped. My nose had long since lost all feeling and I massaged it back into life. Tony gave me his thoughts on the situation – about how pleased he was to be wandering around at four in the morning, in the pitch black, in deep snow, in the cold, in the wind. I told him I was pissed off too. We lounged about and waited. The wind was worse now and Hafþor's anemometer was showing gusts to 60 kph. It only worked when he was stationary, but that was often.

By the time his ready smile reached us we were glad to see him and retreated to try to get warm and ask a few questions. There was, he said, a bridge about 300 metres away. If we could get to that things would be easier on the far side. So we got out and walked again. We walked 300 metres, then another 300, then several more. By the time we had walked half a dozen or more lots of 300 metres, we were losing enthusiasm. Tony offered to walk back towards the vehicle, now a long way off, and left me to think about it all.

To my left the shallow ridge that formed an edge of the valley rose up to finish at a shallow bump. It looked a reasonable enough distance, so I made my way towards it. The snow improved as the slope steepened and I made good time up the 100 metres to the ridge top and along to the 'summit'. I sat down on its rounded hump. The wind was still banging away, but there was an inner calm that was at variance with the agitation I had felt below. It may not have been sensible to climb alone up here at this time in these conditions, but it was little enough, and that straightforward. In exchange I had a view over the wide, flat-bottomed valley, a view that dissolved into the fish-fin ridge on the far side. To my other side the ridge tumbled away from below my hump. Below in the valley the yellow lights of Hafþor's truck jiggled up and down with his frantic efforts to ease it through the snow. Any noise it made was lost in the wind. Speaking of the wind, it was getting stronger and I was getting colder. Time for a little activity.

Back at the truck all was despondency in the gathering gloom. We abandoned the attempt to reach Hveravellir, accepted that the weather and conditions were against us and retreated back down the valley towards civilization. Morning found us at Gullfoss hastily trying to organize sleeping and eating. It was hours now since we had last eaten, hours more since there had been any sleep. Outside the wind grew even more savage and we cut short the one doomed attempt to raise the tent, retreating to the truck for a few minutes of poor slumber.

I woke stiff and cold, feeling as though I had been scrunched up like a paper bag. We decided to walk to the waterfall to see what Gullfoss, well known to us in the summer, had to offer in winter. The snow had drifted deep over the path that has been carved down to the chasm and we soon lost it, progressing by kicking steps into the hard snow. Above the chasm we stopped and I kicked out a shelf for the camera bags. Tony stomped past, stopped and peered into the chasm, setting up a shot. He turned back towards me, opened his mouth to speak and was gone. His feet had slipped from the kicked steps and he was sliding down a steep slope that ended, abruptly, at the chasm about twenty-five metres below. The square toe-cap of his Lundhag caught in the snow about two metres down. He teetered backwards, got close to topppling over, fell back into the snow, looked up and hissed *Jesus* through clenched teeth. He kicked good steps and we thought about it. A couple more feet and even if the toe had caught he would have gone over backwards. Then it would have been twenty-five metres of snow slide and a final trip down a thirty-metre vertical chasm into a mix of ice and ice-cold water. The Gullfoss gorge is – certainly in winter – a stopper. We would have fished Tony out two or three kilometres down after the water had knocked him around a bit, and given him a dreadful bootful since he was wearing his Lundhags.

'Jesus,' he whispered again when he reached me. 'We'll go,' I said, and we did. 'What would you have done if I'd gone down?' he asked when we were back on level ground.

'Put the Bronica in my rucsac and claimed it went down with you.'

Still, it sobered us a bit, and after we had taken several more shots we decided that we needed some sleep, to try to get our minds back in gear. Hafþor said he knew of a little hotel, and would we like to go there? Silly question. Offered a free bed and nosebag, Tony is there like a rat up a drainpipe. So we slept well, in a warm room with sheets, with a loo and a shower, and water that smelt of sulphur. Good place, Iceland, you can spend lots of cash on accommodation and finish up smelling like a boiled egg.

The following morning the room looked as though an expedition had broken out in it, so we fought all the bits back into the sacs, smiled sweetly at the girl on reception and left. Outside the wind had had its cutting edge dulled – possibly against the bones of my shoulders – and was wimpering miserably around the building, occasionally offering an aggressive bark. We leaned against the woodwork, noting that it needed a coat of paint. The receptionist, we decided, definitely needed a coat of looking at. Hafþor arrived.

He took us to the Þingvellir National Park where the clouds parted and the sun shone on square kilometres of snow that was so clean and pure it made me weep for all the time we had lost on the trip, and for the pleasure of being where I wanted to be.

Tony and I unpacked the Upski parachutes that we had so lovingly tended all the way from the UK. John White, loaner of the kit, had given Tony all the instruction we possessed on how to use them. The lesson had been given in a lay-by near Kendal on a soaking wet afternoon in February with an audience of coach-trippers on day release from the Satanic Mills. The lesson had started at 2.30 and finished at 2.38 with both instructor and pupil wet through and hacked off. Tony gave me the benefit of his wisdom as we stood on the edge of a mile-wide snow field and waved goodbye to Hafþor. See you on the other side, we called. Could be a long walk.

My lesson lasted about half the time of Tony's, terminating as he was explaining the purpose of the deadman's handle to me when a gust filled his chute and hauled him off in fine style. I adjusted the position of my skis, laid out the chute lines, hauled in the centre cord a little, clipped the controller into my climbing harness, thought about it a bit, hauled the lines up to give the nylon a bit of air, closed my eyes and gritted my teeth.

After a few hundred metres the pleasure overcame the apprehension. God, this is the way to travel. The chute is a perfect dish hovering a metre or so above the snow and hauling me downwind at a speed that would be unthinkable on Nordic skis. We go up a long, but steepish, slope and pause to catch our breath and share the experience. After only half an hour we can tack left and right – a must in general, as going downwind puts the canopy between you and the way ahead giving you no chance of avoiding rocks and ruts – so that we can move almost anywhere in an arc that is up to 45 degrees on either side of the wind. John had claimed it was just possible to go backwards (as it were), but you must talk to him about that. Suffice it to say that if the wind is going your way, get yourself a pair of skis – which must have a metal edge, and a fixed-heel binding – and a chute.

We were carrying light loads because it was our last day, but we averaged about 25kph with ease, and for a long while. At the far side we used Hafþor's truck to speed-check us, and in the light wind were easily making 45kph. Given a fair blow much higher speeds must be just as easy. After a while you lean back and enjoy the ride, letting the canopy haul directly from your waist to release all strain on the arms. The legs and knees take a belt – you are, after all, suffering most of the strains of downhill skiing and for longer at a stretch – but the distance travelled more than makes up for that. By the time we were packing the chutes we were both hooked and planning another trip. It is amazing what one good day will do.

SCANDINAVIA

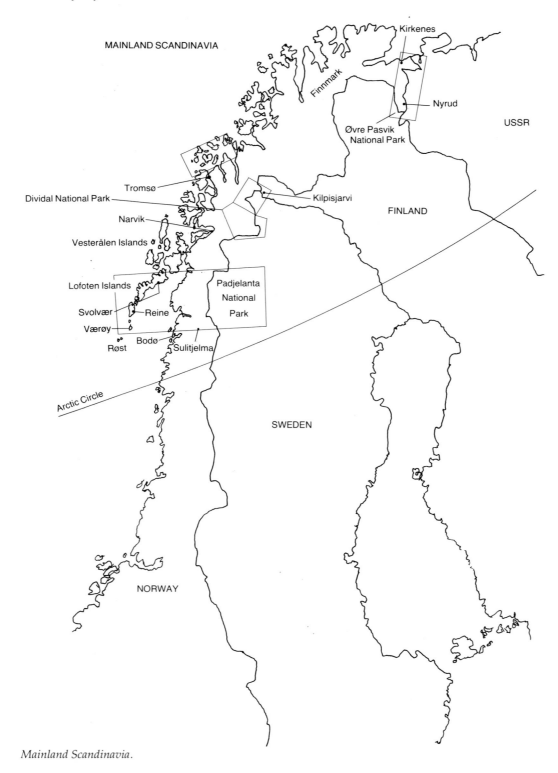

MAINLAND SCANDINAVIA

Kirkenes

Finnmark

Nyrud

Øvre Pasvik
National Park

USSR

Tromsø

Dividal National Park

Kilpisjarvi

FINLAND

Narvik

Vesterålen Islands

Lofoten Islands

Padjelanta
National
Park

Svolvær — Reine

Værøy

Røst   Bodø

Sulitjelma

SWEDEN

Arctic Circle

NORWAY

Mainland Scandinavia.

Technically, Scandinavia covers only the four mainland countries of Norway, Sweden, Finland and Denmark, even though most people also add Viking Iceland to the list. Of the four mainland countries, three have land above the Arctic Circle, and Norway is the most important of these.

Norway is a long thin country, only about fifteen kilometres wide near Narvik and Fauske, yet 1,800 kilometres from nose to toe measured along the crow-flying line. This is easy enough, but measuring along the coastline requires a *very* long ruler indeed. Norway, excluding Svalbard, is a third as big again as the UK with a population of only four million, most of whom live in Oslo, a fine city with one of the best museum complexes in Europe. All visitors to Oslo should see the Viking ships at least and Arctic travellers should make a point of going to the *Fram* museum, which pays homage to one of the most remarkable men and expeditions in the history of polar exploration. Between 1893 and 1896 Fridtjof Nansen attempted to reach the North Pole by deliberately entombing his ship, *Fram*, in the ice near Ostrova Novo Sibirskiye (the New Siberian Islands). Nansen, an excellent scientist, had realised that the polar ice drifted from east to west and reasoned that if he chose his entry point correctly the ice would tow his ship over the pole and release it near Canada. He and his men spent three winters trapped in the ice, but sadly the drift was south as well as west and the ship was released north of Svalbard having reached a point no closer than several hundred miles from the pole.

North of the Arctic Circle Norway has some fine mountainous country and Finnmark, an expanse of flatter tundra that offers a very different and, in winter, a very cold trip. East of Tromsø, the 'capital' of Arctic Norway, is Lyngen, a superb area of jagged peaks that is near paradise for the climber in winter. Southward the Øvre Dividal National Park offers excellent treks in both summer and winter. Further east, the border area with Russia is an interesting area, particularly within the Øvre Pasvik National Park where the quiet visitor can see brown bear and elk.

Sweden is a larger country than Norway with a compact Arctic region dominated by a mountain chain that runs along its western edge, near the border with Norway. This chain includes Kebne-kaise at 2,111 metres, the highest mountain in the Scandinavian Arctic. (There are higher mountains in southern Norway and in other parts of the Arctic, including Iceland.) The peak can be climbed as part of *Kungsleden*, the King's Route, an excellent if over-populated route and one of the very few waymarked trails in the Arctic. The route starts at Ammarnäs, south of the Circle, and traverses the Peljekaise National Park. It skirts the Sareks National Park to the east, reaches Kebne-kaise and ends at Abisko. Abisko lies on a lake and near a National Park that is famous for its animal and bird life and its woods of birch and pine.

The southern mountain parks of Södra Storfjället, Sareks and Padjelanta have a limited flora and fauna, but some fine rugged scenery. Sareks is especially good, but is difficult to reach and explore. Further east, Arctic Sweden is flatter and less inspiring, although the Muddus National Park between Jokkmokk and Malmberget has fine forest and marshland. Elsewhere these plains are home to the great grey owl and the shy brown bear.

Arctic Finland, in contrast to both Norway and Sweden, is flat, a vast tundra forest with lakes that is ideal country for the pulka-pulling skier but a little less inspiring for the walker. Organized ski treks exist, their routes following set trails with accommodation *en route*. One, the Border-Border Trek, is claimed to be the world's longest ski trek. It goes from Tornio, near the Swedish border, to Kuusamo near the border with the USSR. The fit and competent should cross the 360 kilometres in about seven days.

Other treks cross the two fine Arctic National Parks, Uhro Kekkonen to the east, and Lemmenjoki Park in the north, a park that links with the Øvre Anarjokka Park that lies in Norway, to the east of Kautokeino, capital of Norwegian Lappland. The capital of Finnish Lappland is Rovaniemi, home of Father Christmas – or so it is said – and a town that easily overcomes the embarrassment of having everything but the airport lying south of the Arctic Circle. To the north-east of the town is the Pyhätunturi Park, another fine unspoilt forest area. Elsewhere, the Malla Park near Kilpisjärvi is famous for its flora, and walkers can reach the three-countries stone, where the three Arctic Scandinavian countries meet at a single spot.

Summer – Lappland

Many years ago Tony and I sat drinking coffee and swapping experiences. Tony had just returned from Iceland, his epic cycle tour, and I was back from Switzerland, buoyed up by time spent working at the Research Station on the Jungfraujoch. I told him about the sunsets, when the Jungfrau had turned pink and I was the only person on the Aletsch. He told me about the Icelandic landscapes, harsh yet wondrous, of the coloured rocks in Landmannalaugar and the emptiness. Time we did something together, I suggested. He agreed, but we had some difficulty in deciding what. My conversion to the Arctic was still a little while away. I talked of Via Ferrata and Alta Vie, he talked of Lofoten and the Padjelanta Park. Ultimately it was decided that we would try *Kungsleden*, the long-distance footpath through Arctic Sweden. I could tell he was keen from the fact that he didn't mention it again for a couple of years. We went here and there, but *Kungsleden* lay fallow. Until 1985 that is.

———— ◆ ————

At the time I almost lived up to my nickname, Bone – close to Tone, and closer still to bone idle. This idea of a walk that was twice the length of the Pennine Way – or so Dick said – sounded horrid. I'm a *cyclist*; four weeks of tramping with a rucsac would crease me. The nickname was also used by those laughing at my structure – totally devoid of superfluous fat, so that any backpack was uncomfortable. As Dick often pointed out, he had seen more flesh on a wooden leg, and more fat on the breakfast bacon. Today rucsacs can be delightful to carry, a world apart from my heap of the 1960s, but in those days I really did not like backpacking. I stayed quiet.

In the mid-1980s it was trendy to ATB (all-terrain bike) up famous mountains. The purpose of such deeds seemed obscure – why carry a bike up a mountain only to have to push it down again? Mountains are for walking, ATBs are for paths and tracks. At the time I was writing for *Bicycle Times* and one day Dick's Arctic footpath came to mind. Why not see if ATBs were any good for *real* wilderness touring? Why not cycle up *Kungsleden*? I could knock up some lightweight special frames and do a positive test on their value. Pete, the editor of the magazine, and Dick were both keen. We met and a plan was conceived: Pete and Dick would get the next round in, then organise the logistics of food, route and transport. I just had to supply three bikes. Easy. Maps of Lappland were fingered and any snippets of information gathered. I begged and was rewarded. Reynolds, manufacturers of quality bicycle tubing, came up with some special stuff. The bikes had to survive a six-week tour in total wilderness, with fifty kilograms of camping gear, and they *must* not break. They didn't. The final creations weighed a mere ten kilograms, about the same as a top-class racing bike and about half the weight of most ATBs.

Information, even from the Scandinavian tourist boards, was difficult to obtain. You are cycling through Lappland? It cannot be done. You must have a sprocket loose. We carried on and eventually devised a plan. It took about a year to organize, partly because the idea blossomed in the summer, too late for that year; it is not the sort of place to go cycling in the winter.

Just in time, Dick developed a viral nasty that made him lethargic. I couldn't see the difference, but his vet insisted he wasn't fit enough, even when summer came. His disappointment at missing out added to the way the illness was making him feel. His absence necessitated some quick adjustments to strategy. We continued with our three-man tent, a Phoenix Phor-3, and I must say, the extra space was much appreciated on several occasions, not least on 6 August when it snowed all day and I thrashed Pete at cards.

The final plan deviated from the original and we decided to go from Sulitjelma in Norway to Abisko, at the top of *Kungsleden*, in Sweden. This allowed relatively easy access from Bodø, the start of *Kungsleden* (Ammarnäs) being a sod of a place to reach. Because of a combination of so many unknowns, we, or should I say they – Pete and Dick did all the work, I just made the bikes – made

The Lappish church, Staloluokta, Sweden.

a total cock-up of ability and distance. One stretch took three overnights where the great plan allowed just one. But so what? We had five more weeks and there was definitely no rush. There was nothing to rush for and nowhere to rush to.

———— ◆ ————

Staloluokta, our first place of rest, is an oasis of delight. Four days from the nearest tarmac discourages the average vandal, factory unit or traffic warden. On the southern shores of Virihaure, a huge lake rimmed by glaciers and wildnerness, is this stunningly simple Lappish community. Although it boasts little in the way of modern conveniences, it offers many services: mountain hut, camping area and thunderbox, basic shop – in truth very basic and equally expensive – bakery, fish, fish and more fish, church and pure honesty.

Aches and anxieties are dissolved in the *bastu*, the village sauna. To the mountain people this

The Lappish church, Staloluokta, Sweden.

53

daily pleasure is a social event where visiting travellers are welcome, but experiencing the *bastu* requires some tough decisions. The heat can be intense for those not used to saunas, so intense breathing becomes difficult. Some of the local hard cases delight in the sadistic pleasure of ousting strangers by continually watering the stones. Relief waits outside, but it is a masochistic type of relief – icy-fresh river water that is cold beyond belief. Between the two lies a jetty, home to millions of razor-sharp fangs waiting just for you, and your delicate, softened-up softer than usual, parts. You know where I mean. After leaving the hut, hesitation is *not* recommended. The thermal shock is, by comparison, bliss.

A real mountain *bastu* is one of those experiences not to be missed, and all you could want after a hard day's toil, a wonderful relaxant. However, becoming accustomed to the Scandinavian way takes some adjustment. Nudity to them is a much more relaxed affair. We Brits are terribly prudish and you may be, as I was, a little uneasy at first. Not to worry; the welcome and conversation soon takes over as you mix with the whole village: small kids, their little old grannies, Lappish reindeer herdsmen and the odd Swedish blonde. I was worried about the latter but I can assure you here that there is little cause for concern. The thermal shock of zero degrees water is so intense no one can tell how pleased you are to see them.

Another rarity at Staloluokta is the church, even to a heathen like me. Its charm lies in its basic simplicity, a hemispherical structure of birch trunks, wind-proofed around the outside with turf bricks. In contrast, light comes through triple-glazed window units (those bloody salesmen get everywhere). On the floor birch twigs and greenery are over-carpeted with reindeer furs. A wood fire in the centre adds to the warmth, the smoke exiting, together with yet more of those mosquitos, through a central hole in the roof. It was a well-attended service, families coming both from the village and down from the hills. The minister strummed on a guitar to the wailing and life felt wonderful. The praise was complete and we all departed, the minister helicoptering off to the high mountains to give worship to the farmers herding their stock. It was a peaceful day.

The journey so far had been an eye-opener. The mountain range along the border between Norway and Sweden is wild and wonderful with 2,000-metre peaks soaring over seemingly endless glaciers with romantic names like Blåmannsisen and Salajekna. I totally lost myself in the remoteness. The Sorjus pass, 1,000 metres high, gives (relatively) good access to Lappland from civilisation. Just down there is Sweden, we concluded in amazement.

We had decided this part would be tough, and for once we were right. One steep 330-metre climb had to be done twice in order to lift all the gear. Karrimor had made two special rucsacs, the bike's top tube clamping on to the reinforced cover flap so that the whole bike sat across your back. Putting your head through the main-frame triangle, or carrying the bike over your shoulder is uncomfortable in the extreme. My method, although no good in woods, is comfortable and keeps the centre of gravity close to your back. The pannier bags normally stay on, but this climb came only one day into the trip and with a fortnight's food on board I couldn't even lift my bike. After eating most of the load the method is wonderful and wholeheartedly recommended.

Our journey was now planned as downhill all the way to Vietas, some six days away. It was pretty good, but we left the rugged mountains with mixed feelings. The vast openness of Lappland may be less spectacular but the trails are flatter, well-trodden and rideable, sometimes. One thing we knew for sure – beyond here was the unknown, and it looked big.

The outflow of Sårjåsjaure (*jaure* is Swedish for lake), at its eastern end, forms a spectacular waterfall, the spectacle being the volume rather than the length of descent. The backdrop of the lake and the distant Sorjusjokka glacier is breathtaking, helped by the fluffy puffs of cloud stuck to the sky. I like it here. Last night we camped a metre short of the border, a beautiful spot between the upper and lower Sorjus lakes. It was a time to dry out, three days of solid rain having dampened all but our spirits, and to finish our excess of the other kind of spirits before attempting to cross the border. The border is spectacularly unimpressive. A small cairn is the only evidence, making passports a waste of time. Never mind, maybe later I will get a Swedish stamp to add to my collection.

Our evening meal was disturbed by a lone walker, a young German lad, extremely knowledgeable and pleasant. He walked by night and slept by day, the midday sun being too hot for him. It was a novel idea and one we appreciated later when the weather improved. He was reluctant to admit his nationality, and usually claimed he was Austrian to save any possible embarrassments of the truth. He too had discovered that the Nordic people have long memories. He sampled some of Pete's brew and continued his walk.

At the time Pete was fifty, making the challenge of his biking this wilderness more meaningful than my personal quest. He had brought with him a wealth of experience and he shared many a story of his love of the outdoors. In practical terms an experienced camper is obvious; there is no need to issue orders, each knows what has to be done and when, without debate. Arriving at a suitable pitching site, I would erect the tent and Pete would fetch water and have a brew ready by the time we piled in. His kitchen area was out of bounds to me at cook times so I was forced to use the (extremely useful) rear door of the tent. Tidiness is not a fetish but a necessity in a confined space. I would win no prizes for being tidy, but the main aggravation was the fact that we had, between us, eight identical black Karrimor pannier bags. Never, ever was the item you desperately needed in the first bag, second bag . . .

Pete's cooking was obviously the result of many hours over a hot Trangia. His pride in being able to cook three hot meals a day for two of us, on just one litre of meths in six days, was shattered when one pensioner told us that two weeks was more her time scale for such a luxurious amount of fuel. They exchanged recipes like a pair of old women and we departed.

Food was mainly dehydrated but Pete would pep up meals by mixing in spices and niceties he kept in redundant Kodak film cans. On miserable days when both of us were low, he would delve into the depths of a pannier and give me a mini Mars bar or some peanuts. The old man looked after me well.

There were many obstacles to tax our resolve and our language. Bridgeless rivers were waded, often several times, back and fro until all the kit was safely across. Sometimes we had to rope up, sometimes we were frozen numb. Snow fields were ploughed through and ice cliffs were given absolute respect. Rain that made Scotland seem like the Sahara was no sweat, but the midget trees! They were even worse than the mosquitos. You can, up to a point (and we did up to that point), protect yourself against them with jungle gels and mustard gases, but the trees give no mercy and there are hours of them between Staddajakkstugorna, a

River crossing, Sweden.

mountain hut on the side of Kapasluoppal, and Staloluokta. Walkers with rucsacs have created a path through these Arctic forests, a highway that reflects the profile of a backpacker – narrow around the legs and very wide around the rucsac. A bicycle is not profiled the same and the pannier bags were constantly grabbed, causing many a rude word. Progress was very slow, so slow we were genuinely concerned about the possibility of getting much further. We had no idea how much of Lappland was covered with these nasties. Luckily it turned out to be an isolated incident but we had nightmares about a recurrence.

A similar problem occurs on bridges, wire rope and wood affairs that swing, like a worn-out bra strap, in the slightest breeze. The smaller bridges offered just a single plank of wood, too narrow to cycle across and too narrow to push the bike from the side. A tight rope act is required but this is restricted by the near-vertical suspension cables. Oh God, not another; perhaps it will be easier to wade the river, but then again perhaps not . . .

Carrying a tent where mountain huts are prolific may seem an unnecessary burden, but it allows total flexibility and we soon discovered the

The waterfall at the exit of Sårsjåsjaure, Sårjåsjaurestugan, Sweden.

benefits of camping where we chose. The huts are predominantly in valleys near rivers, and invariably the local area was swarming with mosquitos. Camping high, between the huts, we enjoyed insect-freeing breezes and spectacular night views of the midnight sun. We weren't alone in having such ideas; many Swedes prefer this philosophy because it also gets you away from the Germans. No matter how hard you try, they always beat you to the huts.

Isolation and wilderness travel require a special attitude to life. Decisions can have alarming consequences and non-decisions can be fatal. Choice of company is desperately important. Can you share the same confines, for long periods of time, and where does your tolerance level lie? Group

On the spongs of the Padjelanta National Park, Sweden.

Mountain hut, Norway.

travel can relieve some of these pressures but it can also result in 'ganging up', for the silliest of reasons. Unlike the kids in *Lord of the Flies* we had no real problems, but the remoteness does make me anti-social. Both Pete and I found mountain huts overwhelming. It was like being in a super-market during late-night shopping, with that overpowering sensation that you are losing your space. The occasional meeting of a backpacker on the trail was different, and friendly words were always exchanged. Weather, where to pitch and where to fish are typically topical. One meeting half-way across a stream led to a drinking session. I spied a 'Backpackers Club' sweatshirt. Are you English? I enquired. Oh no, I run the Dutch section of the club. Well, I explained, the old codger with me is one of the founder members. He'll be along in a minute. The nearest bank was headed for, and out came their supply of local moonshine. It tasted far worse than I imagine my four-day-old socks would – a memorable moment remembered for the wrong reason, not least for the expression of anguish on Pete's face as the brew hit his tonsils.

Most impressive was the number of retired peo-ple we met backpacking. They came mainly from Stockholm or, at least, southern Sweden and most had been trudging these paths for decades. They seemed to know everything and anything about the area: the names of butterflies and Arctic flowers flooded out from their memory banks. One old fellow told me, apologetically, that he and his wife only did ten to fifteen kilometres daily these days. He added quickly that there was no hurry any more. Don't apologise; I think that is fantastic and I hope – I pray – I am able to enjoy a similar style of retirement. Also notable was the number of fathers and sons out together, for perhaps three weeks with a tiny pack of basic provisions – a tent, survival knife and a fishing rod. This is country where it is easy to live off the land, or out of the rivers, and to learn about life.

Most encounters started in the same way, with a question about the bikes. 'Why the bikes?' 'Why do you carry such loads on your back?' was our most popular response. It's easy to push a bike and it belts downhill. The truth is that uphill the extra weight made it a little harder than walking, but the weight was not directly on my back, a fact that I appreciated. We could push our laden bikes at a roughly typical walking pace up passes. On the flat life was in our favour and we left most walkers behind. Downhill we were in a different league. On one occasion, on a 300-metre climb from the spectacular bridge over the Härrakalou, a green, algae-filled river that drains a huge area of the Sarek National Park, we were accompanied by two fit Dutch lads, who maintained a similar pace. On the descent that followed, leading to Låddejåkkåstugan – *stugan* is hut – about six kilometres, we beat them down by forty-five minutes, freewheeling all the way. Mountain bikes are good.

The going was often helped, considerably, by *spong*s, wooden walkways built over boggy areas by the Lappish people. The quality of these 'roads' varies with their age, the newest three-plank *spong*s allowing us to maintain incredible speeds. However, occasionally the *spong*s also bridge ravines making for brave crossings especially when you have no idea of their quality. The *spong*s are home to another source of interest – food – if you are desperate and very quick, because lemming live beneath them. They are boring, grey-coloured, hamster-like devices that scurry away at the first sound of our Michelin Interroutes; I suppose I would leg it too if some mad giant was riding his bike over my roof. What I would have given for a sesame bap. Dehydrated packet breakfast, dinner and supper drives me potty.

The trails of Padjelanta are not that tough, which is ideal for our bikes. We are now getting close to the flanks of Akka, a seven-peaked mountain that has been visible for four or five days. Now I can

Ninety-year-old Lapp, Sweden.

understand why travellers rave about its obviousness. We camped about five kilometres north of Låddejåkkåstugan on the open moors by a stream that thundered towards the distant watershed from Virihaure. Coffee was followed by yet another sunset, the best possible after-dinner entertainment. More stories, more coffee and another try with Pete's transistor radio. We have tried to use it before but the mountain reception is far from good. I am going to tell Roy Plumley's successor where he can stick the one luxury he allowed us to bring. The only programme our free-with-petrol tranny would pick up was Soviet propaganda, in English, late at night. In desperation we dug a hole, a big hole, in the depths of the night – brilliant sunshine at one in the morning – put the radio on full and buried it. That shut it up.

We didn't make Abisko, chickening out as the weather worsened and the forecasts began to sound even more dire. At last we had reached a road that led to a place called Ritjemjokk where we telephoned home and did all the civilized things in life; like sitting on a loo seat, for a long time.

From Ritjemjokk our maps and information showed ferry routes along Sitasjaure to the Norwegian border. This was an alternative route we had considered in planning so we were dismayed by fresh news. The boats are there to serve Lappish communities, or rather they *were* there. Sweden has gone anti-nuclear in its power-generating policy and consequently vast hydro-power stations have been built in the northern lake areas. For reasons better known to themselves, the Swedes made no provision for salmon runs so the huge lakes are now devoid of fish and the Lapps have left. The ferries have left too.

Controversy is rife this year, the first summer after Chernobyl. This is radioactive reindeer and salmon country. The Lappish diet is restricted to these basic foods and the result has been both anger and concern. However, the Lappish people are more concerned about the plight of their traditional fishing waters, the loss of which is forever,

much longer than it takes contamination from Russia to decay. The Lappish understand that the levels of radioactivity will eventually decay; they are far from happy about the fall-out but it is secondary to their fish problem. But this is not news. Did you see any post-Chernobyl documentary about the lifetime plight of the salmon lakes? I didn't either, but then anti-hydro protesting is not vogue in these 'green' times.

Our chief problem is where to go from here. We have three basic alternatives. One, to bike up *Kungsleden* to Abisko and get wet; two, to cycle 600 kilometres around the road via Kiruna and Abisko to Narvik for our journey home; or three, hire a plane to take us somewhere else. At this stage we had discovered that *Kungsleden* is a motorway for German 'Pennine-wayers'. No thanks, that's not for me; I'm even more of a recluse now. So we hired the *fiskflug*, a float plane used to take fish from Lappish settlements to market and the outside

On the rocks of Muokkeris, Sweden.

Midnight, seen from a sleeping bag, Sweden.

world. Negotiations complete, we sardined our dismantled bikes into the Cessna. Up, up and away, through the valleys to the north end of Sitasjaure and just into Norway once again.

The contrast was stark, an area devoid of anything green, or so it seemed from the air. On landing we saw that small flowers and dying orchids line the rubble road, but the landscape was dominated by huge folds of dark grey rocks. They resembled whales lined up outside the headmaster's office – huge humps sprawled over many kilometres. They made a pleasant change, their undulations much easier to negotiate than the bogs of Sweden. Here it was even possible to freewheel at speed without the risk of the front wheel submerging into a pool of smelly black moss. Time and terrain allowed some short walking, the mountains being steep, yet rounded, firm rock with interesting views.

It was time for reflection: are these mountain bikes any good or are we totally crazy? Well I think the answer was yes, to both questions. There were times when the bikes were a pain but also times when they were of great benefit. On the whole the trip so far was a success. We had cycled on the road from Bodø to Fauske and on to Sulitjelma; pushed the bikes over to Sorjusjaure; ridden and swum our way to Staloluokta within the Padjelanta National Park; and then thrashed our way on the faster tracks through Arasluokuoktastugorna, Låddejåkkåstugana and Kisurisstugan to Akkastugorna and a ferry to Ritjemokk, before cycling by road to Vietas; and gone by plane to Sitastugan at the north-west end of Sitasjaure. We had covered large distances both on-road and off the road, totally independent of public transport. The physical and mental experience had made us healthier people and proof of the excitement and joy of the trip is that I have now become one of the greatest bores on mountain biking in the Swedish Arctic.

Fishing boat, Lofoten.

At last we were back in the mountains. Sadly, the forecasts came true, with sleet and snow making views vanish forever. *Kungsleden* must be hell in these conditions. We escaped just in time and it was downhill all the way to Narvik.

The hydrofoil left Narvik in the early evening bound for Svolvær, on what turned out to be one of the loveliest journeys I have ever taken. The day was idyllic, with clear blue skies and temperatures up in the shirt-sleeves. Our 'bus of the sea' was off, skimming the waves and rearranging the dancing patterns of the evening light. We were travelling along the Lofoten Wall, an apt description for the mountains protecting this huge sea

fjord. The mountains hang everywhere, big vertical peaks just waiting to be climbed. Perhaps next time. Lofoten is a small group of islands sticking out off Arctic Norway rather like the Outer Hebrides do off Scotland. I've heard they are quite beautiful, and I hope so. I hope too that this weather holds. To our right, off the tip of Tjedløya, sea eagles bask in the sun, a great pack of them. They look mean. Oblivious to us swanning by, they show no emotions, unlike me, all full of excitement at so many and so close.

Later that evening, after a brief stop at Lødingen, the Arctic light was once again tantalising. Four Spanish lads tried their best to explain why they had returned. It is the sun, they said; it is such a different sun, so much more beautiful than ours, cooler yet with more warmth. I can sympathize; I have often struggled to get this difficult explanation across. The mountains around Svolvær are spiky and big. The back light from the day's end made them even more dramatic and the sea was on fire. Rings of mist were forming as the temperature dropped around the peaks. That's a two-thousandths at f11; where is all this light coming from? I just don't believe how fantastic it is. This is going to be a good trip.

My first sight of a Lofoten fishing port was on a small island off Svolvær. The hydrofoil entered the harbour, revealing the characteristic wooden docks, with brightly-painted buildings sticking out

of the fjord on spidery sticks. Behind there are vertical cliffs, a dynamic backdrop dwarfing the harbour to insignificance. And this place is hardly on the map.

I was sad to leave the boat, we had made many friends despite the trip being only a few hours long. It was a good day and Svolvær looked rather a special place, but we were now tired and a campsite was priority. Kabelvåg campsite is a few kilometres beyond the village, on the flanks of a charming little beach and remarkably civilized. Campers are welcome to use communal kitchens and dining rooms, and there are washing facilities for both us and our clothes, each of which are in need. I haven't been to an organized campsite for

Get yourself a Tony Oliver! Reine, Lofoten.

Boats at Nusfjörd, Lofoten.

Evening light over the salmon pens, Svolvær, Lofoten.

The Arctic Ocean near Bodø.
Evening over Kirkefjorden.

perhaps fifteen years, so all this is new to me. I do not know what to do and sneak looks at everyone else, while the 'real' campers pause to stare as we sit on Karrimats eating supper. We soon learn that the huts give relief from yet more mosquitos, but compared to central Lappland insects these are either timid or full-up.

Lofoten is the most beautiful place I have known, yet I find it one of the most difficult places to write about. Clichés and superlatives are rampant in the log that I kept on the trip. What do you say when you actually go beyond the realms of astonishment, amazement and incredibility? Each day there was a new sight and each day I was pushing the ability of these words to cope with my thoughts. Every bend reveals another staggering visual feast and it is all to do with the light, the dynamic mountain ridges, the pure white sandy beaches and the undisturbed peace. Each day is too short. There is so much to see, even though it is all basically made of the same ingredients. Perhaps I am abnormal in my endless fetish for light and patterns, but I don't give a damn.

The most beautiful evening (perhaps of my life) was on Flakstadøya. Pete and I took an afternoon ferry from Leknes to Napp, and sweltered the bikes over an unnamed pass to Vareid. We were on the south side of a small sea fjord, the head of which formed a junction for the road to Nusfjord. The setting sun – it was now mid-August, so the sun just dipped below the horizon – would round the headland of Flakstad village and dance over some tiny skerries off the shore. We were only a metre from the only road, but the number of cars that passed was easily beaten by the number of coffees drunk. Yet another master meal was prepared by *le chef*, Pete, and we ate and drank, and watched an incredible show of lights, all of it free and just for us. Divers worked around the fjord and we did absolutely nothing, and said almost less. Speech wasn't necessary; we were both absorbed, miles away, perhaps with loved ones, perhaps . . . well, who cares? Ten o'clock, time for a swim in the Arctic Ocean – well described as bracing – more coffee and then more sky watching. The sun slipped over Flakstad church and the light show began. Even after the sun vanished, amazement continued. Flakstad was drowning in mist, backlit from the northern sky. We fell asleep wondering what we might be missing.

Arctic sunsets can last many hours; I once watched one sun take four hours to touch the sea, and then it immediately started into reverse and rose again. In equatorial areas the sun drops like a lead brick into the sea, light to dark taking only minutes. Here the sun, if you stand still all day, will just circle the sky around you. Unless it's raining of course . . .

Henningsvær, Nusfjord, Reine are all the way the picture postcards show them, and a great deal more besides. The fishing villages only come alive for the season when frantic fleets of boats fill their harbours to the brim. For the winter traveller the climate is harsh, very cold, very windy and very close to the sea. A nasty combination. Now, in summer, the attitude is relaxed. Henningsvær is so quiet, and the sun so warming that a beer is absolutely necessary in a rather super establishment. The locals have obviously never tried a good pint of 6X; how can they drink this stuff? And it's £3 a glass.

On the other hand, food in cafés is excellent value. Whilst suffering another scorching day, we sought refuge in the eating house at Ramberg. There was no menu; you simply asked for what you wanted. The hostess suggested plaice, a less common fish for these areas, and not a particular favourite with my palate. We settled for salmon – bloody salmon again – which arrived as three huge steaks complete with white sauce, carrots and new potatoes. We then had a bowl of fruit salad, and there was change from the price of a glass of beer. This left me staggered as well as very satisfied.

Reine is phenomenal. It is said to be the most photographed village in Norway. I find this hard to believe; it sees little good weather and the trigger-happy Japanese and American tourists are down south. But forget all that, this place is exquisite. Little red huts stick out in the sea, the backdrop is spiky Snowdon-sized mountains straight up, and the place is deserted. The surrounding hills offer fine walking, scrambling and technical climbing. (Take care in planning a walking tour: one guy we talked to came across an impossible cliff which required a two-day detour.)

Reine was our base for several days. From it we cycled to the end of the road, a village called Å; yes, just the one letter. There are, apparently, three such places in the world and I wonder how the others compare in magnificence. From here, the south-ernmost tip of Moskenes penninsula, we took some fine walks.

The most spectacular of our walks was from Reine itself. One of the joys of touring unusual places is the variety of accommodation. Like most of the fishing villages, Reine offers summer travellers the use of the vacated fishing huts, called *rorbu*s. Rechristened 'Rambos', a reflection of their basic and rugged form, they offered us refuge from a rare rainstorm, and gave us a safe place to store excess baggage. We left the *rorbu* and attacked one of the 1,000-metre peaks overlooking the village. A long climb through short vegetation was not helped by my taking my mountain bike. I had come to Lofoten to photograph these beasts in real mountains for my forthcoming catalogue, so I pushed away. The shots were going to look terrific, but this was ridiculous – the very thing I had been cynical about and did not wish to do I was doing; carrying a bike both up and down a mountain. What a waste of time.

The view over Reine, Hamnöy and Kirkefjorden from the top of the climb is incredible, making an unreal backdrop for my equally fantastic work of art. Right, a roll of K25 I think. Where the hell is my film? Christ, I've forgotten it, it's back in the *rorbu*. I can see the hut down there, just a tiny pimple. Four hours of hell for nought. Pete finds this hilarious; he has been dying to get his own back for various things for ages and this comes close to the perfect opportunity. I am quite a pleader at times and this occasion surpassed all previous pleads imaginable. Pete had a roll of Ektachrome 200 and a Gold 100 print film. Hobson's choice really, so I had both.

After the photo session we ate and sunbathed naked, taking advantage of the amazing heat and the warm breeze that kept away the mozzies. Who will ever believe that I lay there, stripped naked, 1,000 metres up on top of a hill that is 300 kilometres north of the Arctic Circle? It was a beautiful place. Below, fishing boats and floating buses ploughed the fjord and seas. The only other noise was from huge bumble-bees, flying like World War II planes, with a low drone that dropped even lower as they shot over my nose. They turned out to be totally placid; just as well, since they are the size of hornets. At five o'clock we wandered back; after all, it might get dark in fifteen days' time.

Each time we crossed the causeway over to the tiny island of Reine, we paused and photographed. The view is as good as anyone could hope, yet each time it is different. The sun on its endless tour round and round the sky gives shadows and hues of infinite variety. If you don't like

Pete at Sorjushytta, Norway.

the lighting, wait, calculate your required angle of sunlight, and return. The morning sun gives direct brilliance, while evening's afterglows offer backlighting and romance.

We left Reine with many memories and hopes of correctly exposed emulsion. However, new things were to come as we departed on the tiny ferry to Værøy, the penultimate island in the Lofoten chain. Only Røst lay further out to sea. Røst is actually a small group of islets rather than a single island, and a haven for birds in the spring. In summer the attraction wasn't so strong and we settled for Værøy. The ferry arrived on Saturday evening and we instantly agreed to stay on the boat and to go elsewhere. Saturday night is racing

Kvalvik, Lofoten.

night, when the youth of the island charge their cars up and down the eight miles of road, the nearest policeman being, perhaps, a whole day away. We later learned that car ferries only arrived some ten years before and the novelty of owning, polishing and servicing cars has not yet been outgrown. There are four taxi-cabs and on average each house has two cars outside. All very well, you might say, but there is nowhere to bloody well *go*. Two cyclists seemed fair game to these pissed idiots so we took off for the hills, only a small range but, we were to discover, quite beautiful.

The north-west-facing ridge walk was simply stunning, with wonderful views in all directions. Down towards the town humps of moraines gave a moonscape appearance whilst back toward Moskenes huge rocks were glistening with cormorants. Towards Røst the sea was a silver reflector, whilst the sky darkened, an Arctic trick we now knew well. The islets themselves thrust upwards, a mass of weird shapes. We ambled with a young German couple to the peak of Værøy, some 650 metres directly above an inaccessible golden beach. There was nothing but height; no fence, no warning of the impending – once-off – leap, nothing. One hell of a place; without words, we concluded Værøy was something else. Ferry timetables forced a quick visit, but it allowed two good days' walking. A third to the far hill range would have been ideal, but something must always be left undone, as an excuse for a speedy return.

Aerial view of Reine, Kvalvik and Hamnöy, Lofoten.

Sea-Kayak

It is high summer, although in the UK only the temperature of the rain would confirm summer rather than autumn to the blindfolded visitor. Tony and I sit in the departure lounge of Heathrow wondering, yet again, how to fill the time between now and take-off. Flying still excites me with that curious mixture of fear – knowing the plane has the aerodynamics of a brick once the forward thrust is lost – and the knowledge that at the other end of the journey there will be new sounds and smells and things to look at. It pumps me so full of adrenalin that I pace in and out of duty-free shops, toilets, coffee shops, anything. Tony closes his eyes and gives the appearance of nonchalance. I am, he tells me, a bloody awful traveller, full or worries about missing flights, losing tickets and the like. Why, he asks, can't I be more like him, calm, assured? And full of bullshit? I ask.

Heathrow has, at least, the marginal advantage of being civilized, in that the cattle are gently shifted from one place to another rather than being herded anonymously. Once, at Milan airport, we were herded to the gate and corralled in an area almost big enough for half of us, then shifted to a bus with six seats and standing room for forty, in which the one hundred and twenty of us stood and waited for the idiot who always arrives twenty minutes late despite having been called ten times and being the subject of an Interpol missing persons search. So we would not overheat they thoughtfully left the doors of the bus open. Outside there was snow in the wind and the temperature was dropping. After a few minutes it was the same inside. After half an hour the bus started and moved us seventy metres, to the nearest plane, the one we could have walked to, with less effort and staying warmer. They got us off and the bus disappeared, but there was still a reason why we could not board – they never let on what it was – and we stood on the tarmac for a long time before being herded to the back entrance. There the lucky ones among us were allowed half-way up the steps before being halted and held in position for twenty minutes while, I assume, the stewardess disentangled herself from more pressing engagements

and tidied herself in readiness. The wind blew and the snow fell, but it didn't matter. The engines were just up there and their noise prevented us from thinking about how miserable it all might be.

Today we were close enough to the front of the plane to have a newspaper in English, and not have to settle for one printed in a strange dialect of Latvian (or whatever it is that they use for those that are always left at the end). We are held briefly at the runway apron, and then we are off. The excitement rises with the plane but soon it is just another flight. Tony and I contemplate the likelihood that on this Scandinavian plane we will have one of those stewardesses you see in the adverts – all blonde hair and curves. Ours has a face like a welder's bench and sounds like the Swedish chef in *The Muppet Show*. Ah, well.

My paper tells me that a dispute over pay between the leading British manufacturer of seaside rock and his chief sugar boiler has left the latter jobless and the former with umpteen sticks of rocks bearing the legend *Mean Bastard* all the way through. I show the snippet to Tony and the resulting peals of laughter from the pair of us bring disapproving stares from all over the plane. There we are, in Lundhags, a Swedish boot that is wonderful for its purpose but looks like a refugee prop from a Boris Karloff *Frankenstein* film, and oddly coloured clothes, rolling about. It just isn't right is it Doris, I mean to say . . .

The alterations in progress when we were last at Fornebu, Oslo's airport, are now completed and we follow the new sign to baggage reclaim. Round the first corner is a corridor hundreds of metres long with a sign at its end pointing left. We go left into another corridor equally long and then left into yet another. Clearly, in order to save some money, the carousel has been set up in downtown Oslo, about ten kilometres away. We arrive exhausted, haul in our rucsacs, check in again and hike back along the corridor to the airport. Two hours later I am mentioning to Tony that I have been to Tromsø airport more times than I have to Gatwick. Not that he is interested.

It is raining in Tromsø. The sky is the colour of

lead shot, with the Arctic Ocean dark and morose below it. I lean against the window of the bus and watch the raindrops spatter down, just as I must have done when I was a kid. Tony sits pensively next to me playing with his films. He does that a lot. This RS1000, he informs me, has already been to the Arctic about six times. Deep joy.

We are grateful for a flysheet-pitch-first tent in the Tromsdalen campsite and as we work speedily on its erection, the man in the camp reception hut watches us through the windows. I imagine he is impressed and that he will invite us for a coffee after, but when I look again he is gone. I peer into the rain for a glimpse of Storskarfjell, but it is all wet misery to the south.

We discuss the merits of lighting the Trangia, but decide that as nobody is watching, a coffee in the camp café will be OK. Later we go to sleep with the noise of rain on the flysheet, that noise that is at one time both infuriating because it means that tomorrow's enjoyment may be curtailed, and soothing in a strange way.

The day dawns bright but still cloudy. A night wind has blown the rain away, leaving behind pale grey rather than heavy grey clouds with, between them, enough blue to make a pair of sailor's trousers – as my mother would say. We sort kit, hanging the tent up in a tree to dry and pouring the rucsacs out on to a Karrimat. I have brought water-purifying tablets which has Tony perplexed. Usually we are melting snow or ice so we don't bother, but this trip could see us near stagnant water. He shrugs. I tell him that a friend who is even now in the Karakoram had been told that in Pakistan it was advisable to double the suggested dose of tablets and then to boil the water for twenty minutes. That should, it was suggested, reduce the likelihood of any problems by about fifty per cent. Tony is amazed that anyone should want to go there at all. Why, he asks, don't they just pour the water on the floor and machine-gun it? Tony's devotion to the Arctic is single-minded. I have tried once or twice to get him to the big hills, or to the Dolomites, but he sees no reason to waste time that could be spent in Norway or Greenland. The last time, when I suggested a climb of Ararat, he asked where it was. Turkey, I said. He considered for a long time. No, he said at length. Why not? I asked. They eat a lot of foreign food there, he said.

In Tromsø Tony searched out a coin so he can call Christine to report the fact that another interesting trip is about to start. I stare at the Ocean. It is still clear, still wonderful. I poke a finger into it; still cold.

Later that day we are at Belvik loading sea-kayaks into the ferry for Vengsøya. With us are four members of the local sea-kayaking club who have agreed to act as guides and mentors for our first couple of days. Tor Edgar is a giant man peering out shyly from behind glasses bequeathed by John Lennon. His shoulders suggest he can paddle all day. He can. He is not much of a talker; a longish sentence for him is *um*, his standard reply to most questions. Eventually, when he has decided that we wish to learn and that we love the Ocean as much as he does, he teaches us things that it is important to know. Leila, his girlfriend, has John Lennon's other pair of glasses, but behind her pair are sparkling eyes set in a face that is always cheerful. She is a teacher of primary school kids and decides, probably rightly, that these two English boys are really only ten years of age and should be treated as such. Don't forget your paddle, Tony. And what will you do if it rains and you haven't got your anorak on the deck, Dick? Sorry, miss, I didn't think. That's your problem, always has been . . .

Per Ivar – and woe to him who shortens it; just like Odd-Knut, he wants you to say his name properly – is blond and cheerful, ashamed of his English (God knows why, in comparision to our Norwegian), and shy of the camera. Bianca, sitting boldly upright in her kayak *Svalbard*, is suspicious of us and aggressively protective of Norway and all things Norwegian. By the time she is leaving us she is wondering why she came.

The sun shines on the ferry as we do the last of the packing. The kayaks have lifted snouts and two holes, one at each end, closed and sealed by hard rubber covers. Into these we store kit; rather like trying to push a piano through a thirty-centimetre hole. The hard bits that will not go are tied to the deck fore and aft of the paddler. I contemplate the thought of days spent looking along the length of Tony's tripod bag.

As the ferry nears Vengsøya I talk to Tor about our chances of seeing an orca, a killer whale. During our last dog sledge trip I had talked of my love of whales to Odd-Knut. He tells me that a girlfriend of his was fishing, with her mother, from a rowing boat in the fjord near Tromsø one day. As dusk fell they decided to go in. Odd-Knut's girlfriend lowered her oar into the water and it hit

Vengsöya.

Campsite, Vengsöya.

something hard. When she looked over the side in surprise, to her horror a huge orca surfaced just a metre away. It turned lazily around and peered at her. This eye contact unnerved the girl and sent the mother near hysterical, but having decided that they either meant no harm or, alternatively, that they were no good for eating, the orca lost interest and left. I should be so lucky as to get that close. Um, said Tor, but then went on to explain that only a week or two before he had been within a hundred metres or so of a school of orca. Was he afraid? Um, he said, thought a little and then said no, he didn't think he had been afraid. Um, I said.

The inhabitants of Vengsøya – or, at least, those near the ferry quay – watch us struggle on-shore with the kayaks with that curious air of pity, fear and interest I have seen before. These people are going paddling on the Ocean. Children wrestle to free their hands from their parents; Mummy, please let me go and throw stones at the idiots. One comes and stands next to Tony, watching as

he secures the last bit to his boat. Hello, says Tony, affably, how are you? The kid grows wide-eyed; Mummy, mummy, the idiots talk all funny.

I learned to canoe years ago when three of us put borrowed boats in the water at Glasbury and pulled them out, finally, several days later at Tintern, having gone down the Wye. For many hours on day one the river seemed amazingly narrow, one bank of it always being on the front end of my canoe. By the time I reached Tintern I could go in straight lines easily and had a right wrist the size of a tennis ball that was painful to touch and crackled ominously when I flexed it. I hope that it was all good practice for the sea. There is, true enough, no bank to poke into – get round the first headland and the next bank is the shore of Svalbard – but it would still be a good idea to be able to go in a straight line. How do you do this? Tony whispered as we carried our boats to the sea. Calmly and quietly I suggested.

Sea-kayaks are unstable in comparison to river canoes I decide. I ask Tor what the survival time is in the sea at this time of year. He eyes me, thinking that, although I might have done a few things in the Arctic, I am still a tiny lad without any fat; he decides that it will be just a few minutes. Comforting.

The Arctic Ocean from this distance, about a metre from eyes to surface, is even more wonderful than it seemed in Tromsø. It is so clear that to look into it takes your breath away: there is no sense of depth and the rocks could be two or twenty metres away. When I was a kid I loved the seashore for its mix of beautiful, subtle colours and strong smells. I recall how disappointed I was in the morning to discover that the pebbles I had collected so lovingly the evening before were just a pile of dull stones now that they had dried and were away from the beach. Still, that discovery never stopped me from making another collection of the glistening best ones that same night. Here the rocks and pebbles on the Ocean's floor are the same glistening colours, permanently etched because they can never dry. The sea is calm, but such ripples as there are flick the light from the sun about and refract the view of the pebbles so that staring over the edge of the kayak is like peering into a kaleidoscope over whose speed of rotation you have no control. Often I find that I am many hundreds of metres behind the party when I escape from the trance of pattern-watching and childhood recall. I paddle quickly, aware too that the Ocean's cold has gnawed its way

uncomfortably through the thin GRP of the kayak and into my poorly protected flesh.

Tony waits for me, to point out a small brown duck that is lurking among some rocks to our right. We paddle over to investigate. It is a female eider, duller and browner now that the mating season – for which she did not, in any case, dress up – is over. With her there is another bird which at first and with excitement we take for a king eider, but closer inspection reveals it to be an immature eider drake still paddling along near his mother. Ahead and to our right a head breaks the surface. The seal, too far away to be identified with certainty but probably a grey, peers myopically and is gone. I suppress an evil wish that an orca will be drawn in by this moving lunchbox of an animal.

We round a headland and I am behind again because of staring downwards and then towards the horizon, willing an orca to break surface. It is late and the sea is a little rougher so Tor decides to head for a sheltered inlet that he knows. The inlet is an almost perfect semi-circle of sand backed by huge cliffs whose vegetation-hung rocks defy their position. How can it be that here, on a north-facing cliff, with nothing between it and the North Pole and situated more than 300 kilometres north of the Arctic Circle, the vegetation can look like that?

A few hundred metres off-shore we congregate so that Tor can explain the best way of going ashore. It is straightforward – you paddle like hell straight at the beach and with luck and strength can get the boat far enough up to ensure dry feet when you get out. It works too. Tony and I drag our boats up the beach and head off to the rocks, our balance oddly disturbed by the many hours afloat. The vegation turns out to be more sparse than we had imagined. It comprises stunted birch trees in the main, each tree with a mass of leaves. I am puzzled. Surely here, with day-long sunshine, there is no need for so many, and surely they just add to heat and water losses? Under the trees there is a luxuriant mass of grass and moss beneath which numerous streams flow. We discover this when we try to walk towards the cliffs, our progress hindered by the occasional disappearing foot and accompanying staccato shout of *Shit*!

We camp Lappish style in a *lavvu* that Tor, he of the wall-to-wall shoulders, has paddled here on his deck. He has also brought a paraffin pressure stove (though if Optimus or Primus I am not sure)

Sea kayak.

Sea kayaking, Kaldfjorden.

of such proportions that correct plumbing would allow it to centrally heat a sizeable town. I fetch water – an easy job, just grab a kettle, head for the cliffs and fill from the first stream you fall in – and offer it to Tor. Almost by return I get a mug of tea.

We eat bread and the marvellous brown Norwegian cheese that looks and tastes like fudge. The best is made from goat's milk, although the goat–cow milk mix offers a smoother taste. I cut the cheese with the Lappish knife I acquired last time out; it has a 25-centimetre blade and can open

cans, cut fire-wood and generally keep misery at bay. Tor is impressed. He takes it and examines it keenly. Um, he says, and goes on to explain that in Norway a small, useless knife sometimes seen about the person of hunters and campers who have little idea is known as a 'mouse castrator'. Our knife, he decides, does not fall into that category.

Later we all climb to the top of the cliffs behind the bay, an arduous scramble up step, stream-washed scree. At the top, perhaps three hundred

metres or so above the camp, the view is phenomenal. Flat-topped Sandøya rears up out of the
sea, with, behind it, the tent-like shape of Sør-
Fugløya, a bird reserve. Per Ivar tells me his
mother comes from Sandøya. Life there was hard,
especially in winter and today no one over-winters
on the island, islanders preferring to fish and farm
in summer and to retreat to the comforts of Tromsø
in winter. I suggest that it is sad that a way of life
that is so ancient is ending, but Per Ivar is less
convinced. It is easy to be romantic about a way of
life at one remove. Maybe if I was on Sandøya

when winter came, when the sun went in for two
or three months, when all the water froze, when
ice covered the ground and fishing was a risky
business of frozen fingers and ears, on water in
which survival was measured in seconds, I would
be less romantic about it. Probably I would be
more convinced that Tromsø, with its snug
wooden houses, its thick air-spaced double glaz-
ing, its heating systems, its hot water from the tap,
its colour televisions and supermarkets, was not
just a retreat from reality.

The Norwegians choose a long ridge walk to go

Sör-Fuglöya and Sandöya from Vengsöya.

back to the camp and by the time they have arrived Tony and I have decided to take the kayaks out on to the Ocean. Tor looks at his watch. It is approaching midnight, but he agrees it is a fine idea. Minutes later we are heading for a small island group north of Vengsøya, to round that and head on for the next. The trip is one of the most beautiful I have known. The sun is setting now, midnight sun ending a few weeks before, but it only disappears for an hour and even then it leaves behind its mark of golden twilight. I sit on the first island to photograph the kayaks heading north into the last of the sun, then refloat again to join them. The low-angle light smears colours, so that the Ocean is uniformly dark brown. Above, the sky is yellow and yellow-orange, a thin band of cloud on fire with the red of the dying sun.

The Ocean is calm, so calm you could believe it to be lacquered wood rather than water and that if you were in a hurry you could leave the boat and walk to shore. The sun disappears, leaving behind its glow on the horizon as if the colour is in my head, burnt in by gazing too long at the red sphere. We stop paddling and rock very gently. Tony paddles over; the dripping water from his paddle ends, and the suck of water into the holes they leave behind are the only sounds for miles. We talk, using the hushed tones you would reserve for a furtive conversation in church. Time passes. I gaze at the island, a dark mass against the still-light sky. The highest point on Vengsøya, a little over two thousand feet above the Ocean's surface, suddenly turns pink. Not green or brown, but pink. We watch, and the pink spreads downwards as the sun rises behind us. We are in the wrong position to see the flash of light as the sun erupts again, settling instead for seeing it emerge from behind the northward island as we paddle slowly in.

I try to sleep, but cannot, and go for a walk along the shore and on to a ridge from where Sør-Fugløya is thrown into relief by the blinding sun. Life is a privilege.

The privilege lasts through a good period of fine weather. We paddle on seas the green of cat's eyes, and seas as clear as mountain streams. We are watched by seals. We see through jellyfish that are ghostly pale blue outlines in the water. One day we see not one, nor even one pair, but two pairs of sea eagles lift off from the cliffs under which we are paddling. One bird drifts overhead and I swear it is gazing at my quill-like yellow boat

as I am gazing at its white tail. Black guillemots (*teiste* in Norwegian) dive and disappear as we approach. A shoal of fish jumps out of the sea, a sight to quicken the heart as Tor says this often happens when the fish are being chased by orca. But there is no orca.

The fine weather brings out butterflies – something else to surprise the infrequent Arctic traveller – and mosquitos with jaws like drills. For days after we are all victims to the angry itching bumps they leave all over us. They drive me to distraction: at first I refuse to fight back, on the grounds that life is sacred and it is not their fault that they are mosquitos, but I eventually join in the swatting that punctuates the quiet every so often. It is, I decide, not my fault either that I am a human being who does not want to be eaten alive. During one meal I swat one off my arm and ask Tor if he knows what was the last thing that went through the mozzie's mind. Leila helps translate this for me as she, but not he, understands the colloquialism. No, he admits, when he understands, what? His ass, I suggest, wondering how the bluntness of the joke will go down. The taciturn Tor falls off his log and eventually complains of painful stomach muscles. All over north Norway now this characteristic English reply is a trade mark of those who know the mighty Tor.

Finally, we make for home, heading past Vengsøya towards the mainland. All morning it has been calm but now we are threatened by a storm that has been brewing out to the west. It hurls itself around the island and in seconds the sea is alive, ugly waves crashing over the boats, white horses flicking over the surface on the hooves of the wind. The sea worsens, the waves rising in height, and to add to the misery a sleety rain starts to emerge from the wind. Unable to stop paddling for fear of capsizing, Tony and I cannot put on our anoraks and within a few minutes we are soaked by the freezing combination of sea and rain. My glasses are creased by running water and I can no longer see past the end of the boat. I ask Tor, who has come across to see how I am coping, if this is normal, a guarded, off-the-cuff way of informing him that I am shit-scared and would like the weather to change. It is, he says, pretty bad. Can it get worse and still be survivable? Yes, he says, he has known it a little worse, but not much. It is rough, he says, very bad. He is glad, he says, it is not too far.

Sunset.

Loading the kayaks at Belvik.

Midnight launch.

Not too far is about eight kilometres, a distance that takes us well over an hour, although time is irrelevant. We are paddling at 45 degrees to the sea so on every wave the paddle must be just so to stop the boat going over. It is a wearying business, and I find myself thinking again and again of the lecture I went to on surviving in dangerous situations. The lecturer gave his definition of stress – a sense of impending incontinence. Never before today have I realized that the man was offering a Great Truth. Tor suggests we try to stop in the small bay where we will touch the mainland. If we can go ashore we can have coffee and Tony and I can put on our anoraks. Sounds good to me. As we near the bay, Tony and I draw level. How is it going, can you see yourself going all the way? Well, I take every wave as it comes, Brian. But they do win through. The lads done well.

Getting ashore is tricky, with the sea threatening to destroy the boats on the boulders at the edge. I haul my kayak up with what seems to be the last of my strength. I am soaked, cold and not a little lacking in enthusiasm for the next try. Tor goes off to a cottage up the hill from the bay and comes back disconsolate, having been told to 'piss off' by the occupants who were robbed last week and are not in any mood to offer the traditional Norwegian hospitality to a motley collection of bedraggled canoeists.

All the matches are wet, so we cram down a few handfuls of cheese and boiled sweets. We change into drier – not dry – kit and go again. The storm abates a bit, and there is no problem in reaching our start point. Taking the boats out of the water and loading them on the cars is a chore. Then everything must go in plastic bags so the car doesn't get wet. Leila drives, a remarkable performance given that we are so wet and steaming that she must peer through condensation thick enough to carve.

She has, she says, only enough petrol to reach the first garage. It is closed.

Winter – Sledging

'Good afternoon, ladies and gentlemen, this is the captain speaking. We are flying at a height of 11,000 metres and at a speed of just under 750kph. We expect to be landing in Oslo in about fifty minutes. It is a good day in Oslo. The temperature is 2°C (36°F) and it is raining'.

No one seemed to think this an out of place remark, but the three of us fell about.

Tony and I had organized a dog sledging trip which we hoped would take us from Dividal in northern Norway through Sweden and into Finland. After his good showing the previous autumn Nathan was coming too. He and Tony got on well: they started arguing over whether it was better to have two bits of black pudding rather than two sausages in the terminal café, and when that battle was over they started another about who was going to have the window seat on the plane. Tony's meal was a revelation – solid cholestrol from first forkful to last. It brought a new meaning to the phrase 'terminal breakfast.'

At Oslo the performance of transferring the kit was an epic. Tony's cameras were in three largish bags and each of us had a very large rucsac. In addition there was a roll bag that our 'tidy' stuff was going in. We were a two-trolley group. Tony was bearded for the trip. Having decided that he was very unlikely to shave for next sixteen or so days he wanted his beard to be at the past-scratch stage when he arrived. I had my Arctic haircut, long and rat's-nested. Nathan had needed no special arrangements: when very well dressed he looks scruffy – I suppose it must be a gift; it is certainly true that he couldn't give it away – and today he was not very well dressed. We were, therefore, a to-be-avoided, two-trolley group. Mothers kept their children away from us, and were grateful when we had checked in and gone for a coffee.

Tromsø had no more snow than we had seen in the autumn, but it was colder. It was a raw cold too, the cold of being close to the ocean, a wet cold – if that is not a contradiction for a temperature down around −12°C (10°F). It was a shrug the shoulders, sink the hands deep in the pockets and

be fed up about the running nose cold. It was too late to go to the campsite, or even to get a bus out of town, so we stopped at a hotel where they worried about us and charged too much for Coke. We rang our dog man, Odd-Knut Thoresen, and told him we had arrived. We had not yet met Odd-Knut, but his voice was friendly and competent.

He knocked on the door of the room I was sharing with Nathan while I was repacking kit. Nat let him in and went to fetch Tony who appeared wearing a pair of boxer shorts and a big smile. It turned out that he had locked himself out of his room which was likely to be embarrassing as I, for one, was not about to go down to reception for a key for him.

Odd-Knut had a Viking shock of blond hair, but little other resemblance to the Hollywood Norseman. He was slight and short-sighted, with a gentle smile that belied an amazing toughness and an ability to withstand cold that was to beggar our belief. He eyed Nathan suspiciously, clearly wondering whether he would survive the trip, but gave a reassuring 'impressed' look when Nat told him about our trip over Tromsdalen. We went for a coffee and Odd-Knut explained his ideas for the trip. He would pick us up tomorrow early and we could help buy some last bits and pieces. Then we could go to his place and learn to sledge. The day after it was off to Rostadalen to start. We asked about going into Finland but he shook his head. Rabies had reached southern Finland and there was an embargo on cross-border dog movements. True, the disease would sooner or later reach Norway after travelling up through Finland, but the Norwegian government had decided to stall it as long as possible. Who could blame them? Odd-Knut – whose English was good enough to know that he did not want us to call him 'Odd' – suggested that he could leave us near the Finnish border and we could ski or walk the last bit. We talked about the wildlife of the area and what we might see. Odd-Knut smiled at us. Later we were to learn that if you travel with two dozen sledge dogs you see no wildlife.

We drank coffee and talked some more. Odd-Knut rolled a thin cigarette and poured himself yet another coffee. Tony bought him a whisky and then bought him another. Outside the café the night sky was filled with the pale light of a ripening moon, invisible from here except as a shimmer on the quiet ocean.

Several months later, Nathan wrote up his dog sledging trip for a school project. He was having some trouble with one section. He was describing Odd-Knut's Volvo which arrived the next morning, the like of which I have yet to see again. It was an estate, the hatch door being held down by gravity. There were sections of smooth plate occasionally between the dents and here and there paint of an ancient Volvo hue showed through a patina of decrepitude. Nathan thought hard and finally wrote that the Volvo was 'old and depressed'. I can't improve on that.

We loaded our kit into the car and went into the town. Odd-Knut dropped us off so that he could go and get the last of his dog food. I casually wondered whether this meant 50 tins of Pedigree Chum and then ambled off after Tony who was being shown the Arctic Ocean by Nathan. Tony set up his tripod in a snow drift and started to contemplate a shot, so we left him to it and visited the town's Polar Museum. It was an intriguing place, full of photos of early explorers and of Roald Amundsen, who left Tromsø for his Arctic nemesis. Nathan was intrigued by a polar bear trap used when the Norwegians saw the big white bear as target rather than as tourist attraction. The trap was hideously unpleasant and, probably, equally hideously effective. Elsewhere there was a reconstructed hut which came alive with sound when you walked through a hidden beam. There were dog howls, wind howls and ice creaks. The suggestion was that Arctic travel was a miserable journey into a land of cold and fear.

Odd-Knut picked us up again and we went off to buy him and Tony some beer, available in Norway only at government alcohol shops. Then he took us to the university where a friend of his, an Englishman, was studying the local bird life. He was a fascinating man who shared with us some of his delight in Arctic birds and animals. As he spoke I noticed, over his shoulder and out of his study window, a large grey bird go past, moving quickly with the wind. I asked him what it might have been; after all, if he was an expert on the local birds then he ought to know. He looked puzzled and asked for a better description. Well, I said, it was about so long – hands out at just beyond

shoulder width – and about this much across the wings – hands now indicating a fair wingspan of several feet – and it was grey, well, greyish. He shook his head. No, no that didn't fit the description of anything we had ever seen or heard about. Was I sure it wasn't white? No, grey. And that big? Yes, perhaps even a little bigger. He shook his head again. The others joined in the story. Was I sure I had seen it at all? Of course I was. Well, perhaps . . . and so on. In the end, to draw matters to an unhappy conclusion they all agreed that it had probably been a bin liner.

Odd-Knut Thoresen was the Tromsø dog collector and owner of the local dog hotel. In midwinter – it was the first week of February – there were few dogs in his compounds, although there was one large, affable-looking but wholely terrified cat. Outside, doing their best to frighten the cat spitless with their howling, were fifty sledge dogs, each chained to a kennel, well separated to stop their most frequent game, that of tearing lumps out of each other. We called them huskies, as you might expect, but Odd-Knut was not happy with the name. They were a cross-breed, Alaskan and Greenland. Since Greenland dogs were always dogs not huskies he preferred that name. The Siberian animals, beautiful silvery creatures I had worked with once before in Switzerland, were huskies.

He took us inside and introduced us to Kjell-Arne, a lanky, shy youth who worked for him and was told to make coffee, and Tove, the kennel girl. Her moon-shaped face was always split with a smile, even when she was scooping up dog turds with a device the handle of which was at least two feet shorter than I would have wanted it to be.

We were shown our sledges. Not for us the tourist sledge of the one- or two-day package visitor, a short contraption, more tea tray than means of transport. Our sledges were long and sleek, with pine-resined or PTFE runners and compartments of wood and nylon for our kit.

First we will learn to harness the dogs, said Odd-Knut. He took off his shoes, climbed into a chair, rolled a cigarette and poured himself a coffee. We waited. And three hours later we were still waiting. The best time of day to ride sledges is at night, and shifting Odd-Knut in daylight needed explosives.

Nathan turned the conversation to the bear trap in the museum, asking Odd-Knut if he had seen it, and soon we were talking about the killing of

View west from Blåmannen on Kvalöy near Tromsø.

animals. Before we had left England the Lindberg film on seal killing had been shown, an indictment of the Norwegian sealers. Odd-Knut said that the locals, many of whom were in the fishing and related trades, were incensed. They insisted that the film had been shot in Canada in 1987, despite what the voice-over said. On Norwegian ships, if someone was a bad killer they would be locked in the holds, they said. If Lindberg was to come to Tromsø he would be hung from a lamp-post, probably by his balls. This last comment was the only one I could feel was definitely true.

The conversation drifted to whaling, where the Norwegian record also seemed lacking in compassion and common sense. Odd-Knut found that record harder to defend, and ultimately gave up trying. To lighten the proceedings he told us of an incident some years ago when there had still been a whaling station in the town. A group of Germans – 'fat Germans', he insisted – was being shown around when an ancient whale carcass, blown big on decay gas pressure, exploded. The visitors were covered from head to foot in over-ripe whale bits. With great glee Odd-Knut told us that the fat Germans showered ten times every day for a week and still reeked of rotten whale. This was not the first time I had noticed the old enmity of the Norwegians for the Germans. Once, I had inadvertently called Nordic skiing *langlauf* and had been lucky to escape alive. Old memories die hard, especially in a town like Tromsø which was home to a large contingent of the German navy. *Tirpitz* lies at the bottom of the local fjord, and every year the local diving club goes down to it on New Year's Day to retrive a handful of bits guaranteed to fuel the old fires for another year.

Odd-Knut showed us a video of the Iditarod, intriguing for what it didn't tell you which, as it turned out, was quite a lot. He told us about the longest race in Norway; he had taken part and had done very well, finishing very close to the front of the 'amateur' racers (as opposed to those who race dogs for a living). Norwegian television had followed the big race the previous year and about 100 kilometres from its end had stopped the leader to interview him. The man was not wanting to be interviewed, but such is the power of television that he had to agree. They did a take, and then another. It was cold and the man's dogs lay down to rest and stay warm. By the time the interview was over the dogs were all asleep and refused to wake up. The sledger shouted and kicked, he cursed the dogs and swore at the television crew. The dogs slept on and the race went past him.

Odd-Knut explained the theory of dog sledging. Keep your lines straight and taut and your dogs will go faster. Keep one eye on them at all times to avoid problems. If one stops for a piss the rest might catch up and if they do they will either fall straight over him so that you finish with a ball of dogs that will take forever to unwind, or they will take lumps out of him. When feeding your dogs don't hand them their meat or they might take it from your elbow down. When your dogs are eating it is not a good idea to pat them; if they think you are trying to take their food they will defend it with your life. It was sobering.

At the front the sledge has a semi-circle of lathed wood hinged to it. This piece allows the dog line – the tow line – to operate in a different plane to the sledge and also absorbs some of shock of towing. Each dog is attached to the tow line twice. To get the sledge ready you anchor it firmly; this is vital because once you have attached your first dog he will start to tow and the whole shooting match will be long gone by the time you get back with your second dog. To fix the sledge you use the snow hook, shaped like a double fish hook but about a foot long and wide. You use this both to anchor the sledge during a trip, by stamping it into the snow, and at the start of each day to hold the sledge, by clunking it on to a tree trunk.

Having anchored your sledge you fix your tow line to the front hinge piece, using a karabiner. The snow hook is actually on the end of the tow line so that in the unlikely event of the karabiner unhooking – as it did once on me – the hook stays close to you giving you an outside chance of holding on to the team. Next you take a lead dog and put on its harness of padded nylon; this goes over the head and the front legs poke through stitched loops. Down the dog's back runs a nylon tape with a small karabiner at its ends, which hooks on to a tug line that is crimped on to the tow line. Both tow line and tug line are wire encased in nylon; if they were just nylon the dogs would chew through them. After the dog is clipped to the tug line it is clipped to a neck line so that it is held tight in position relative to the tow line. If you are running with one lead dog then it attaches to both the front tug lines and has no neck line. If you are running with two lead dogs then you clip one on each of the front tug lines, and neck line them together.

Now you attach your lead dog to a tree, or the sledge in front, or anything to keep your tow line taut. If you forget, as you turn to go for another dog the lead dog, being a friendly creature, will come with you. It will probably then go round the other side of the sledge and might even go over the snow hook line. Give him thirty seconds and you will have knitting.

After your lead dogs are guyed out you attach the next pair, the point dogs. There could be several pairs of these. On one part of our trip Odd-Knut, for all sorts of reasons, ran with eight dogs. Finally you attach your closest dogs, the wheel dog pair. Now you are ready to go. Now comes the dodgy part.

But we are still drinking coffee in a dog kennel. The evening wears on and we all shuffle impatiently. Suddenly Odd-Knut gets up and asks if we would like to go dog sledging. We dress up like bit-part players in an epic on Scott and go out into the night where the air bites clean and deep, and the snow crunches in that beautiful cold way. After the horror stories about the dogs I hesitate to go near my first one, but with us they are just big balls of fur. They are chained separately only to keep them clear of each other. I move in on a twenty-kilogram monster, all bark and paws. *Nice doggy, good doggy.*

Doggy leaps up on me and tries to wash my face with a tongue like a coarse bastard file. It bone breaths all over me. Jesus, what does he feed them on? That was 'orrible.

The dog seems anxious to get the harness on; indeed, all through the trip the dogs are always keen to pull and seem miserable when they are tied off for the night.

Between us we harness two teams and go out with one of us sitting in a sledge driven by Tove, one on the back of Odd-Knut's Sno-Go snow scooter, and the other tentatively riding the second sledge. With a team in front, life is easier as the dogs follow and all we have to do is keep the tow line taut and holler the occasional encouraging word, as much to each other as to the dogs. Riding in the sledge is an experience. Encased in pile and nylon, hoods drawn tight, it would be easy to forget the world in a welter of sensations, were it not for the running commentary that Tove keeps up.

'Hold on to the sledge rails here – keep a loose grip or your hands get tired – try not to keep your foot on the brake [a miniature snow hook held off the snow by an elasticated octopus grip] or your

Sledge dog.

other leg will get tired – don't shout too much at the dogs or they get confused – the occasional quiet word is helpful – on downhills brake gently if you need to so that the line stays tight.'

And there is much more advice that I did not take in, except that later I remember it when a new situation arises. For the moment I am concentrating mostly on the fact that I am riding under the Arctic sky, a very black sky, heavily overcast, being pulled across the ice by a team of dogs. They are silent. Only during a stop do they howl or yelp, as the frustration of inactivity gets to them. They are moving at good speed – we are on one of Odd-Knut's prepared training runs – perhaps topping 30kph on the level sections. When you are held in tight beneath the sledge's nylon coverall

Taiga.

Dawn sledging, Rostadalen.

that feels very quick. Occasionally the front of the sledge runner, about 2 or 3 metres in front of me, hits a hummock of snow and my face is thwacked by a handful of icy flour. I spit it out and flick it from my eyes. It adds to the exhilaration, bringing a smile rather than a frown. Next backwards comes a waft of dog fart. In the days that follow we learn about this smell, which varies from *ugh!* and a turn of the head to really gut-wrenching. Tonight it is just another sensation.

When it is my turn on the sledge the experience is incomparable. Not like learning to drive a car, not even like riding a horse. There is a sense of isolation from the rest of the world, a sense of the power in the dogs, and a wonderful feeling of being in control, but only just. It is perhaps like being on top of a big wave in a canoe or on a surfboard, but to try to describe it is to fail.

The following day we packed Odd-Knut's depressed Volvo. On its roof there were four sledges – three ordinary ones for the three of us, and a monster for Odd-Knut, built, it seemed to us, to carry everything including the proverbial. In the back of the car was our kit. The overspill (considerable) was packed into what space was left on the roof (inadequate). Hooked up at the back was a double-decker dog carrier, each deck having four holes to a side, giving a total of sixteen holes. Twelve of these were packed with two dogs in each, two dozen dogs. I was not looking forward to the packing. The second row of holes was at chest level. Hands up those wanting to lift a twenty-kilogram dog into a 25-centimetre hole at that height. In fact, the dogs could not wait to get in. Each time we went for another animal all those left howled and fought their chains to get close to us so as not to be left behind. As we collected a dog it would lurch towards the car, the rest falling silent in their disappointment. Our only problem was with the doubling up. Get the wrong number two dog in with a number one and the cuddly koala in your arms turned into megatooth.

We filled the spare holes with harnesses. As I loaded them in there was a sharp reminder of the night before. The harness stank of dog, that unpleasant smell which big-dog owners never seem to notice in their own house. Here it was again, but so strong as to be an insult to the word stench. Later during the trip I noticed that one morning the smell hadn't registered with me. It took me a while to cotton on. By then everything I wore smelled of it too.

With 500 kilograms of dog, about the same quantity of dog food, sledges and kit, plus the four of us on board, we made our way out of Odd-Knut's drive. The main road was ice-covered. Why not? Everything else was. Odd-Knut had studded tyres and Alain Prost delusions. Tony sat in the front. He was used to this sort of thing, he drives a big motorbike. When we went round the first corner at about 90kph Tony went very quiet.

It was a long trip, not helped by a tyre that cried 'enough!' in the middle of nowhere and required changing – a job made more difficult by the fact that Odd-Knut had no spare – but ultimately we arrived at the entrance to Rostadalen. The snow was so deep we could make no progress, so we went around into Dividal instead. It was late when we finally eased our stiff limbs into the night. The sky was clear, the stars were beautiful and the snow creaked underfoot. Our breath made huge clouds of steam which hid our faces as we talked, and we hopped about and shrugged elaborately to ward off the penetrating fingers of cold that probed at our necks and hands.

The sledges came down first and were loaded with tents, dog food and our kit. The dogs grew noisy with excitement, and each wire door was now filled with the pressed muzzle of an anxious face. Carefully we laid out the tow lines and attached our snow hooks, Tony to one roadside fence post, me to another, Nathan to the bumper of Odd-Knut's car. Odd-Knut was ahead of us, so that nothing would stop him being first away.

The unpacking of the car and the packing and preparing of sledges took a long time. It was dark, and all the fiddly jobs like clipping in the dogs or tying kit on to the sledges meant taking off gloves. After just a minute or so, especially if we were handling metal, we would need to stop and huff on to frozen fingers, standing around with pained expressions while circulation returned. During one such stop I looked up. In the lead-up to the trip I had been telling Nat about the Northern Lights and how wonderful they were. Now the sky above Dividal was filled with the most glorious Lights I had ever seen, a shimmering waterfall of green light.

'Nat, look.' I pointed up.

He stopped packing rucsacs on to his sledge and looked. He did not say a word, just stared at the sky. For once, the product had turned out to be even better than the advert. Tony and Odd-Knut stopped work too, and there was a silent time, broken only by Tony's mad rush to find his camera and tripod. We had chosen our visit to coincide with the full moon, but it also coincided with a period of maximum solar flare activity, and on every clear night the Lights treated us to a spectacular show in green and red.

As we watched, a man arrived on a snow scooter and he and Odd-Knut talked long and quietly. When he left Odd-Knut told us he was Lappish, and that when asked if the trail to our campsite was piled high with snow he had said yes it was, but that he would break it for us if we were willing to pay. Odd-Knut, not willing to spend our money and not inspired by his attitude, declined. In that case the Lapp had said he would do it for a few drinks if we had any with us. Odd-Knut agreed, but only if the bottle was found tomorrow rather than today. The Lapp shrugged and left. Odd-Knut did not know if he would break trail. The next day the Lapp arrived for his drink, but we had seen no evidence of a trail.

At last everything was ready. At close to midnight, when the three of us were already tired, Odd-Knut slipped his snow hook and was gone, so fast I was stunned. Tony, over to my right, shouted something to me, released his hook and was gone. My dogs were straining against the sledge now and yelping as if badly hurt. I took hold of the snow hook, but to release it meant hauling in some slack on the line. The five dogs on the other end of it were not impressed with the idea of going backwards and battle was joined. There was a loud *whoaa!* to my left and Nathan shot past. He shouted something at me or at his dogs, I don't even now know which, and was gone into the night. My dogs were frantic, and so was I. I hauled one last time, the line came back two centimetres, the hook came free and the dogs roared away. From standstill to top speed was, it seemed, instant, with me fighting to stay in balance as the sledge buckled over the rough trail.

The journey started easily enough, the way going up a track that in summer is an unsurfaced road used by tourists. Soon the going became very rough, with deep snow that constantly stopped Odd-Knut's dogs. Frequently we stopped, turned and went back for another try to the left or right. Our order did not change, with Odd-Knut out in front, then Tony and Nathan, and me bringing the line to an end. At the back, sometimes out of sight of the others, I became engrossed in my own problems. I was tired, very tired. I was also sick and tired. Sick and tired of stopping and starting, of going up banks only to go down them again, of being whacked in the face by the branches of trees that the dogs ran under, and of not knowing where we were going or why. Why were we in this bloody forest anyway? Why did we not just stop and camp? Up front Tony was asking the same questions. We were in the forest to try to get less deep snow, he was told; we were going to a campsite that Odd-Knut had prepared. Nat turned and shouted this garbled message to me and I hooked my dogs to a tree and went forward to talk to him.

In the light of my head torch I could see that Nat was grey-faced with fatigue, his eyelids drooping, his mouth surrounded by frost that he had not had the strength to wipe away. Snow from the trees had fallen all over us and his arms and shoulders were covered in a white dust that sparkled in the light from my lamp. I could not see his feet as snow ploughed up from his brake when he had last stepped on it reached to about mid-calf. I was appalled. What right had I to bring him here and to inflict this sort of suffering on him? Are you OK? I asked. He smiled. Fine, he said, this is great isn't it? His face lit up suddenly, he wiped his mouth and shook his feet free of the snow cocoon. Back there, he said, did you see me go over that bump? I went right up in the air. I could have held him tight and told him I was proud of him and that I loved him just for being there, but he would have struggled free. So I settled for dusting off his shoulder and giving it a quick squeeze. He smiled again, and then was gone, off in pursuit of Tony who had started moving again.

By the time I am ready to move again everyone has gone. The dogs follow the trail, so there is no problem, but it does mean that I miss seeing the sudden three metre drop that we go down to reach a frozen river. The bottom is reached with a mind-numbing crash that jars every bone, but at least this thaws out my brain. We follow the river, very easy going, and then leave it to go uphill through very deep snow that means we have to push the sledges rather than ride them. The country is more open here, with fewer trees and flatter ground. Ahead I can see that Odd-Knut has stopped and is off his sledge. Tony stops too. Oh Christ, not more delay.

But no. In the centre of the clearing where they have stopped is a Red Indian wigwam, the one

Lappish lavvu.

Odd-Knut erected a few days before. We have arrived. I look at my watch. It is just past three in the morning, and the journey here has taken a little over three hours. I am dog-tired, as are the dogs. My legs are stiff with inactivity and cold and my breath freezes in front of me to obscure the view. It is groaningly cold, possibly as low as −25°C (−13°F), although we cannot be sure as Tony's thermometer is buried under a mound of tackle.

We unharness the dogs and attach them to a chain that Odd-Knut fastens between two trees. Even when they are off the sledges the dogs are kept apart. OK, says Odd-Knut, we must pitch the other tent and get some food. When we have the chance we will camp Lappish style, with *lavvus*, the wigwam tents made of birch poles and reindeer skins, but tonight we are using a modern *lavvu* of canvas and aluminium poles. Tony and I

dig a platform for the tent, lowering the snow by about seventy centimetres to give us a nice protective wall. The *lavvu* goes up, the canvas at the bottom held down by shovelled snow. While we do this Nathan is off cutting birch twigs. Odd-Knut has given him a hunting knife, and pointed him at the trees. I go over to help and find him upright but asleep, his head against the trunk of a tree, the knife, evil-looking with a thirty-centimetre blade, half held in his hand. I wake him gently. We cut small branches between us and these are laid on the floor of the tent. Next on go reindeer skins, then our own Karrimats and sleeping bags. Nathan needs to be helped from his shell clothing he is so tired, but we insist he must stay awake to eat. Tony and I cut wood while Odd-Knut erects a wood-burning stove in the tent.

The fire is soon going and we have tea and eat

something – God knows what. Nathan is propped up against a rucsac with a cup, plate and two glazed eyes. He eats mechanically, because we say he must. He finishes and asks if he can sleep now. I say yes and he keels over, being asleep before his head reaches the floor, his shoulders and arms still out of the bag. I ease him into it and then make for my own. I assume I must have made it because when the noise of movement outside wakes me four hours later that is where I am.

The *lavvu* is a shambles; everywhere there is clothing, the nylon stiff with cold. Nat's Dachsteins, dropped on a piece of exposed ground, are frozen solidly to it, have to be prised free, and will need to be thawed over the stove. Words are exchanged, and there is a tense moment or two. Tony, ever sensible, ever the peacemaker, suggests that we were all tired, still are, and it might all look better after a cup of tea. He hands me a billy and suggests I get some snow for water and a few twigs to start the fire. He also suggests that it

might be a good idea if we move one at a time to avoid a ridiculous crush in the tent; I should get up and move out, then he will get up and start the fire, then Nathan can get up last. Agreed.

Getting up is purgatory. I have slept in a full set of thermal underwear, but the cold gets to me as soon as I leave the bag. I hastily dress, but there is a limit to how fast you can put on two or three layers of clothes. Outside Odd-Knut is feeding the dogs in miserable weather. It is not snowing, but there is enough wind to be chilling and the day is grey and misty, so I get little sense of where the camp is, with visibility only a few tens of metres. I collect snow and start off for the nearest dead tree with the big knife and an axe. I come back with an armful of dead birch to find Tony digging films out of a snowdrift near the tent. He takes the wood and disappears back into the tent. I amble over to Odd-Knut to ask a few dumb questions. He answers patiently.

Breakfast is tea and muesli, the muesli made

Avoiding a tree.

with hot water and milk powder. Nathan gets up and goes off in search of somewhere quiet, clutching a toilet roll and anxious anticipations. Odd-Knut makes coffee using the method we have become familiar with – chuck the coffee in a pot, add snow to taste, boil on the stove, when empty add coffee and/or snow as necessary. After the third filling it was a treacly mixture that certainly woke you up. Nathan returns, suggesting that you need to be in a sheltered spot for minimum discomfort; he thinks that constipation is to be feared almost as much as the wind. Tony asks him whether he dug a hole, but he says no need, the stuff just melts its way down. Odd-Knut is much amused by all this talk, and tells us that in Greenland the sledge dogs will eat it if they can get at it. Will they really?

Odd-Knut produces a bottle of Wolf's Paw, a local spirit drink, and offers it around. As the non-drinker I get first go (why?) and it takes my breath away. Tony tries and with his eyes watering declares it a good noggin. Thankfully Nat declines.

We tidy the tent, sort our kit and the light starts to fade. Odd-Knut thinks that it might be best to make a night trip with empty sledges, returning to the camp, especially as a friend of his is likely to arrive for the night. We all agree. More tea is drunk, food is eaten. We stretch out in the *lavvu* which is pleasantly warm now after a day of the stove being ablaze. Odd-Knut's friend Tom-Frode arrives, a perpetually smiling man with hands like dinner plates.

It is past nine by the time we start to harness the dogs, and the sky is a little clearer, the temperature a little cooler. Again, when we move off the speed startles me. Apparently, the tow given to old whalers by a harpooned whale was known as the 'Nantucket Sleighride'; I haul back on the line, release the snow hook and take a similar ride. We move through a band of forest and then start to climb steeply, going up over 300 metres at a good steady speed. Nathan is behind this time which means I can have the occasional shouted conversation with Tony. This is fantastic, he shouts. This is unreal, he continues. No one will ever believe us.

He's right. It *is* fantastic. Under the Arctic night sky we are going gentle uphill without effort, hauled by dogs whose only noise is a gently effort-driven panting. The whole thing does seem unreal. It is so far removed, not only from my normal run of experience, but from anything I have ever done that it seems beyond the realms of reality, a fantasy production, a dream come true.

A far shout calls me back to truth. Behind me Nathan is having problems, his wooden runners sticking in the snow and causing him to go slowly. We wait, he catches up and we go on again. Again he falls back and at the top of the climb we wait again. Below us the forest of Dividal is visible. It is an illusion that the Arctic is dark in winter. The snow is so white that it reflects any available light. Above us there is a full moon and the light that is forcing its way between the clouds is quite sufficient to provide a picture. The picture is in black and white – there is never enough night light for colours to emerge – and this adds to the unreal quality. Far below us now is a hurricane lamp that Odd-Knut has hung from a tree knowing it would be visible from the hill.

Nathan arrives and Odd-Knut inspects his runners. They need a touch of resin he decides, but as he has none it will have to wait until we get back to the camp. To save time we hitch Nat's sledge to a tree, distribute his dogs among the three of us and put Nathan in my sledge. He is not pleased. With Nathan on board my dogs move more slowly, and we trail off from the others as we climb up above the tree line. The clouds clear and the moonlight sparkles on the snow. Ahead, as they swing away from me, the other sledges look like commas on the writing paper of the snow. The temperature falls and Nathan pulls the nylon sledge cover up over his head, peering out through a narrow slit so as not to miss anything.

Tom-Frode, Odd-Knut and Tony wait for us to arrive. Tom has to get back tomorrow, so Odd-Knut decides to circle the peak ahead and rejoin our outward trail to pick up Nat's sledge on the way back. I let Nat have my dogs and sit in with Tony. Odd-Knut lifts his snow hook out of the snow and with a *swish* is gone. We follow. From within the cover the ride is impressive; closer to the ground, I can hear thumps and bangs as well as the runners hiss. I can hear the dogs panting ahead and occasionally I am flurried by snow kicked up from a runner. Tony talks to his dogs all the time, a *hup, hup* here, a *go, Brussie* there, and he shouts down to me too. We pause again and swap passenger so that Nathan takes Tony round the edge of the peak into a long and narrow, and steep valley. The wind is whistling up this and within seconds my face is frozen. It is so cold I am going numb. We all stop to cover our faces with our balaclavas, haul in the drawstrings on our anoraks and clamp snow goggles over our eyes. Because I wear glasses, there is a slight air gap and soon my eyes are watering with the cold. The wind-chill temperature that night must have been way below the −25°C (−13°F) of the air temperature. It was a biting cold that almost turned the pleasure of the ride into a chore, or a want for it to end.

Back at Nathan's sledge he is too cold to be bothered to ride again so we hoist it on to Odd-Knut's sledge and ride on. Nathan and I bring up the rear, and soon we are alone, with Nathan buried deep beneath the nylon sledge cover. We are going down towards the forest and the Arctic night is awesome. The trees and mountain ridges have a magnificent stark beauty. And it is so quiet. The dogs never bark on the move, so there is no noise but that of runner on snow, and it is a warm, comforting sound that amplifies the silence.

My goggles ice up at regular intervals and I wipe them with my glove, afraid that I will miss the trail – a groundless fear as the dogs follow the pack scent. The trail goes steeply down and the speed increases, and I let go of the sledge rail to wipe my goggles – a fatal move. The sledge bucks on an uneven hummock and throws me off. I hold on with one hand, landing in a fast-moving heap that upsets the sledge's balance. It turns on to its side and as I cling on for dear life I hear a startled cry from Nathan. Cocooned in the nylon sack, from which he could escape only with difficulty, he is suddenly on his side heading downhill at speed. He struggles to escape, alternating shouts of *Stop!* at the dogs and shouts to me to see if I am still on board. Odd-Knut said that you must never let go of the sledge, I say again and again to myself as I am pulled through snow heaps and ruts. Something bangs hard into me and my arm is almost wrenched free, but eventually the dogs stop, no longer interested in dragging the overturned sledge and me. Nathan and I are quite alone, many miles from civilization and, apparently, lost, the wind having blown snow across the tracks ahead of us. Nat suggests that we just let the dogs lead us towards the others, a well-reasoned idea that works perfectly. By the time we meet Odd-Knut coming back to find us we are only a few hundred metres from the camp.

The Arctic dawn is stunningly beautiful. One day Tony gets up to watch and witnesses one of the few times when the sun travels across a blue, cloudless sky. It moves slowly, wearily and as if to ensure that you understand that it is tired; it goes only a few degrees above the horizon, making a long, low arc. Even its light is tired, a pale yellowy-orange, nothing like the vibrant light of the south where the tireless sun goes high and stays high. Tony is entranced. The low angle means that all shadows – ours, the dogs', the trees' – are long and ghostly across the ice, and the orange light wraps itself around everything so that all things seem to be part of one thing. He shoots tree stumps and furrows in the snow. He shoots the dog's paws, too hairy and with huge hooked nails, yellow, hard and shiny. Eventually he turns to me smiling broadly. That's another roll finished, he says. God this is great.

We leave base camp on a day that is grey and oppressive, the air full of snow. Packing is miserable, nothing is the right shape to fit the sledges. How did we get it all here? Odd-Knut discovers that his dogs have been hauling a full, 5-litre can of chain-saw oil around. This amuses him greatly. It is as well the dogs do not speak English.

Wiggen, one of my wheel dog pair, a monster of a dog weighing nearly thirty-five kilograms, jumps all over me as I go for him. Yesterday I fed him the bony scraps from my reindeer stew and he is now mine for ever. Thankfully, he has seen this simple act as one of friendship rather than for what it really is – I am afraid of him and I want him on my side. He paws at me, licks me, nuzzles me and I talk back. Harnessing the dogs is routine now, with Wiggen, with them all, a mixture of soft words and cold fingers.

We are ready. Odd-Knut slips his hook and we head for Sweden and some Lappish people he knows. It is the first pull of the day so we all know what to expect. Odd-Knut feeds the dogs on a high-fat, high-protein mix of cow's stomach and other offal, fish, blood and oil. With the first morning pull the dogs become so excited that they shit within metres. The output is an evil treacle, black and vile. When you see it coming – remember that they do everything on the move – you jump on to the runner on the opposite side from the dog, take a deep breath and hope the runner won't kick it up. Even the dogs don't like it and will avoid the mixture from the dog in front at all costs. Tony always says that you can tell a happy motorcyclist by the flies on his teeth. His latest joke is that you can tell a happy musher by the dog shit on his teeth. I remember this and smile, clamping my mouth shut as Wiggen goes into action.

Dawn, Dividal.

We pause while Odd-Knut peers at his map and then ahead into the greyness. The stop sets one dog off barking and others join in. Since I gave Wiggen the reindeer he runs with his tail up, happy to be part of my team. I notice, in a matter of fact way, that before he wuffs his gruff, low wuff, Wiggen's ass contracts. Jesus, he's sucking in air at the back and wuffing it out at the front. Now, he half turns and looks my way, love for the reindeer bones in his eyes and woofs merrily at me. No hi-fi speaker maker has ever come up with a woofer that low and resonant.

We are off again. We take a frozen river for a long way, a bumpy ride that keeps you concentrating, and when we eventually come off it, there is a lone tree that the dogs pull towards despite our efforts. One by one the dogs on the left of the trace anoint it, the ones on the right going frantic in their efforts to reach it. Later in the trip we pass a lone Nordic skier. The man jabs his left ski down as Odd-Knut goes by, gets the ski between dog and trace and is hauled over and forwards. He falls in a heap, and as they pass every dog on the right of the line raises a leg and pees on him.

The Lapps are a curious people, pragmatic almost to the point of unfriendliness. If you can't eat it or, better, drink it then they don't want it. Odd-Knut tells us that in Tromsø there was a notice on the only bit of grass in the town. It said 'do not go on the grass', translated literally from the Norwegian – somehow the story doesn't work so well in English. One day a policeman stopped a Lapp who was striding across it. I am not going on it, said the Lapp, I am coming off it. End of discussion.

One Lapp shows me his reindeer skin boots, and shrugs when I ask him why the toes curl up. Because they do. In early winter, when the first snows come, he wears socks in the boots, but when it gets cold he takes them off and replaces them with grass. The grass is harvested in summer from the bogs at the edges of lakes, and smashed flat with a knife butt. It is very warm, he tells me, but you must replace it when it is wet. The following day, in a temperature down around −20°C (−4°F), I am wearing loop-stitch socks and Lundhags, and he is wearing reindeer skin boots and grass. The boots are finished with a long, broad ribbon that is wrapped around the ankle, being raised to go over the join of boot and trouser if there is a danger of wet snow going down inside.

Nathan asks how many reindeer the Lapp has and is rewarded with a piercing look. Odd-Knut tells us that to ask a Lapp that question is like asking an Englishman how much money he has in the bank. There has been a move by the Norwegian government to try to tax the Lapps on the basis of reindeer numbers, and almost overnight the Arctic was denuded of animals, at least on paper. Our man is not poor though. He has a snow scooter, and enough cash to hire a boat twice a year to move his reindeer on to an island. We never have a satisfactory explanation of where it comes from.

Old women knit and sew outside their *lavvus*, bare-handed even in this temperature; one, with fat, gnarled hands, uses no gloves all day. It is, we hear, one of the worst winters on record, with heavy autumn rain saturating the ground and early winter cold – the cold and snow that caught Nathan and I in Tromsdalen – causing the ground to freeze early. The consequence is that the reindeer feed is buried not only under a metre or more of snow, which the reindeer can cope with, pawing away at it to reach the lichen that is reindeer moss, but under many inches of solid ice. The animals cannot always break through this, and they struggle away, pawing and moving in frustration, pawing and moving again. Two kilometres or so away, over the Swedish border, the conditions are worse and these Swedish Lapps have come over to find better feed. This *should* make no difference with the Lapps, the Same (prounounced Sam-ay) as they now wish to be called, being all one race. In fact, there is considerable aggravation, with the Norwegian Lapps complaining to the government, and demanding that the police be moved in to catch and deport the interlopers. There is talk of night-time raids between groups, of harsh words and harsh actions.

Later in the year, when we visit the area again, we heard that the Swedish Lapps had fenced off an area of the Dividal National Park, with over five kilometres of wire. The incensed Norwegian Lapps called in the authorities, who had to hire a helicopter to go in and confiscate the wire. The Swedes were moved out, but were back the following day. The day after that they hired their own helicopter, landed in the local village, repossessed their wire, flew it back in and re-erected it. And how much does it cost to hire a helicopter for a day?

I lie in my sleeping bag, listening to the shuffling of reindeer hooves, and thinking this over.

Conventional wisdom tells us that it is the lure of civilization that breaks up the old life, Tromsø's video games and bars pulling the Lappish kids down out of the forest into the town. What about the effect of such arbitrary things as country borders on the way of life? Here in a land where you expect Lapp to fight Norwegian for the privilege of staying Lappish, Lapp was fighting Lapp for the privilege of being Norwegian rather than Swedish.

We leave, saddened by the plight and determined to come for longer the next time, to stay through a winter and spring, to find out what that old woman had really been up to holding that white sheet up to the Northern Lights. They give me a reindeer hood that they assure me will be warmer than my silk and fleece and wool. They do not give me a carved wooden cup though, something we all covet. You must make your own if you are to be a Lapp.

We move on next day over hard packed snow that has been wind-blown into flutes and columns. This is the most beautiful place I have ever been, a land of snow that is so fresh and clean that to ride over it seems criminal. I try to ride last so I can stop now and then to be alone, to look back and be glad that I have been able to come this way, but Tony has the feeling too and has bagged the back spot for the morning run.

We ride a long way and in late afternoon (sun time rather than clock time, which has long ceased to be important to us) we stop for coffee so that Odd-Knut can work out a route. He wants to go back to the base camp before we push on towards Finland. There is a problem that way, as he cannot take his dogs over the border. Technically that offers no problem, as there is no border in the accepted sense between Norway, Sweden or Finland, but rabies has reached southern Finland and Norway has placed a restriction on dogs coming back. We have no problem going in, but if we are caught or seen then Odd-Knut will not be allowed to bring his dogs back without a lengthy and expensive quarantine. He wants to get us close enough so we can ski over the border, but needs to find a road so he can field the dogs before collecting us. He pores over a map while I collect wood for a fire and Nathan digs out a seat for us all. Tony announces that he is off for a crumble, an expression that has taken his fancy and replaced the computerese of going for a 'system dump.' Relentlessly, every day, he tells us when, presumably fearful that we will follow him, camera in hand. He

comes back as Odd-Knut starts making the fire. He uses the conventional method for these parts. Not for him the Baden-Powell approach of rubbing two Boy Scouts together; he liberally douses the twigs with paraffin and throws in a match. If it looks good he throws on more wood, if it looks bad he throws on more paraffin.

Blackie, his lead dog, watches passively. I wonder if she has yet worked out that for every douse she has to pull less load; probably not, or she would be pissing on the wood. She has, after all, pissed on everything else all day. Odd-Knut collects a kettle of snow and has settled into Nathan's seat with a roll-up. I sit down too. The smoke blows in my eyes making them water and sting, so I get up, move and freeze my ass off sitting beyond the smoke in the wind up the valley. I move again and try to write some notes, but it is cold enough to freeze the ballpoint off my biro. Tony measures the temperature and tells me it is warming up. No it isn't. Give me that thing, it must be wrong. Why doesn't it have a mark on it for absolute brass monkeys? I sit disconsolate in the snow. This place isn't beautiful, it's miserable – bloody cold, bloody windy and no I don't want any bloody smoked reindeer. Tony brings me a cup of coffee and tells me that the tracks we crossed a while back were, Odd-Knut says, *jarv* or wolverine. I have to admit grudgingly that this is interesting, and I trudge up the path with Tony just behind. Why is it only me that gets the rats? What keeps this bastard so cheerful? Then I remember that time when the tent blew down in the snowstorm and his sleeping bag went in the slush. That didn't cheer him up. And there was that other time when . . .

My mood improves. By the time we get to the *jarv* tracks I am over it, putting it down to a poor night's sleep and a wearing day that have combined so that I am feeling the cold more than I normally do. The tracks are indeed of *jarv*, a shy, elusive animal that neither Tony nor I have ever seen. Odd-Knut has never seen one either, but that is less of a surprise as the noise and smell of his dogs frighten most animals away long before he spots them. Later in the day we spot the tracks of elk (what the Americans and Canadians call 'moose', although, as might be expected, theirs are bigger).

We move on, with me grabbing the back spot. Rayo, who is running lead for me today in harness with Kaisa, gets her leg caught up in the trace. I see it happen but wait, hoping that as usual she

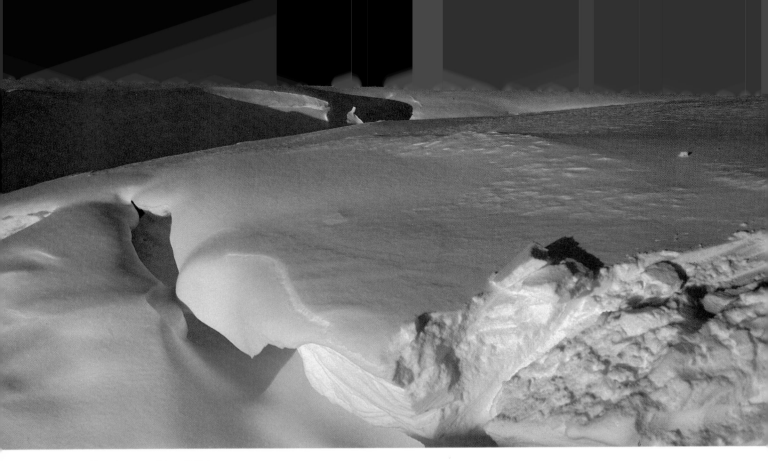

Evening near Liggafjellet.

Full moon above Liggafjellet.

will jump out from it, but it just gets worse and she slows almost to a stop. The wind picks up some snow, or it is snowing gently, as I snow hook the dogs to sort her out. Hey, good dog Rayo, have you got your leg caught? There, there it's OK. And I untangle the mess. Kaisa, bored by the proceedings, takes advantage of the slack trace and goes over to have a look at a tree. I let off the snow hook, Rayo heads for the tree, Kaisa leaps out of the way, Sunniva follows her round and it's back to knitting in seconds. It takes me many minutes to sort it out, as each released dog shows marked enthusiasm for getting tangled up again. The snow is much worse as I finally move out, and the only consolation for the time it has taken is being alone, and arriving late so that the others have already begun on the tent and wood collecting.

Odd-Knut calls for a volunteer to help feed the dogs in the gathering storm and I don't step back quickly enough. The dog food comes in frozen slabs that must be cut up with a felling axe. Normally we heat it first and add biscuit so that the dogs have a warm, mixed meal, but tonight Odd-Knut is considering giving it to them frozen to save time. Finally his conscience gets the better of him and we break out the large billy from his sledge and light another fire in the lea of a sledge. It is miserable work as the snow is now falling thickly, the wind blowing hard. We put on the billy and head for a coffee and warm, pausing at the tent entrance to brush off the snow that is heaped on our jackets and hoods. Tony and Nathan have made tea and soup and we have some before going out to feed the first batch of dogs. They feed from steel bowls that must be filled by dipping. It is a gloves-off job to avoid getting them soaking wet and the combination of cold steel, snow and wind, and wet dog food is bad for the fingers. While the first group of dogs feeds – it takes just a few seconds for them to finish the bowls, right down to the lick clean – I huff on my fingers, more hopefully than knowingly. By the time we have fed the second and, thank God, final group of a dozen we are frozen.

Back in the tent there is more soup, coffee and a hunk of smoked lamb that goes down well. Tony finds several packets of banana custard that is hot and sweet; it tastes bloody awful and neither Tony nor I like it, none the less he fights me for the last helping. More tea, then more coffee. I have a headache and am concerned that the wind has dehydrated me; it is so important to pour liquid

down in the Arctic, especially in winter. We drink some more, eat some more. The stove warms the tent up and we become drowsy, and oblivious to the storm outside. By the time I am curled up in my bag I am totally content, warm and well fed, exhausted but not wanting to sleep for fear of missing these moments of happiness. The tent is warm, and I have taken everything off, even though it has been the norm to sleep in our thermals and a pile fibre hood. What a day.

I wake suddenly in the night, aware of the others breathing and the wind banging the tent fabric. I need a pee. If only I hadn't had that last cup of hot chocolate. I lie still hoping that I will be able to fall back to sleep, but knowing it is a waste of time. Slowly I get out of the bag. It is perishing in the tent, but I can't be bothered to dress – it will only take a moment, I tell myself. I open the tent door, already cold. I leap outside into the snow,

High speed sledging, Sördalen.

stand ankle deep in the snow and strain frantically at the same time trying to remember which direction I am pointing so that I can give instructions about where not to get the snow for tomorrow's tea. I start to shiver. The wind howls through the trees, the wind chill temperature must be *low,* and I have no clothes on.

No clothes on, do you hear? I am cold. COLD. Give me a c, give me an o . . .

By the time I am back in the tent I am on the borderline, cold enough to wake Tony with disjointed movements. OK? he asks. Yeah, OK. And into the bag and who cares if I'm wet.

It takes a long time to warm up, a very long time, but then I sleep as though practising for death. The storm rages through what is left of the night.

*Lavvu*s have a hole in the top to let smoke from the wood fire out. The modern version we are using has the same hole, and our wood-burning stove has a pipe that goes through it, while the rest of it is closed with a cowl that is a bitch to fix. Last night in the cold and dark we failed to fix it properly again, and when I wake up there is snow all over us and our kit. I look sideways at Nathan who is lying motionless in a bag covered by an inch of snow. The snow has penetrated everywhere, hiding gloves and socks, filling boots, even packing five centimetres of itself into the stove. Tony and I get up as quickly as we can, brushing the snow free from clothes before putting them on so that it will not melt with the heat from our bodies. We tell Nat to stay where he is, brushing the snow from his bag to try to minimize how wet it will be. The advantage of the temperature being so low – although it has risen several degrees with the cloud over – is that the snow is like dry flour and brushes off easily.

It was late when we woke, and by the time we have cleared up the mess it is later still. Working outside is difficult in the fresh snow and when the wind picks up again we admit defeat and agree that we will stay another night. We fix the cowl in the twilight and prepare the evening meal. Nathan goes outside with the kettle, anxious for some activity, having spent most of the day inside. We turn in, with the wind picking up even stronger and threatening to blow the *lavvu* away. The rearrangement of the kit has pushed me close to the side, and just above my face the fabric cracks and bangs in the wind. Far away we can hear the noise of the wind forcing its way up some narrow

gully then bursting free to hurl itself across the plateau we crossed yesterday. Tony tells us about his lone stay in the Westmann Islands off Iceland when I had to leave four days earlier than him. The wind blew down the tents of the other lads he had joined in camping on an apparently sheltered spot in a hollow above the sea. Tony sat it out – in my tent I feel obliged to tell him – listening for the noise of a train, a noise that meant the wind was coming up the defile between him and the sea. He counted the seconds, one, two, three, four, and then it hit the tent with a fury that he had never known, he inside in his sleeping bag with his feet braced against the dome pole facing the onslaught. He painted a vivid picture of apprehension and tiredness. His storm lasted two and half days, leaving him ragged and with only enough energy to get to the airport to be ready for the first flight out. Nathan asks me if our storm will last two or more days. I say no, and hope that he doesn't realize that I really have no idea. Tony takes the hint and decides not to wax equally lyrical about the Svalbard storm that kept everyone in the tent for seventy-two hours, unable to go out for *anything.* Thank God for dome tents with two bays: you collect snow from one end for tea, pass it through the middle-man, and then deposit it at the other end.

Next morning the worst is over. Outside there are scudding clouds, but they are high up and the sun occasionally breaks through. Down here there is a metre of snow on the windward side of the *lavvu,* and I fall over a small rucsac that had disappeared. Well, Nathan, you have survived your first Arctic storm. Not so bad really, eh? Go and fill the kettle to celebrate.

We pack and move on, the dogs finding it difficult to move in the fresh snow. In desperation Odd-Knut suggests we go down on to a frozen lake, Devdisvatn, the Lake of the Dead Man. It is an ancient Lappish name, and Odd-Knut is not sure of its origin. There is, he says, an old Lappish church near its eastern edge; he has never seen it but he has been told of it by an old Lapp who lives near the lake's western edge. Perhaps we go and take a look? Sure, anything is better than man-handling the sledges through waist-deep snow.

The lake has been swept clean of snow by the wind, the sweepings making a huge bank on our side that we have to negotiate. It is topped by a wind-blown crust that almost holds our weight as we descend. The ride across the lake gives us our best sledging for days, but the search for the ruin is hopeless, an endless toing and froing among trees and too-deep snow. The last remnant of the storm hits us, thick snow blotting out the view of anything, so reluctantly we call a halt and go back down on to the lake. The snow stops and Odd-Knut suggests we try a little fishing. Fired by his own enthusiasm, he stops his sledge and gets out a huge snow drill, like a brace and bit but capable of boring a twenty centimetre hole. Nathan grabs the drill: this will be great for his project. He and Odd-Knut shovel away the snow to reach the ice, making a large hole about a metre deep, and Nathan jumps in and starts to brace and bit with enthusiasm. The ice is thick and he is a good deal less enthusiastic when the tip breaks through. What Odd-Knut has not told him is that the water under the ice is pressurized, and it wells up out of the hole. Nathan is now experienced enough to know that wet feet and the Arctic are a poor mix and is out of the hole like a rabbit. The water pours on until a few inches has collected in the bottom. Odd-Knut rigs a fishing line and offers it to me. He seems to think that it is fair that I should have first crack since I am the one who has carried the worms about for the last umpteen days. On the first day Odd-Knut gave me a tobacco tin of worms and told me to keep them warm, and they have travelled the Arctic inside my second layer of clothing ever since, even sharing my sleeping bag at night-time. Now their time has come. And a bloody good job too.

My opinion has always been that fishermen, at least those who fish to catch and return, are on a par with the hunting fraternity. Killing things for fun seems to me to be so immoral as to warrant no discussion at all. It is wrong, end of conversation. As a result I undergo a bout of conscience, taking the short rod only when Odd-Knut assures me that we will eat whatever we catch, and that we will probably not catch anything. Odd-Knut smokes a pensive roll-up, I fish, Tony photographs, Nathan wanders off with a shovel and ice drill. My father, a Desert Rat, tells me that in the North African campaign you never asked a man with a shovel where he was going, so I let Nat go. Soon he is digging like a whirling dervish, the impressive show ending with another frantic leap. Ice fishing, I find, is as cold as anything I have ever tried in the Arctic, and after a few minutes of unproductive ass-freezing I pack it in. Tony has a go and I mooch over to see how Nat is faring. Badly.

We freeze and drown worms for a few more minutes. A sudden snow flurry gives Nathan his first-ever view – if that is not a contradiction in terms – of a white-out. The two of us stand next to his second hole unable to distinguish sky and lake and cut off from the other pair. It lasts an impressive minute or two, then whirls away. We pack in the fishing; Odd-Knut pronounces the last of the worms dead and suggests we all come back for another go in April. If only we could.

We camp, and to compensate for the fishing Odd-Knut suggests he will cook us another of his specialities, *blåbærsuppe*, a fish stew. He disappears to collect the ingredients from his sledge, Tony and I start feeding the dogs, and Nathan decides to show Odd-Knut an English dish – pancakes. Odd-Knut has given him some eggs that turn out to be frozen. Nat tells Tony, expecting sympathy and assistance. He gets neither. When he has thawed his ingredients Nat cooks the way he dug the snow hole – frantically. Odd-Knut's soup is incredible, a mixture of different fish and shellfish.

When the meal is over we notice that the sky is clearing; now there is enough cloud-free sky to show that the Northern Lights are out. We drink coffee outside, leaning against trees to watch the free show. The Lights are a shimmering green waterfall that grows in intensity, then dies slowly to be replaced by a separate show in another part of the sky. There it is a plaited rope, moving sinuously. The colour is very bright, and occasionally there is a splash of red, rarer, at the edges. We watch for a long time, Tony catching the show on camera, then notice that the temperature has plummeted with the clearing of the sky and turn in. During the night I hear the harsh squeal of a fox, a long way off, answered by a staccato bark from one of the dogs. The bark starts them all off and they howl at the moon for a few minutes. Odd-Knut calls out sharply and they fall silent.

In the morning there is a centimetre of ice on the tent pole to the side of my head, probably from my breath while I slept. Outside the weather is beautiful, blue sky and rising sun. We decide to go for a ride on the lake and rush to harness the dogs. Use Rayo as your lead dog today, Odd-Knut tells me. OK, I say, which one is Rayo? She is next to Kala. Thanks Odd-Knut, thanks a lot, which one is Kala? I hope that he will not say that Kala is the one next to Rayo. He doesn't.

We ride across the lake on one of the best trips we have had. The lake is flat, its hard crust free of

Ice fishing.

fresh snow. The weather is perfect and we are now experienced enough mushers to be able to enjoy the high speeds without anxiety.

Venstre, Rayo. *Høyre*, Rayo. Go left, go right.

So good am I that I turn round on the runners to photograph Tony. The sledge hits a bump and I am off, using my camera as a snow hook. So much for experience. Tony races past, laughing his head off. Give us a lift, you miserable bastard. Ho, ho . . .

They field my dogs and we ride on. Odd-Knut finds a steep up-slope where a river joins the lake and we play for a bit going up and down steep slopes. When we ride away from the river Odd-Knut stops sharply. The river has curved round and Odd-Knut has drawn up a few metres from the edge of a very steep drop. We investigate. There is a wind-blown cornice of about one and a

half metres overhanging a sheer drop of about eight metres. I ask Odd-Knut if sledgers often go over cornices. Again, he misses the answer – which is, of course, 'No, only once' – and says with a grave look that usually the dogs see it even in poor visibility, but in white-outs it has been known.

We call in on Odd-Knut's Lappish acquaintance – not 'friend', because the Lapps rarely make real friends with non-Lapps. He lives in a glorious wooden hut with several equally attractive out-buildings. In a small enclosure three reindeer sniff the air, detect dog, either from the dogs them-selves deliberately left many yards away, or from our clothing, and shuffle nervously as we approach. Nathan, anxious for a closer look, goes over and the animals go mad. We call him back.

The Lapp speaks no English and we have a stilted conversation through Odd-Knut. Yes, it is a bad winter, the worst he has seen in sixty-five years of herding reindeer here. Sixty-five years? How old is he? He is seventy-nine. Good God, he looks about fifty. He has a straight back and huge arms that betray a phenomenal strength. When he walks with us he is out ahead, large, confident strides. How does he feel about the Swedish Lapps? He shrugs. How can the reindeer tell which is Norway and which is Sweden? It is the animals that come here, and the Lapps just follow. So he is happy to see his Swedish brothers here? Well, he understands that those Norwegian Lapps that are closer to the border than he is might not be so keen. Norwegian Lapps? Does he not just see Lapps? Don't they all talk the same language? He changes the subject awkwardly. Would we like some smoked reindeer (not that you can make good smoked meat now, not with all the air pollution, the acid rain and the like from the UK). I ask what the charming little wooden shed down the track is for – tools and things? No, he says, it is the toilet. That's a hell of a way to go, I say. True, he says, but it is a fine place for the smell.

Tony has been outside photographing the Lapp's hut and comes in raving about its beauty and position. Ask him if he would like me to send him a print of his hut, Odd-Knut. The Lapp is puzzled. What would he do with it? He could put it on the wall here, explains Tony. The man is still puzzled. He says something to Odd-Knut who turns to Tony. He asks, explains Odd-Knut, why should he want a picture of his hut on the wall when he can go outside and look at it? Tony looks at me, for once lost for words.

We talk some more. I am intrigued by this old man who seems so unimpressed by everything we find attractive and interesting. Reindeer? You eat them. A frozen lake? A nuisance if you want to eat fish. A good-looking dog? A dog is just a dog. It is not that he doesn't care, just that his sense of values are different – not better, not worse, just different.

Outside the light is fading. A flock of Siberian tits twitters away above us. Tony and I pause to watch. Not until now had we realised how much we had missed birds.

On the drive back to the camp one of Odd-Knut's lead dogs, Stig, trips in a dark section of woodland. The point dogs catch him and one of them nips him on the leg – take *that* for being more popular with the boss. By the time we get back to the tent Stig is limping badly and when Odd-knut looks

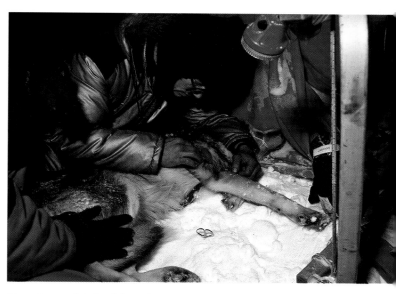

Operating on Stig in a blizzard.

he finds he is bleeding profusely. Odd-Knut fetches his first aid kit, and I get ours. Odd-Knut muzzles the dog with a piece of trace line, ties its front and back legs together and lies it on its side. The wind has picked up a bit, and there is a light snow falling. We turn a sledge on to its side for shelter, and by the light from our head torches we examine the wound. It is long and deep, the flesh pulled off the meat. I clean it out with antiseptic wipes, passing them to Nathan to finish the job when Stig starts to buck and fight. I hold him down, Nathan operates the most stable of the head torches, Odd-Knut operates the needle and thread and Tony takes the photographs. The stitching takes a long time and hurts Stig a lot more than it hurts the rest

Stig after the blizzard.

Crossing a frozen lake.

of us. I wonder whether the cold is much of an anaesthetic. Apparently not.

In the tent that night we eat smoked trout and Odd-Knut tells us that the previous year there was a fight on his team and after it was over and the dogs were moving again he saw blood on the snow. He stopped the team and found that Brusie, now Tony's lead dog, had a serious stomach wound, one of her teats having been almost torn off. He fought to staunch the blood and stitch the wound, with the dog slipping towards unconsciousness. Finally her eyes turned grey and rolled, and Odd-Knut thought she was dead. He worked to revive her and eventually she recovered enough to be wrapped and put on the sledge. Exhausted, Odd-Knut cut short his trip and went home. He was met by Kjell-Arne, his kennel boy, who told him that when he was eating his lunch he heard the noise of a dog scratching against the door. He went out, but there was nothing there, just the rest of the dogs on their chains. He went back in, but the noise started once more. Again Kjell-Arne went outside, this time checking everywhere for a dog off its chain or a stray. There was no dog anywhere. He became very nervous, and was glad to see Odd-Knut come home. Odd-Knut asked what time it had been when Kjell-Arne heard the noise. It was at exactly the time when Odd-Knut feared Brusie was dying, as she became unconscious.

The next day Stig, kept away from the other dogs on a separate chain, but not under cover, is stiff-legged and looking mournful. He gets an extra ration from Odd-Knut, who is clearly worried about him. Stig was due to lead in the *Finnmårrks Løpet*, Europe's longest sledge dog race. The Iditarod is closed to most European mushers as there is rabies in Alaska, so Odd-Knut is hoping to break into the top five of the European one, and the loss of Stig will be a serious blow. All day Stig rides on the sledge, a real sledge dog. He is upset at the lack of activity and howls appallingly, but when Odd-Knut tries him on the trace he is clearly crippled and in pain. It is four months before Stig is well enough to walk properly, and by then winter is over and the race has passed, with Odd-Knut making the top ten but no higher because of the loss. Stig makes a full recovery which is some compensation.

Our ride with Stig is the last ride we make. The loss of the dog means that we cut short our projected trip north, and go down into Dividalen, to the south. We go the long way; who knows how long it will be before we come this way again?

The last sunset is orange and yellow, then shades of purple. I see the way the snow is kicked up off the paws of the dogs, the way their breath explodes around their heads. We round a corner and the way goes downhill steeply into the valley. The last of the light is directly ahead, painted sky between dark hills. The descent is never-ending – I am glad – until Tony comes towards me. Hitch to the sign over there, he points, Odd-Knut is arranging for a car. The dogs howl and whine at first, then realize that they have finished for the day. It is all over.

Tri-Point

Odd-Knut Thoresen pointed east. It is that way, he said, you just follow the Swedish border. He forgot to mention that the border hereabouts between Norway and Sweden is unmarked. This section of the border runs almost due east-west, as though the border-makers were fed up with the toing and froing they had been forced to put up with further south and had just decided to rule a line across and have done with it. There was a small squabble over the ruler so that it pointed very slightly north. Perhaps this gain of territory by Sweden was the reason why the Norwegians tell Swedish jokes the way the English tell Irish jokes.

Odd-Knut was pointing towards the three-countries stone, the point where Norway, Finland and Sweden meet. You must remember to do as I said, he reminded us. Anxious for another fine story about Sweden to tell his friends, Odd-Knut had made us promise to stand with one leg in Norway, one leg in Finland and to pee into Sweden – OK in principle, but at −40°C (−40°F) it is difficult to find anything to pee with. And I will see you in the hotel at Kilpisjärvi, on Friday at two o'clock.

Hey, Odd-Knut, I called as he prepared to leave, cuffing his dogs into silence, how do we recognize this stone? Is it big? Will it be covered with snow? No, no, it will be obvious; it is very big. This big – well over his head – and this round – from here to the sledge there. It is painted. It is . . . he fought for an English expression of obviousness. It sticks out like dog's balls, Tony suggested, seeking as always to improve Odd-Knut's vocabulary with the very best of English expressions. Odd-Knut had been taught enough alternative words – and been a dog owner long enough – to fall about, the cold air crackling with his rich, deep laugh. He repeated the expression to be sure it had lodged well.

None of this gets us closer to knowing what the stone is really like. Odd-Knut goes, so do we.

We have been living in tents for several weeks now, in the Arctic mid-winter, and we have become almost blasé about the temperature. We know that the thing to fear is the wet; if you are wet at about −2°C (28°F) life is cold and miserable, and more so if there is a limited chance of getting dry. The best temperature is, funnily enough, around −10°C (12°F). In that you can work comfortably without gloves for a long time, leave your hat off for a bit, and if you do get covered in snow, brush it off because it is dry like flour. Of course, if you have your gloves off for a long time, or if the wind is blowing, you will be cold. Of course. Between −15°C (5°F) and −20°C (−4°F) life becomes more difficult as you need to keep covered most of the time. But we still photograph without gloves – although usually in a pair of silk or thermosilk inners – and sit outside to eat and drink. Below −20°C (−4°F) life gets more tedious, and interest in survival takes over from enthusiasm for working as the temperature falls still further. The worst job of all, Tony tells me, is changing 120 film as it can only be achieved gloveless and he occasionaly finds that his saliva has frozen before he has got the sealing tab to stick.

On the Friday we are to meet Odd-Knut in Finland the day dawns beautifully, perhaps the bluest sky we have seen. It is cold, very cold. I woke in the night, pulled on my pile jacket and, very unusually, put on a silk balaclava. Now that I wake again I am still noticeably not warm. My breath produces huge clouds of mist. The remains of last night's water have frozen in the Trangia billy. It's so cold my fingers stick to the aluminium, which sparkles with a smear of hoar frost. I get back in my bag as the Trangia starts work on the ice. The problem with boiling snow at −20°C (−4°F) is that you need mounds of it to make tea. (Ice is easier in one sense as it produces water on a one-for-one basis.) The heat input to melt the stuff is about half the total heat needed to boil it, so you sit, or in this case lie, and wait apparently for ever.

Dropping the tent is not easy. The aluminium poles that hold up the flysheet dome decline to come out of the pouches in the stiff-with-cold nylon and then stick to most things, including gloves and sore fingers, that they come into contract with. We are still in our Lundhags, so have to use a bear-trap-type ski binding. The metal of its

Nordic skiing, Finland.

sprung end has to be hauled into place, a miserable job that is the worse for having to be repeated too frequently, the heel cut away on the boot being not quite deep enough to hold the wire securely. Skiing has the advantage of warming us and by the time we reach the three-countries stone – the *Treriksröset* in Finnish – life is becoming more reasonable. Tony puts the thermometer in the snow – upside-down so it will measure air rather than snow temperature – and climbs the stone, a jelly-shaped lump of concrete, by way of the conveniently placed ladder. Yes, it really is that big. On the top he lies his passport on the actual meeting point and photographs it. Very chic.

In bright sunshine, and now at the 'hottest' part of the day, the thermometer is reading −34°C (−29°F), which excites him no end as he has no photos, as yet, of a thermometer reading below −30°C (−22°F). Carefully he supports the tube on ski poles and clicks away. I fail to see what all the

fuss is about, as the shade temperature is several degrees cooler. Nathan, who has plodded around the stone half a dozen times in the hope that he can win credibility with his schoolmates with tales of having been to Finland at least six times, claims that he has seen a shade temperature of −41°C (−42°F). This is possible, as the radiation effect on a day like today could well be worth 7°C. Even with gloves on, sufficient heat leaks away from us to raise the temperature each time we lift the thermometer. By the time Tony has finished his shot it is reading −28°C (−18°F).

Near the stone the country is superb. When you approach Finland, especially in the north, it starts distinctively. Suddenly you are in a forest with lakes and small rounded hills, and the high angular peaks of Norway or Sweden are gone. Here the effect is similar. Away to our left we can see the last hills of Norway, hills we have so recently left behind, while behind us is a birch forest and

Skiing near the Three Countries Stone.

View west into Norway from the Three Countries Stone.

beyond that a frozen lake. The stone itself stands near open water in summer. Today that water is indistinguishable from the snow fields at its edge. The birches are sugared with ice, a curiously exaggeratedly shaped ice that is sharp and fragile. If you brush a branch the ice decays and falls like mist, each crystal that catches the sun exploding into light, like the parts of Nathan's Tromsø snowballs.

The pause at the stone chills us all. Nathan is frozen virtually into immobility by the inactivity and is beginning to lose all enjoyment in the scene.

I manipulate the icy bear-trap on my skis and leave my fingerprints behind on the metal. My camera has stopped working, the amps frozen into the batteries, but Tony takes a last few shots. As we start to move we catch the noise of a snow scooter. We have gone only a little way when it comes into view, driven by a smiling man in a bobble hat. In halting English he asks us if we are the friends of the Odd-Knut. *The* Odd-Knut?! Yes. *Hyvaa*, good. Odd-Knut, fearful of the cold today, has sent a friend to see that we are all right, bless him. The man has a sledge behind his scooter. You ride here? *Joo*, yes, we ride here. Climb aboard, lads.

And so we cross the Kilpisjärvi lake in style – almost. Up front the Finnish driver has a huge wind-protecting screen and heated hand grips. The sledge, on the other hand, is exposed. On the lake – miles of it – we are travelling at perhaps 40 kph, perhaps more. I do a quick sum; −35, +7 for radiation, minus something for the wind chill. But my brain is seizing up. In minutes I can only think about how cold it is. The wind-chill temperature is difficult to calculate for well-clothed people with unexposed flesh, but it must be around −60°C (−76°F). Nathan, hunched into me as far as he is able, closes his eyes in the hope that when he opens them it will all be over. When he tries to open them he finds he cannot, they are frozen. Tony's nose freezes and he has to break out the ice to free an airway. My nose freezes too and for weeks after loses skin like a moulting snake.

But Kilpisjärvi arrives and there is Odd-Knut standing, tactfully, outside the hotel door, alerted to our arrival by the noise of the scooter. We break free of each other and the sledge, bang about to clear the ice and regain a little circulation. We follow Odd-Knut in. I have coffee here, he says. Dick, you want milk? It doesn't matter, Odd-Knut. I'm going to pour it into my boots.

Russian-Norwegian Border

The dog sledging with Odd-Knut had been terrible. Not that we had suddenly grown to dislike our musher or the countryside, but after the previous year's trip when we had good, crisp weather, the winter had been unseasonably warm. Only on the last day had the temperature finally fallen, and then only to −8°C. For the early days it had been around zero, making the snow wet, making us wet. One thing Tony and I had learned was that getting wet in an Arctic winter was not to be recommended. Staying warm became a problem, and getting dry more of a one.

So we packed up, borrowed some skis and flew north to Kirkenes. We had no real plan, just a vague interest in seeing the Russian border and in visiting the Øvre Pasvik National Park. A few hours later, as we were skiing across some rather dull country, we decided to see if there was a stone where Russia, Finland and Norway met, the way there had been where Norway, Sweden and Finland met. There was, but there was no way we could dance around it as we had further south. This stone, a smaller, physically less significant object, was wired off. So too, surprisingly was the Norwegian-Finnish border. It seemed that the Norwegians, a little afraid of aggravating their Russian neighbours, had decided that Finland could sort out its own problems, and that no one pestering the Russians from that country could escape into Norway. Further along, more evidence of the Norwegian worries surfaced, with notices that told us in several languages that we must not photograph Soviet territory, or throw stones at the Russians, or urinate over the border, and so on.

The border was a fearful place, marked by pairs of tall pillars, tall enough to be in no danger of being called insignificant. On 'our' side they were yellow with black tops and the Norwegian coat of arms; on the Soviet side opposite there was a red pillar with a green top. Where the border was on opposite banks of a river or lake – which it usually was – the pillars stood on the banks, the border running along the bed of the stream. On dry land the pillars were a few yards apart, the border bisecting them. At one point, to the east of Kirkenes, there was a small section of wicker fencing about two metres long and sixty centimetres high between the pillars, marking the exact position of the border. It looked ridiculous. In the main the fences – sometimes a bit forlorn – were on the Norwegian side.

The sun went down as we skied quietly up the border again. We skied on, but eventually, concerned that if we flattened the batteries of our head lamps we might have problems later with cooking, we stopped. We pitched the tent in a hollow in the snow excavated with shovel heads attached to our ice axes. Soon the Trangia was boiling water and we were sorting out our kit. To save weight Tony had brought plastic cutlery. It was white. He put it on the snow and we never saw it again. What sort of idiot takes a white fork and spoon to the Arctic?

Tony had also brought a small radio, but we soon found we could only find Russian channels. These were exclusively filled with a Russian female 'singer' who had recorded a huge number of LPs while her hand was trapped in the studio door. We turned it off. The silence was extreme and yet now and then there were odd snappings and cracklings. The park bears were hibernating, surely, although there were probably other animals about like elk and foxes. Everywhere we had been these noises had accompanied us, so why did we feel so nervous here? It was straightforward really; neither of us could escape the notion that out there in the night soldiers and other ne'er-do-wells were criss-crossing the area intent on no good. Sooner or later one group would find our tent and kill us in the night, or kidnap us. Neither of us wanted to finish up teaching physics in a Soviet school in Uzbekhistan, and Tony did not fancy the idea of trying to find good-quality bike frame metal in the Urals. We spent a nervy night and woke with miserable heads and eyes, a need for a cup of something hot and a desire to be moving on.

At length we reach Nyrud and an affable

Skiing at the Finnish border.

the area. Clouds of gas and steam from the industrial city of Nikel had accompanied us as we had travelled south, and for many miles the red glow from the city was like a misplaced dawn. East from Nikel, he said, the forests were dead for seventy-five kilometres, the water was poisoned, the people were sick and pale. It is a holocaust, he said; thank God the winds blow from us to them. He hoped Gorbachev would be given the time and peace to sort the problems out before it was too late.

We moved north over snow so dry and powdery that even our skis sank into it on occasions. At one point I took mine off to try to follow a flock of Lappland buntings that elusively flitted among the pines, and almost disappeared from sight. We skied over yet another large snow field that had once been a lake and into another pine forest. The only break in the flat landscape were the mountains of Russia to our right.

Campsite near the Russian border.

Norwegian policeman who pointed out a Russian observation tower and politely explained that new regulations meant we could photograph with up to 200mm lenses, provided we did not use tripods, photograph the tower or include Soviet territory in the shot except as a background. I asked how far the border was away from us, as there was no intervening fence and the boundary river was frozen. About two hundred metres, he said. And if I tried to walk over, I asked, what would you do? He gave me a real beaming smile. I would stop you, he said. And he clearly meant it.

We talked of bears – last year he had fed one near his tent over a period of several weeks – and snowy owls that occasionally visited the area. We spoke of the ecological problems Russia caused in

Night skiing in the Øvre Pasvik National Park.

Campsite, Finland.

When night came we moved inland, away from the border, to reach less nervous ground. The night was calm and we sat outside the tent to eat. Tony set his thermometer upside-down in the snow to measure the air temperature. He peered at it: −18°C (0°F), he said; not too bad. I nodded and offered him tea. He took it and as he moved away to stretch his legs, he kicked the head off the thermometer. I suggested that the temperature – or at least part of it – seemed to be falling. He carefully dug about in the snow to retrieve the bits and for a moment I really did think he was going to drink the alcohol, just as he told everyone he would if he was ever down on his uppers.

We turned in early, tired out by the soft snow. Tony made hot chocolate and then thawed snow, kettleful after kettleful, filling our plastic bottles and passing them to me so I could stuff them in my bag. Long since we have learned to sleep with the water in our bags so that in the morning we are spared the effort of melting ice and can reduce the time spent waiting to pour liquid down throats parched by breathing cold, dry air all night.

Unhappy with the new bag I was trying, I pulled on a silk balaclava. Bad bag or not, I was asleep before I had time to think about it. In the morning I saw that Tony had also pulled on a hood in the night. We must be getting old and past it.

Tony looked very peaceful, snoring quietly. It seemed a shame to disturb him, but I needed a tea, so I gently slammed into him with both feet. Wake up, you idle bleeder and get the Trangia on. He was not too pleased and told me, amongst other things, that I had the matches. Bullshit. Any old excuse for not having to bother to do anything. It turned out to be true which placed me in an awkward spot. It hardly, I observed, detracts from the fact that you are an idle bugger. Bollocks, he said.

We skied for another day or two, digging a snow hole for sleeping one night when the terrain had beaten our brains into insensibility and we needed activity and novelty. But in the end we gave up, went to Kirkenes and did the tourist bit. There is a shop that sells postcards, a nice café where they charge an arm and a leg for two coffees and two doughnut-type things. There is a ginormous factory of some description. There are a lot of fed-up-looking kids. There is a bus station. There was a bus to the airport. We got on it.

GREENLAND

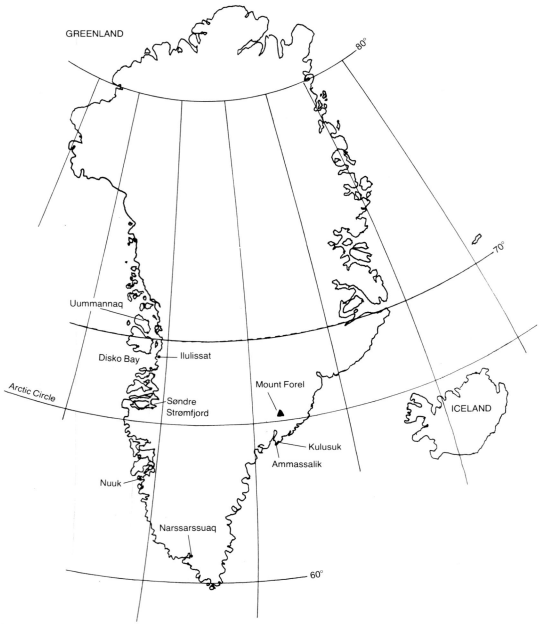

GREENLAND

80°

70°

Uummannaq

Disko Bay — Ilulissat

Arctic Circle

Mount Forel

Søndre
Strømfjord

ICELAND

Kulusuk

Ammassalik

Nuuk

Narssarssuaq

60°

Greenland.

Despite its inhospitable reputation, Greenland has been settled for a long time, and there is evidence in the north of the country to suggest that hunters walked over the land bridge from Canada as long as 4,500 years ago. These earliest peoples, of the Saqqaq culture, lived around Sisimiut, among other areas. They were replaced by a quite different people – known as *tunits* – before the appearance of modern-day Greenlanders, Eskimos who crossed the Bering Straits perhaps 1,000 years ago. At roughly the same time Erik the Red reached this island, the world's biggest, on his way to discovering Vinland, North America. Initially, all the settlements on the island were in the north, but as the climate grew colder the settlers retreated southward so that today most settlements are in the south, and the north of the island is left to nature.

Greenland – named, it is always said, by Erik the Red to persuade settlers to come to the country – is covered by an ice sheet that, at its maximum dimensions, is 2,250 kilometres long and 975 kilometres wide. The ice, at its deepest, is nearly 3 kilometres thick and the whole cap covers two million square kilometres. Like the football matches of inadequate commentators it is an island of two halves. In the west the Inuit peoples want to be called Inuit and, while accepting their ancient culture – go into any town and they will sell you a *tupilak* – they are anxious to be seen as western, and neither Eskimo (a term almost of abuse), nor Danish. Calling them Danish is particularly unpopular as the Greenlanders desperately want home rule and insist for example on the use of Greenlandic names for towns in favour of the Danish equivalents. On the eastern coast the Inuit people still live the ancient life. You should not go there hoping for wildlife if you are planning to stay close to the (few) villages, because the local hunters will shoot anything that they can eat. There is likely to be little about, and what little there is will disappear at your approach. Here there are no shops, let alone shops that sell *tupilak*s, and the people have no interest in what you call them. Eskimo, Inuit, it is all one to them. They are reserved, almost to the point of being disinterested in you, but if you do speak they are friendly and polite.

West or east, the traveller is restricted to a very few sites and a limited range of activities, real expeditions requiring a great deal of planning, and permission from the Danish authorities in Copenhagen (*see* the appendix on regulations). Near Nuuk a good couple of days' walking can be had by following the spur of land that ends at Ulajuk, or by going inland to the peak of Store Malene which, at 833 metres, offers superb views towards the interior. North from Nuuk, Maniitsoq places its emphasis on skiing with, it is claimed, over 150 kilometres of ski tracks.

Sisimuit lies on a rocky fjord, the rock being hard gneiss and marble that gives an uncompromising landscape and offers hard days in tough country. The good expedition from here is to go west to the airport at Søndre Strømfjord, a distance of about 120 kilometres, four good days over ground that is, surprisingly, undulating rather than mountainous as it is closer to town. There are lakes and streams for water and there will be reindeer and sea eagles to see. There may even be a herd of musk ox to avoid.

North again is Disko Bay with its peppering of villages. The best is Ilulissat, a large town of over 4,000 people. The name is Greenlandic for 'iceberg' (very appropriate), and superior to the Danish 'Jakobshavn', which derives from nothing more romantic than the name of an eighteenth-century Danish merchant. Inland from the town there are excellent opportunities for the walker, with possibilities ranging from a few hours to several days as the shoreline of Disko Bay is reasonable along much of its length and is visited by any number of small boats. The boats will also allow close-up shots of icebergs the size of blocks of flats.

North of Disko Bay Uummannaq is a town that gave Tony and I lockjaw; I cannot understand why the Greenlanders did not go all the way and call it 'Uummaannaaqq'. The town offers tremendous boat trips out into the fjord and beyond, searching for seal and whale. At the end of the island on which the town sits is a 1,333-metre peak which should not be attempted by any but the very experienced climber. On the mainland close to the town those not wanting to camp can rent small mountain huts. The mountains themselves vary from the very shaly to the very hard, and walkers should be cautious as the change from one to the other can be very quick.

South of Nuuk most travellers will fly into Narsarsuaq and so will visit that town, or the nearby small towns of Narsaq, Qaqortoq and Nanortalik. The waters here are whale country, and there is plenty of scope for trips among the tight, jigsaw fjords. But it is also good walking country – it is about seventy-five kilometres overland from Narsarsuaq to Narsaq, about 105 kilometres from Narsarsuaq to Qaqortoq. Either route is straightforward as the fjord edge acts as guide. But do remember that if you get it wrong, or if something goes wrong, the fjord will look more like the proverbial creek, and you will be, literally, up it. And in a barbed wire canoe.

On Greenland's east coast the visitor is very restricted. Ittoqqortoormiit, to the north, is difficult to reach, while the wondrous country north again, around Mesters Vig and Ørsted Dal, is all but off-limits. Most people fly to Kulusuk, a small village set on an island from which the larger town of Ammassalik/Tasiilaq can be reached. From there the walker can, and must, head for the Valley of the Flowers.

# Summer

One autumn, for reasons of recce, Tony and I split up in Reykjavik, he took the long flight to Nuuk, heading north, while I took a shorter flight to Kulusuk. Tony's was a colder, less enthusing trip.

———— ◆ ————

'Where the hell are those matches?'

It is so cold that I am talking to myself, a sure way to get some quality conversation. Desperation? Yes, must be because I am near to causing an argument – with myself.

'I must find those matches. Shall I have chicken or tomato soup?'

The debate is irrelevant if I can't find the matches, so where the hell are you? The icicles are waiting their pleasure, lying in the Trangia to be transformed, just for me, into soup. Nice, warm, thick and delicious soup.

I have pitched north of Illulissat/Jakobshavn overlooking Disko Bay. The sunset has been spectacular, the fluffy cloud base underlit by the fiery ball of sun. It was gorgeous. I do enjoy the simplicity and freedom of camping. No hotel could offer an equivalent serenity. My bed was soft; as in Lappland the mosses and Arctic flora (all in brilliant colour) almost make a Karimat redundant. However, the clear September night is cold. Even at this ungodly hour the icebergs creak around the bay. They creep like huge ghosts following the fetish of winds and currents; it is pretty eerie out there and minus Christ knows what. I need warmth, but my sleeping bag is not good enough tonight. It is hardly the bag's fault, since I have underestimated the clime by at least one sleeping bag season. It is a mistake not to repeat, and after all these years one I should not have made.

The latent heat of melting is 80 somethings – BTUs per fortnight? – I forget, but melting takes an age. And then it will have to boil. I'm impatient on occasions, like now. Once fulfilled with internal heat I'll venture out of the pit, put on another set of thermal underwear and my fibre pile coat. Hey, I've got a balaclava, dry gloves and another set of thermals. Perhaps then I can sleep. Perhaps then I will survive the night. But only if I find the matches.

Illulissat/Jakobshaven is a traditional Greenlandic seaside town some three hundred kilometres north of the Arctic Circle. Most Greenland places have two names – Greenlandic (Inuit) and Danish. Illulissat means iceberg, an apt name for this, the third largest town in Greenland. Although a modern centre for trade and industry, traditional methods are still used, usually connected with harvesting from the sea. The sea provides a livelihood for most, and there is a perpetual toing and froing of craft around the bay. Winter causes some inconvenience – the sea freezing is the worst – but activities continue, with seal hunting and fishing under the ice. Traditional transport is used in the winter, dog teams bringing catches from the ice edge back to town.

Now, I'm a master musher, with plenty of dogging in Scandinavia. My memories are of the real delights of sledging, and of something none of the brochures tell you about – the smell. Illulissat is said to have 4,000 sledge dogs, all Greenlandic huskies. For a town of about 4,000 people the ratio of dog to his best friend, man, is, therefore, a little above the average. It is not a place for cats.

Despite the numbers of dogs, and the fact that they all live outdoors, the pavements are clean. Well, in truth, there are no pavements, but still there is no evidence of the dogs. There is the occasional stream of frozen yellow piss, very slippery and most definitely not to be fallen on to, but, thankfully, there are no smells. Controls by law are strict and adhered to. Loose dogs were rare, as escapees are soon caught by one of the town's professional dog catchers, and the attitude towards the animals is rather more civilized than that of British suburbia, where dogs wander and mess at random. But then these aren't pets. They work for their living, and if they don't work they usually don't live. It is, by our standards, a hard attitude, but in this harsh environment sentiment has to come second to the realities of life.

The town has much to offer, hotels, shops, a museum (well worth a visit) and a bus service. Perhaps 'service' is not within the spirit of the trades description act; the bus is certainly an

Ilulissat, West Greenland.

experience. The driver goes around at random, with no set route. He obviously knows everybody and where they want to go. The occasional tourist has little say, but it can be a fun way to see the town. The single fare, for any ride, can last from seconds to tens of minutes. In the end you often aren't where you hoped; on your second lap the tedium can get to you and you choose to get off rather than have to suffer it all again.

The geography of the west coast is based on a very old and hard rock, amongst the oldest in the world, one of the Isua super group. This makes walking pleasurable, particularly when compared with the country of Svalbard, an archipelago of coal-tip screes. Within the towns, homes are built around huge boulders which form patios for packs of pissed off-looking huskies who long for the winter ice and some sledge pulling. Filleted fish hang on the clothes lines to dry just like your smalls back home. Dog teams have right of way on

the road and tourists, in September, are as rare as cats. It is a weird place that is quite delightfully different and a good place to refill my larder.

I took a trail south. From the hill top immediately west when leaving town there was a fine view back over civilization, Disko Bay and the mountains inland and to the north. It was quite an impressive sight following the overnight snows, with everything clean and fresh. The town's cemetery was surprisingly fresh too. The mix of winter chills and bright arrays of flowers were as ponderous as its location. The site was a good hike from the road's end at the old heliport, and not an easy journey for those tending a grave, particularly considering the state of the path. I resisted the temptation to suggest that many coming here need not bother about the trip back, and continued to

121

the wilderness beyond the cemetery where all tracks lead, initially, to Jakobshavn Isfjord (ice fjord).

Here, calving ice from the most prolific glacier outside Antartica can be spotted. In fact, the whole seascape is full of glacier calf-ice, icebergs and nothing but. It is incredible, beyond the realms of amazement: huge icebergs crash and fall about like ninepins. The Isfjord is some fifty kilometres long and full of moving calf-ice. The inland glacier, Jakobshaven Isbræ, moves at an impressive 20–30 metres per day and is seven kilometres wide. The fjord is some 600 metres deep but for a sea-bed hill (the iceberg shoal) at its mouth, which gives only 200 metres of water. The icebergs get stuck at this point until the pressure of ice behind is so great the bergs inevitably fall over. The sight of a 100-metre-high iceberg toppling is awesome, as is the sound.

The path was wandering, often hidden by the autumn fall. A steady but disconcerting northerly wind cleared patches of ground where red and brown contrasted with the cold blues of the season. The Arctic tundra is always surprising, the flora warming the spirit even though their shades announce their forthcoming death. The crunching snow disturbed snow buntings, removing my sense of loneliness. They were busy gathering any available food to secure them through the quickly approaching winter, and worked among Arctic grasses bowed in the wind, some frozen in lakes of solid ice, crystal-clear ice, with just their heads sticking through the surface. I felt at peace with the world and despite the weight of my rucsac the burdens of life had gone.

I could not travel too far; after all, this was wild country known for sudden changes of weather and with limited rescue services. I had left information as to my route with the Greenlandic Travel Company, where the previous day I had discussed the problems of Greenlandic tourism with delightful people. I was now on one of their recommended tourist walks and was pleasantly surprised to find that tourist trails in Greenland are quite unlike those found back home. I saw no little acorn signs and huts selling Taiwanese junk. This is a virgin wilderness. It is wonderful, but I imagine it could be easy to underestimate these trails; some are quite strenuous hikes.

I enjoy my own company to a certain extent, as long as there is interest in the day and a goal. There are times when I need to be alone, especially photographing wildlife. Whoever is with me often gets bored and their presence usually frightens off my prey. There is one exception. While I was photographing puffin on Ingólfshöfði, Dick helped me by sneaking up from behind (he is good at doing that) to make the dozey birds flap their wings. They were so tame that otherwise they just sat there looking ordinary. Today I was ideally alone with all the time in the world to do not-a-lot. But there was actually not a lot to do, and to make matters worse there was no sun to sparkle up the fantastic autumn colours; perhaps I would have to try some flash.

The following day new snow made the walking more serious as it hid crevasses and ice ponds. I wandered off, singing 'tip-toe through the tundra', knowing full well that the chance of anyone hearing me was small and that even if I was heard the chance of my audience being British was even smaller. And guess what? Yes, I met no one.

I slept furiously after a hard day's walk and took some waking, but eventually the thunder and a quaking earth disturbed even the deepest of my dreams. Camping by Jakobshavn Isfjord may remind you of a railway line but the visuals are a good deal more spectacular. Every year sixteen cubic kilometres of ice float into the Davis Straits – that would complement some tub of whisky, I think, although quite what volume I cannot calculate or imagine. It is, in fact, more than all the water consumed each year by all the EEC countries put together!

Apart from the grind and creak and bang, camping at the mouth of Isfjord is quiet; the closest neighbours have been silent now for nearly 3,500 years. Sermermiut is the premier of 122 registered archaeological sites around Ilulissat, and here there is a four-metre tall slope showing impressve culture layers of civilizations (unless, of course, it is covered by snow, as it was when I tried to find it). This is also the site of an ancient Inuit settlement. Within the municipality of Ilulissat there are traces of Independence I and Independence II cultures; pretty old. As a consequence many areas are protected from the over-zealous digger or rampant archaeologist.

It was just north of here at a place called Qilakitsoq, near Uummannaq, that two brothers, while out hunting ptarmigan, found a grave with eight ice-preserved mummies. It beats the hell out your average Sunday afternoon stroll, but it is not actually my idea of fun. In 1978 the mummies were carefully moved to the Greenland National

Museum in Nuuk/Godthåb. Carbon dating estimated the bodies to be from 1450, which is quite remarkable as the mummies are complete with skin and clothes. A visit to the museum to see them is essential, but not for the faint-hearted. I am definitely no anthropologist. I am not really into history either, but I was fascinated by these chilly finds.

More up my street is the wildlife. But where is it? One of the problems for the likes of me is that all animals in Greenland are terrified. The Greenlanders shoot anything that moves, and the hunted certainly know it. At least all that is shot is eaten and is shot only for that purpose; shooting here is not a privilege sport, but a way of life and survival. I understand that, but the natural consequence is that, as soon as man is spied, any animal with an ounce of brain will run, fly or dive out of range. If you are carrying binoculars this is a nuisance, but it is almost impossible if you are a photographer, particularly nearer the towns. The consolation is that, since towns are few and far between, contact with nature improves the further you are prepared to travel.

The snow and Lappland buntings depart for the winter, leaving ravens, ptarmigan and gyrfalcons – and Greenlandic falcon variants – alone with the polar nights. All the sea birds – gulls, terns, Brünnich's guillemots, cormorants, eiders, mallards and the odd goose – vanish too, as the sea freezes. Seals and whales can often be seen at sea and in the bay close to town, while inland, polar hares and Arctic foxes are common and in some areas reindeer are visible to the quiet, patient and cunning.

'Christ, that's ugly!'

I am talking to myself again but not, I hasten to add, about myself. The subject is a musk ox; a big male, the one with the huge bony bit over its black beady eyes. With this he nuts opponents away from his intended cow, along the lines of the 'Glasgow kiss.' What a way to propagate the species. Sideways on, the long ankle-length mobile shag pile looks like an overgrown Dougal – come on, you remember *The Magic Roundabout*. These animals, I'm told, are rare, yet in this valley there are dozens. What at first sight looks like a rock often turns out to be a dozing musk ox, or two, or even a family group. Here in Kangerlussuaq/Søndre Strømfjord they thrive; it is a safe haven that will ensure their survival in Greenland.

Steen Malmquist is the director of the air base at Kangerlussauq/Søndre Strømfjord, a desperately remote place some 300 kilometres from the coast, and a long walk from Sisimiut. The location enjoys extreme winter cold but little snow, ideal for an all-year runway (as built by the US military) and musk ox. Steen is an interesting bloke; he ran with the Sirius Patrol for several years, a dog sledging army exercise that over-winters up the east and north coast of Greenland where it is really remote. It was there, I think, that he fell in love with the musk ox and became concerned over its plight. The beast originated in Siberia and migrated through the Canadian Arctic to Greenland. It was followed by man and his reindeer, and its existence was threatened by the first European explorers, starting with those racing to be first to the North Pole at the end of the last century. Those animals that escaped being breakfast struggled in the harsh environment up in the north and north-west. The clever ones had previously travelled further south and east, but the south-bound musk ox soon found their limit of travel just past the Thule National Park where a huge natural barrier, a broken glacier range several hundreds of kilometres long, forbids further progress to fresh pastures, the glacier calfing directly into the sea. Along the north coast and down the east coast there were no natural barriers until the rugged sea coast between Ittoqqortoormiitt/Scoresbysund and Kulusuk was reached. Musk ox successfully migrated to these boundaries and can be found today in valleys like Ørsted Dal and around Mesters Vig.

Extreme winters have a dire effect on numbers, burying food under deep ice and snow where it cannot be reached. In the mid-1950s there were three long and severe winters, so bad that there was effectively no summer. All the reindeer in the eastern fjords died, along with most of the musk ox. In order to protect the species from a repeat disaster twenty-seven young musk ox were helicoptered across the ice-cap in slung nets to Kangerlussauq/Søndre Strømfjord, The whole exercise, way back in 1962, was funded by Barbara Hutton, an American millionairess. Today, from these original twenty-seven there are approximately 2,000 musk ox in the Kangerlussauq/Søndre Strømfjord area, with a yield of young of thirty per cent per year. This is unusually high, so I am informed, and here it is common to see twins, and parents which have young each season. In east Greenland twins are rare and the young are

Arctic fox, Søndre Strømfjord, West Greenland.

Musk ox, Søndre Strømfjord, West Greenland.

Calf-ice, Disko Bay, West Greenland.

produced every other year, hence the slow recovery rates. The east to west transfer is a great success story. At the same time animals were also taken to the Thule area in the north-west and to the southernmost peninsula. Those in the north may have survived – it is not known for sure as none have been seen for years, but no one can afford a search without a sponsor, and no sponsor has come forward. The animals taken south all died. The wetter climate was no good for them. They could not handle the summer rains and in the winter they needed hay due to the heavy snow falls. Sadly Greenland could not afford to feed hay to such animals.

Musk ox numbers are only around the 1,000 mark in Arctic Canada, although there are between 15,000 to 20,000 in east Greenland, a huge, place. The Kangerlussauq/Søndre Strømfjord area looks ideal for their survival. They eat anything, unlike reindeer which only eat special lichens. The musk ox does not mind the cold, though he does not like deep snow. To see the musk ox is quite easy, once you have found a way to be allowed to leave the airport complex – the whole location is military and wandering the local countryside is not encouraged. When you do meet your musk ox beware of tell-tale signs. Once he starts to snort and nuzzle his nose with his front hoof, leg it. He has had enough. They are very fast, and will nearly always outrun you, especially uphill. Downhill they are a little more cautious – they obviously understand the physics of gravity-assisted momentum. Prepare your escape route prior to annoying one. Rabies is rampant in Greenland, so if you manage not to be killed by the steamroller effect you must beware of the bite. The animals are strictly vegetarian, but you never can tell! Generally speaking, though, they couldn't give a damn about you, and will ignore you. Just don't get between a bull and his loved ones.

The problem of rabies may not be serious with respect to musk ox, but it is very important when you come close to any Greenlandic animal, especially frightened foxes and dogs. Foxes can be startled, not so much in the wilderness, but while they are scavenging waste-bins in town. And petting town huskies is definitely not recommended.

I fell in love with West Greenland: the wildlife, the moods of light, the peace and quiet and freedom from tourists – the whole country has only 4,000 tourists a year! Walking and backpacking is encouraged and it is OK to camp almost anywhere, as long as it is vaguely sensible. Each town has a helpful tourist organization with simple guides and maps to walks in their area. Away from the vast wilderness the towns offer friendly and interesting contrasts. Their culture is in turmoil, the ancient Inuit traditions threatened by modern Danish Europeanization. Husky mushers wear Sony Walkmans, fish hang to dry from windows of blocks of featureless flats. The mix of times is confusing but creates a colourful essay for the photographer and traveller alike.

Back in the east I have time for reflection on my flight.

When Ejnar Mikkelsen sailed down the east coast of Greenland in 1900 he rounded a headland near Ammassalik. He wrote, 'Then we rounded the last point, the swells subsided, and we glided into the protecting embrace of the small fjord. Mountains with peaks so high and pointed that it looked as if they were piercing the blue sky. They stood as a giant contrast to the low grass-grown land on the left-hand side of the fjord and were reflected in the glittering water.'

I think of this as the plane dives its way down towards the sharp peaks of the coast. Below, huge icebergs lumber their way south. The sea drift takes the ice down Greenland's east coast and round its southern tip so that there is the oddness of ice-locked eastern and southern edges, with an ice-free western and north-western coast when winter's icy fingers stretch down from the polar cap. The bergs below are part of that drift.

The plane lands at Kulusuk, though the airstrip is a little removed from the town. Normally, in spring and summer, I could walk the few kilometres to the village, and in winter I might be able to dog sledge in. This autumn there has been an unseasonally early snow fall, and the snow is

lying thick on the ground. Good for dogs? Well, yes normally, but today's bright sun is turning the snow to mush. So we travel by boat, a tiny boat that has to be dug out of a snowdrift and hauled to the sea where it refuses to start. When, at last, it bursts into life it throws out black clouds of evil-stinking diesel fumes. We board by tightrope, walking over two other boats and pirouetting along a still slippery cabin edge. The boat chugs out on to the ocean, threading its way between the icebergs.

The sea is flat calm, the sky the colour they claim it always is in Provence. The tent-shaped peaks are reflected absolutely symmetrically in the sea. The icebergs are reflected too, and there are also two suns, one above the berg, one in the sea below its reflected image. The boat goes over a shoal of capelin, a vast number of fish, tight-packed, their sheer numbers forcing some to the surface. We pass a boat-load of Greenlanders with smiling faces and all the paraphernalia of the hunt. Ammassalik, the town nearby, is named for the fish, but only, I recall, by the West Greenlanders. The locals (the real Greenlanders?) call the place Tasiilaq – 'the lake' – because of its position on a nearly land-locked fjord.

Kulusuk is reached up a vertical, but short, ladder at the quayside. It is an odd place, the air a mix of fish and dog shit, the former obvious as they hang from every roof angle, the latter oddly absent, at least in tangible form. The village is the standard collection of Greenland houses, high-walled, high-roofed, and coloured. But not brightly coloured as in Reykjavik; here the colouring is more subdued, more in keeping, it seems, with the environment. In the streets young Greenlanders – looking very much like sun-tanned Chinese – laugh and slide. I am nearly run down by a three-kid sledge.

On a hill beyond the village is the cemetery, a collection of poignant memories overlooking the ocean. In the opposite direction is a staircase to a high point from which the village can be viewed, right back to the school from which the day-release kids have come. Beyond is a lake, a pleasant place in summer but today a blue oasis in a white desert. It will be tonight's hotel balcony.

The trip is curtailed by weather that keeps me moving about the island and up some of the closer hills, anxiously waiting for the weather to become colder or, alternatively, warmer. One afternoon I sit looking out over the sea, where glistening bergs

Tupilaks.

amble aimlessly about on blue glass. I decide that Kulusuk is the most beautiful place in the world. Other places have held the trophy before – Lyngen in north Norway, Nordaustland on Svalbard in recent years, and neither is as good as Lofoten, Tony tells me – but I doubt somehow whether there will be many contenders later.

In spring Kulusuk is just a jumping-off point. Your plane will be met by a Glace helicopter which will whisk you noisily across the berg tops to Ammassalik. The town is like Kulusuk, but bigger. It has a bakery and an old folks' home. Be sure to visit the church, a recent addition with fine artwork by Aka Høegh, a Greenlandic artist. The cross and font were carved from driftwood, while the inclusion of an *umiaq*, a boat specifically for women, is in keeping with this centre of religion for a seafaring, hunting race.

But you have come to visit the Valley of Flowers, a broad valley reached by following the river up and out of the town. Here there are lakes and waterfalls and, in spring – the time we came –

there are flowers, beautiful Arctic flowers, more plentiful than on Svalbard or in most places in Iceland, more colourful than in the temperate zones where there are insects in swarms and plants have to work less hard to be visited. Keep walking, until you get out of sight of the skiing debris. Perhaps you could climb Qeqqartivagajik. It will take you about the same time as it takes to learn how to say the name. The reward is a view over the sea and to the mountains at the mainland's edge.

———— ◆ ————

Back in Kulusuk I was fed up with trying to make something out of walking about in slush. I went boating among the bergs, searching – and failing to find – seal. Then I joined the villagers and allowed them to show me some of the ways of the Green-lander, although in a reserved way, in the village square at first rather than in the houses. An old man, with fewer teeth now than he had once had, showed me a *tupilak* he had carved from a reindeer

Sea-ice and mountains near Ammassalik, East Greenland.

Kulusuk, East Greenland.

antler. Many years ago the *tupilak* was a bad-luck sculpture, a Greenlandic form of the Haitian voodoo figures, and the act of carving was the equivalent of the sticking of pins. The carver decided upon his victim and carved the *tupilak* to harm him, the completed figure having to be secretly placed in the victim's home for the magic to work. As with all forms of magic, the evil power could be fed back – if the intended victim was stronger – to the carver and could destroy him. Today, the carving is just an art form. The old man's carving was wonderfully intricate. It was a beast with four legs but a pair of short front arms. Its teeth were National Health dentures, its eye a staring bead. From the front of the head a seal's head grew, from the rear a seagull's head erupted. Another seagull emerged from where a tail might have been.

Another example – carved from a narwhal's tusk – was a pair of skulls on a devilish body. The resemblence of this to a Red Indian totem was striking. Perceived wisdom has Mongol tribes crossing the land bridge from Siberia to Alaska and flowing east and south. Looking at many Greenlandic *tupilak*s it is easy to see a common ancestry.

Camping north of Ilulissat, West Greenland.

Such commonality is also visible in the women's bead work which has many similarities with American Indian work. Today the beads are plastic, but the designs and construction are as ancient and intricate as ever. Many of the designs are geometric but occasionally the spirit of the wild intrudes, with a polar bear or seal being included. Bartering for my own piece – Kulusuk has no tourist souvenir shop and I hope never will have – I am intrigued by the notion that a century or so ago the white man took beads to the natives of many continents in order to swap them for gold, while today I am offering gold for beads.

When it was time to leave I walked back to the airstrip, the melting snow turned grey by the passage of feet. The living here is harsh and unpredictable, but it is also more intensely real than anything I have known in civilized Britain. It does not surprise me that few, very few, of the children born in Kulusuk ever leave.

129

 Winter

Laugh? Well it's about time. Was that a smirk? Pissed off? Too right. At last we were descending to Kulusuk. Today was Monday and the flight had been scheduled for last Thursday, but then travelling Iceland and Greenland in March you must allow for some delays. The wait in Reykjavik was horrid. Rain on the snow caused vast lakes of slush, some so deep they came over the top of our Lundhags, the first time I've had wet socks for years. I am trying hard to forget the weekend. Knowing full well the first flight couldn't be until Monday we hired a car in Reykjavik. Actually it was a Honda Civic four-wheel drive as we planned to go to Snaefellsness, an area with snowy roads and a 1,666-metre conical-shaped glacier at the peninsula end.

The drive was hopelessly uneventful, the weather being typically dull, with the world showing only shades of off-white and mank. It is dull in the extreme, not helped by the thought of what this Japanese wonder is going to cost. Even so, the attraction of Snaefellsjökull is greater. I have been here before, on my bike, but then I saw nothing because of the rain. Now I can see nothing due to the wind-blown snow and low cloud. And even more snow. Does it never stop? Perhaps it will tomorrow.

Near Buðir, somewhere under the vast snow fields leading to the sea, we put up the tent and settled for Pasta Choice followed by semolina and dried apricots, followed by chicken cup-a-soup, followed by coffee, biscuits and hot chocolate, followed by a long irrelevant discussion on how the hell croûtons are crispy in cup-a-soups, and perhaps we should have some more.

The evening mank was clearing, stars were appearing and the glacier was retreating out of the clouds. The weather changes so quickly (when it changes) and tonight was one of those beautiful nights. Tomorrow would be superb. Owls hooted and on the mountains foxes were barking, the only sounds to break the quiet night air. It is at times like these I appreciate the quietness of the Trangia, my old primuses being like central London in the rush hour by comparison.

Morning broke and so had the weather. All my dreams of Snaefellsjökull were again shattered. Luckily the tent had two exits; so much snow had blown to one door we were afraid of avalanche should we open it. Outside was as bad as the inside suggested, so we discuss retreat tactics over breakfast. Dick cooked a bowl of muesli, about the limits of his talent, or laziness, but I must admit he skilfully managed to melt the frozen-solid carton of milk that he forgot to put in his sleeping bag. Over the chewing and munching we discussed the feasibility of becoming millionaires so we could jack this joke in. We decided we ought to go home and design a meths-driven microwave.

Luckily the shovel was still bolted to my ice axe, following the evening's digging in of the tent. I used it to go out and find, and dig out, the car. After all Dick had made the breakfast. I finished just as he finished the packing. We had to be back in Reykjavik at first light tomorrow and there were 250 kilometres to do in white-out conditions. After 500 metres the car stopped. The roads were compacted to hard, icy snow and were easy to drive on, but the verges remained soft snow and then it was digging time, again. The wheels sank so the chassis of the car was resting on an ice shelf. The only way out was to dig away the ice roadway from under the car.

Four-wheel drive, Dick muttered. Oh yeah, the sticker on the go-faster door may say four-wheel drive but where is the differential lock? Or has it got a limited slip diff? A what? Do all four wheels turn at once, you pillock. Of course they don't. This is Japanese four-wheel drive where only two wheels really drive. What a con. Dig on. Only a few vehicles can either lock their differentials or have limited slip diffs thus allowing four wheels to drive at once. This is not one of them.

Once back on the road, an hour later, and much knackered for the pleasure, the return journey to Reykjavik was as uneventful as the drive out. Driving on roads that melted into the featureless verges was tiring beyond belief. We arrived back in town, had a swim and were totally exhausted having achieved nothing at all.

My first sight of Kulusuk was overflying at 20,000 feet *en route* to Nuuk. Kulusuk is the home of DYE4, one of several American navigational aid stations used by this Grønlandsfly Dash 4 from Reykjavik. Then it looked like a fairy story, dark blue fjords with icebergs dotted like dropped ball bearings. Today it looks like a nightmare, bullets of snow rushing past the window as the plane drops towards the runway. Jon, the pilot – Jon Helgison, son of Helgi Jonsson, owner of the plane – scrapes away the ice from the inside of the windscreen with his Visa card and peers out, looking for the runway. We land. We get out. Christ, I think, this is desolate. The other two passengers vanish off on the Glace helicopter to Ammassalik leaving just us and the other passengers – fourteen seats worth of bananas and oranges – to wait. For what? Eventually I discover the pilots have gone off to the airport control centre about half a kilometre down the road. Hot coffee and buns, and I order a taxi to Kulusuk village.

I have been in contact with Jørgen, a schoolteacher in the village, and he and his family have been a great help. Sure enough he arrives, his younger son driving the carriage, an eight-dog power sledge. What a splendid way to depart from the airport, and soon we are drinking more coffee, this time in the warmth of Jørgen's lounge. The town is very different from my expectations. I have seen Dick's autumn photographs but nothing is recognizable. The solid sea-ice and deep snow falls have made the obvious divide between land and sea vanish. Everything is white or a close shade of white and the village rather featureless. I admit I am a little disappointed, given Dick's suggestion that east Greenland was the closest he had yet come to paradise, but by contrast the kids are bright and all dressed in the same flashy, warm, ski-type clothing. The boys play football, as they do everywhere, and the girls play at being girls.

Our hosts are teachers in the village school and as such have considerable respect within the community. Jørgen is Danish and his wife, Helena, is also non-local. She is from Nuuk and speaks west Greenlandic which is different from the local Greenlandic. Their kids, Isac and Aslak, both boys, and Arnannguaq, a young girl, are therefore, trilingual. Nicer people are hard to imagine and I soon learn the open and friendly ways of Kulusuk. We didn't quite get to *all* the homes of the 350 people living within the village, but we probably visited the majority. Open house is the order of the day and visiting is apparently compulsory and delightfully frequent. Our first party is for a small boy's birthday, the tradition being that on a birthday the house is open all day for people to drop in for coffee, cakes and fun. He is a shy lad but a session of peek-a-boo gets me the shot I want, his strong Greenlandic features framed by the tatty woodwork of the open double-glazed window.

Every day at the top of the hill overlooking the village the old boys of the town meet to scan the world. Ask them and they will tell you they are looking for seal or polar bear. In fact, they seem to be more interested in what is going on in the village itself. Wherever we go their binoculars are pointing our way. Well, there are very few visitors in winter, and even fewer that seem to have any interest in the people.

We visit several craftsmen, the best of whom, Thorvald Mikaelsen – a surprisingly Danish name for clearly so Greenlandic a man – offers us coffee and a chance to see him at work. *Kasuutta tamatta*, Thorvald – even with tea and coffee the Greenlandic version of 'cheers' is exchanged. Thorvald is one of the very few Greenlandic craftsmen who still make wooden buckets, producing them only to order. But we have come to see *tupilak*s. The flat ones, we discover, are the traditional type, the ones that stand, being required by the tourists, and so are now becoming more popular. The best are carved from whale tooth which is a more consistent medium and polishes better. The income for the local people has dropped dramatically over the last few years, as whale teeth are now very hard to come by and expensive. Reindeer antler is beginning to be used more frequently. To us they seem almost as good, although the finish is not as smooth, but the carvers are less happy with them as they fetch a lower price for the same effort. Thorvald also carves in wood, not *tupilak*s, but traditional hunting figures. We also see stone carving, the most beautiful of which – and perhaps the best work that we saw in any medium – was of a polar bear with a seal in its mouth. We had hoped that Thorvald's tool kit would be a model of the ancient craftsman's art. It turns out to be western and modern, final polishing of the figures being with brass polish. The only local items are a twiddly thing for boring the eye recesses and a seal-skin thimble for protecting his thumb.

We have come to Kulusuk in winter because Dick has organized us a polar bear hunt. The east

The birthday boy, Kulusuk, East Greenland.

Greenlandic carved wooden figure.

Greenlandic bead work.

Greenlanders are still allowed to hunt the bear, on a quota basis, although very few travel this far south. The rules of the hunt are very strict, the meat from the animal being shared out among the hunters, and the skin going to the man who first spots the bear. Usually the lucky hunter will take the skin to the west coast where the prices are higher. Even with the extortionate price of flying to Nuuk it is still worthwhile. We have mixed feelings about the hunt. We are on the side of the bear, but realise that this way of life is centuries old and poverty in Kulusuk is still the standard way of life, with many families existing at subsistence level on a diet of seal meat during the long, hard winter months. We have come to explore the Arctic, not to impose our ideas, nurtured in the affluent UK, on it, nor to judge it. Later we reassess this idea.

Finding a hunter is easy as just about every man in the village is willing to take us. The only man not available is the one who Dick organized to help

us last autumn. He, it seems, rode out of the village a few weeks ago and has not been seen since. But he will be OK, we are told; he is a good hunter. When we ask Jørgen about this he shrugs. It is almost impossible to plan ahead with the Greenlanders; they are an impulsive people.

To 'guarantee' finding a bear we are recommended that a minimum of five days is needed. However, the appalling weather conditions that held us up in Iceland are still raging here and the top layer of fluffy snow makes travel on the snow-ice slow and dangerous. Never are we sure what we are travelling over; any snow drift might have hidden an open water lead. To make progress even slower our Greenlandic dogs are just not the same as the Norwegian dogs we are used to. Over there the most essential piece of kit was the snow hook to restrain the dogs every time we stopped. Here, every time we stop the dogs lie down and sleep, and are very reluctant to get up again. When they do they travel at no better than a fast walking

Sledging on sea-ice, East Greenland.

Polar bear stone carving.

pace. We rapidly discover that sledging in Greenland is amazingly tedious. We have looked forward to sleding on the sea-ice, but once you have seen one huge frozen-in iceberg you have seen both of them. Eventually, when it becomes clear that we are not likely to be able to go far enough to find bear and, much more to the point, that our 'guide' – possessor of the only driving licence in roadless, carless Kulusuk – is showing no great enthusiasm for the job – did he know something that we didn't – we settled for a slow, meandering tour of the likely seal areas. We have discovered early on that the dogs move so slowly and the ice is so flat that we can light the Trangia on the move. The tea relieves the tedium. We visit several seal holes, or so we are told, but see less than one seal.

Each time we stop we go for a quick walk, choosing a vantage point to search for bear or seal or anything. Walking on the sea-ice is the only good thing about the trip, the ice creaking and groaning delightfully, particularly when we are close to land. The weather, which had been improving slightly, now turns miserable again. The wind picks up and the visibility begins to fall. Our new sledging friend politely inquires whether we are afraid. Afraid? Of what, for Christ's sake? A little wind, a little cloud? But we take the hint and agree to head back towards the town.

On the way back we pass a sledger going out into the wild. He is wearing reflective blue shades and a Sony Sledgeman, complete with aerial poking through his woolly hat. This sight makes Dick and I reassess our attitudes towards the hunt. If the profits from the skins are used to support the old way of life then so be it. But it would appear that the young Greenlanders, as elsewhere, are keen to fill their lives with Japanese goods and Taiwanese junk. If that is the case is it really fair that one of the great animals of the world should die to satisfy the urge?

Frankly, we are happy to be back in Kulusuk, which I, like Dick, am coming to love.

Next day there is a commotion as we walk through the town and a bright red Volvo Sno-Cat comes over the hill, closely followed by a group of jogging men in grey. It is the local fire brigade on exercise. We watch entranced. By early evening the exercise is still in full swing, the team with the ice drill having not, as yet, managed to find water while the rest of the team have still failed to find the simulated blaze. Ho hum.

In the town we hear that the cook at DYE4 has been feeding Arctic foxes; what a chance for some photos, and it's only ten kilometres across country.

Being lazy we opt for the hike up the trail to the airport. It's longer, but perhaps we can cadge a lift because lorries travel this route. We don snow shoes and set forth. The rucsac is heavy with emergency gear and camera gear, including an expensive lens. It will not fit into my climbing sac, so I am forced to take my backpacking Condor.

We are soon knackered and cold, so when a lorry comes along, out goes the thumb. 'Any chance of a ride to DYE4?' I ask, most politely. This huge, gum-chewing gorilla snaps back a 'Why?' I hear there are Arctic foxes and I am interested in seeing them if possible. All been shot. Taken aback by the starkness of reply I shyly inquire if they were communists. At this he rams it into drive, and drives, dummy-like navigator and all, very fast. We do not go to DYE4.

Back in the town our reservations about hunting, tourism, firemen and dead foxes dissolve away. The hospitality of the villagers rapidly overcomes all our negative thoughts. When the time comes – as it does all too soon – for us to leave, there is no doubting that we will return.

SVALBARD

SVALBARD

Woodfjorden

Bockfjorden

Moffen

Amsterdamøya

Gustav V Land

NORDAUSTLANDET

Mosselbukta
(Mussel
Bay)

Wahlenbergfjorden

Andrée
Land

Gustav Adolf Land

Wijdefjorden

Hinlopen Stretet

Ny Ålesund

SPITSBERGEN

KONG KARLS LAND

Templefjord

BARENTSØYA

Sassendalen

PRINS KARLS
FORLAND

Hayesbreen

Longyearbyen

Barentsburg

Svea

EDGEØYA

Agardhbukta
(Agardh Bay)

0

Hopen

Svalbard.

Icelandic sagas, written as the twelfth century became the thirteenth, speak of the discovery of a land north of Norway and four day's sailing from it, a land the saga writers believed was a continuation of the coast of Greenland. Those earliest travellers called the land Svalbard, 'the cold edge', a name at once accurate and evocative. When William Barents came this way in 1596 he knew nothing of the Icelandic sagas and believed he was discovering a new land. As he approached he caught sight of the array of pointed peaks, of

which Bautaen is one of the most striking. So impressed was he by the feature that he called his land Spitsbergen, 'pointed mountains', and it is by that name that it is now generaly known. In fact Spitsbergen is only one of the islands of Svalbard, although it is also very much the biggest, occupying about two-thirds of the total land area. From the southern tip of Svalbard, Norway's mainland is about 600 kilometres away, with only Bjørnøya – Bear Island – to pass on the way. To the east of Spitsbergen are Barentsøya and Edgeøya and, beyond, the small archipelago of Kong Karls Land, a strictly prohibited area because of its importance as a polar bear denning area. To the north-east there is Nordaustland (literally 'North-East Land', a highly imaginative name) where access is also prohibited. To the east Forlandsundet separates Spitsbergen from Prince Karls Forland.

After Barents had discovered Svalbard its importance as a site for whaling stations was quickly seen by British and Dutch whalers and, to a lesser extent, by whalers from France, Germany and Norway. By 1630 British whalers were over-wintering on Svalbard, no mean achievement, and there were numerous whaling stations. Chief of these was Smerrenburg ('blubber city') on Amsterdamøya a Dutch station on a small island off the north-western tip of Spitsbergen. Within 200 years the whalers had succeeded in making the Svalbard whales, particularly the Greenland right whale, extinct. Following this clever venture in commerce and conservation, man did the same thing again. Starting in the early nineteenth century he – this time chiefly the Norwegians – came to the islands to hunt seal, walrus, polar bear and Arctic fox. By the end of the century those animals too had suffered a severe decline, though hunting continued on a lower level and still does.

In October 1899 one Søren Zachariassen (whose name has, thankfully, not become attached to any major feature on Svalbard) brought a load of coal to Tromsø that he had literally picked up on Spitsbergen. Within a few years the island had been settled by many looking to make a fortune from the find. Chief of those was an American, John Munro Longyear, whose Arctic Coal Company worked mines on the southern edge of Adventfjorden, a small inlet of Isfjorden. Soon a city of about 1,000 people had grown up and Longyear, not long on modesty, called it Longyearcity. Only when the Americans had gone, and the Arctic Coal Company had been taken over by Norwegian interests, did the name change to Longyearbyen. It is an evocative name, looking as though it might derive from the long year that the area enjoys, with its 24-hour daylight period – that lasts (at Longyearbyen) from 19 April to 23 August, a total of 127 days – and its dark period from 26 October to 16 February, a total of 114 days. Just as an aside, the reason why these two periods are not equal, as they should be, is that refraction – the bending of light rays by the atmosphere – reveals

the sun to the observer when it is technically out of sight below the horizon, so lengthening one period and shortening the other. Such refraction is normal everywhere, but is sometimes exaggerated in polar regions because the density distribution of the cold polar air bends light more than is usual. It is not unknown for the sun suddenly to reappear at midday several days after it has gone for the winter, a red, oddly distorted ball sat on the horizon.

The Norwegians not only changed the name of Longyear's settlement, but of the coal company. It became, and still is, Store Norske Spitsbergen Kullkompani (SNSK), the company that until very recently owned the town and, therefore, all the facilities on offer, with uncomfortable side-effects for the visitor. Despite owning the company, however, Norway did not own the islands, and there were disputes about sovereignty right up to World War I. After the war the major parties interested in the region, the Scandinavians, British and North Americans, agreed that Norway should be granted sovereignty and this was embodied in the Treaty of Svalbard of 1920. It was further agreed that all signatories to the Treaty – the first group were Denmark, Sweden and Norway, the USA and Canada, Britain and Ireland, Holland, France and Italy, South Africa, Japan and India – should have equal rights with respect to mineral rights. Further, military operations on the islands were banned. Today over forty countries have signed the Treaty although only the USSR – who signed in 1935 – exercise their mineral rights. Norway's representative on the island is the *Sysselmann* or Governor whose word is law even, technically, within the Russian settlements. Today there are five settlements – Longyearbyen and Svea, Norwegian mining towns; Ny Ålesund, a former Norwegian mining town maintained as a research station, and Barentsburg and Pyramiden, Russian mining towns. Barentsburg, the biggest of all these towns, has about 1,400 inhabitants.

During World War II the island was occupied by the Germans, but retaken by Norwegians from Scotland and subsequently shelled by *Tirpitz* and *Scharnhorst*, during which attack Longyearbyen was flattened. So much for Svalbard being a demilitarized zone. Today there is a strange unreality about the place, the visitor rapidly forming the impression that these people are here to make sure that those people are not the only ones here.

 # Summer

Odd-Knut Thoresen, impressed by the scenery near the Øvre Dividal National Park, has moved himself and his dogs to a small cottage outside the village of Øverbygd. I renew my acquaintaince with Wiggen, who looks thin and scraggy in his summer coat. Hey, Wiggen, remember me, the lad with the tasty reindeer bits? Wiggen sniffs me suspiciously. Ultimately he offers to put his muddy paws all over me, but not by way of recognition. I am miserable.

We decide to go for a long walk, linking a section of Kirkesdalen with some of those superb-looking peaks that lie below you if you fly into Bardufoss airport, and finishing at Målselvfoss which, Odd-Knut says, is the finest waterfall in Norway and is likely to be covered in leaping salmon. Odd-Knut will not come. Walking is only for those who have had too much to drink and so cannot drive.

The walk in the forested section of the valley is superb, the air constantly scented with pine resin and needles. The camping is excellent too, with a pine-scented fire sparking away beneath a clear star-sparkled sky. We are supposed to go over those peaks at the back there, but warm, scented air turns out to be a lethargy drug. We drink coffee, talk, lounge about, get aggravated over mosquitos. Tony finds himself disturbed by pine needles that are in food and drink – a memory of the dog sledging days when everything was covered in reindeer hair – in sleeping bags and the cells of Karrimats. He hoovers out the tent remorselessly at every available opportunity, and his right hand is worn smooth by his brushing efforts.

Eventually we tire of the inactivity and push on westward to Målselvfoss to meet Odd-Knut. In this area, we decide, Norway is very like Finland, a forest with lakes, although the view to the hills of the south is very *un*like Finland. Målselvfoss is indeed impressive, but it suffers from being famous. At its base is a caravan park and gift shop, and a nearby car-park allows tourists to reach the site with little effort. The falls are a big version of the Swallow Falls that lie between Capel Curig and Betws-y-Coed in Wales. In fact, they are a *very* big

140

version. We scramble up the side, a climb made very much more difficult by a half-erected new fence being installed, so Odd-Knut tells us, to stop people poaching the salmon. Near the top we can make a way through to the river and we take up a position on a rock platform. Målselvfoss turns out to be at its most impressive from here. The river narrows, throwing the water into a thin,

Pack-ice near Nordaustlandet.

shallow step cut into the rock, beyond which is the fall proper, a couple of hundred metres of not-too-steeply inclined waterway. At the step so much water is funnelled on to the top of the falls that it is forced upwards. From where we are the top of this huge arch of white, noisy water is about level with our heads, the water rising two metres before galloping over the edge.

We clamber back down the side of the falls, Odd-Knut stopping several times to show us salmon resting in pools carved at its side. These seem to be artificial, put there to make life easier for the fish, and at several we wait to get a glimpse of a flashing silver leap. No luck. Tony, who has lugged several big loads of camera kit to the spot, is not impressed. We are unlikely to see salmon here, he decides. He knows rivers in Scotland where they jump every few minutes. And we've carried our kit through half the forests in north Norway, got covered in mosquito bites and pine needles, and for what? I suggest it might still happen. Be careful, he says, you are more likely to step in rocking horse shit than to see a salmon leaping. He is right as it turns out – not about the rocking horse shit but about the lack of salmon.

Tony is quiet all the way to the hotel where Odd-Knut takes us. For revenge he wants to eat salmon but there is none. Bloody typical, he mutters. I wander off and come face to face with a stuffed wolverine near the gents. When I return we have, apparently, ordered elk. It is, we agree, even better than reindeer. Tony cheers up and persuades Odd-Knut to stop at a hostelry for one or two of the low-alcohol Norwegian beers. I drive us home again, the price of sobriety. Back at Odd-Knut's his friend Pal arrives, carrying a bottle of something that takes the enamel off your teeth and decokes diesel engines. Only when I point out that the flight to Svalbard tomorrow is earlyish and from Tromsø does the party end. Next day Tony has a headache. Odd-Knut has promised to get us to Tromsø on time, and he does. It is no longer a surprise to us that Scandinavians frequently win the World Rally Championship.

Approaching Svalbard from the air is one of the great delights of Arctic travel. All flights – except those from Russia which are, in any case, usually filled with Soviet citizens only – leave from Tromsø, irrespective of their original point of departure, and the approach is then along the length of southern Spitsbergen before a final turn, usually close to the Russian mining village of Barentsburg, along Isfjorden and the only airport, near Longyearbyen. From the plane the view is stupendous; the country is a mass of brown rock and ice of the purest white. It is a barren, inhospitable, uninhabited land that would tempt anyone. Our first entry took us over the tooth of Bautaen, an angular peak near the end of Hornsund, a reminder of the name of this unforgiving land.

Longyearbyen airport is chaotic. Few planes are seen here and today's early arrival is also today's late departure. On a trip we made when our departure was only an hour or so after an Aeroflot landing, there were Russians arriving, Russians departing, others arriving and others departing all in the terminal at the same time. It could comfortably hold 50 or 100 people, but there were 250–300 there, the overspill propping up parts of the outside of the building and smiling into the wind.

But we have just arrived. Our rucsacs are hauled in on a trolley that looks remarkably similar to the one that will be hauled out again. I retrieve them quickly. Tony has discovered that we can get a bus into town. He has also discovered that we can hire a car (which seems like a must in view of the fact that there must be at least thirty kilometres of road), and that we can hire mountain bikes. We pile into the bus – I choose my words wisely – and are off down the side of Adventfjorden. Soon to our left there are enormous rusting structures, left over, it seems, from the making of *Star Wars*, while ahead tall chimneys of something belch out smoke or steam. The road is hard, baked clay. To the right there is a jumble of rocks and scree. I am reminded of Scott's comment at the South Pole: 'Great God, this is an awful place.'

The bus drops us in the 'centre' of Longyearbyen. It is a long town. A very long town. The Information Centre – yes, there is one – is at the top of a long hill, almost the last building in the new 'town' of Nybyen. Why, when there is nothing for kilometres in all directions, is it necessary to put the office nearly a kilometre away at the top of a hill?

The bus goes, the people from it all evaporate into the hazy sunshine and Tony and I stand and look around. All over the valley that Longyearbyen occupies there are huge, gaunt towers, the remains of an ancient overhead coal bucket system, now looking more likely to have been gallows from some reign of terror. Uphill, its windscreen glinting in occasional shifts of sunlight, a bulldozer is chugging noisily about in the valley's stream. A partially submerged, still operating bulldozer is not something I see often, and I watch, fascinated. In front of us, raised off the ground a metre or so, is a pipeline. Not until later do we realise that these raised pipes carry water and sewage. Bury your pipes here and your fluids will go stiff with cold. After we have worked it out it adds a piquancy to the occasional rest we take leaning against the pipes. In Ny Ålesund, we discover later, the structure is of wood, so that if you want to you can lift the lid and stare inside. Tony wonders whether, given the right circumstances, you could flush a local bog, hurl yourself down the road, attack the lid with a screwdriver and be in time to give your residue a last wave on its way to forever.

Longyearbyen is quiet. On a later visit we learn to love it, a little anyway, but today it seems to us that Longyearbyen has much in common with Blaenau Ffestíniog on a wet Sunday in November.

Svalbard is not well set up for the independent traveller, although things are improving. Until very recently SNSK owned everything, and since their shop was subsidized the visitor could not use it, meaning that all the food necessary for your entire trip had to be bought in on day one. Now food is available, and the range available in the (only) shop is good. There is a hotel for those not interested in the daily haul in from the campsite near the airport, the only place where tents are allowed near Longyearbyen. There is a shop that will sell you some of life's necessities, together with a Svalbard T-shirt. There is a museum and a bank. There is a café.

The mountains of Svalbard are, in the main, composed of carboniferous rock that is highly susceptible to frost erosion. Summer's water seeps into every crack and pore of the rock, expands on freezing in winter and tears the rock apart. Only on Spitsbergen's north-west coast and along the eastern shore of Wijdefjorden, the huge incut that almost cuts Spitsbergen in half, are there more robust rocks. There granites and gneiss resist the ice and create some stability. Travel in Svalbard in the summer months is a laborious and tedious task. The mountains seem mere scree piles whose ascent is miserable – a walk up a downward escalator – with the constant risk of real stone slides or stonefall from above. Though the mean temperatures in Svalbard are just higher than those in the Arctic to both the east and west, a result of the Gulf Stream that runs up Norway's mainland coast, it is nevertheless a cold place. The mean summer temperature is only about 5°C (41°F), while in winter it drops to a mean of about −12°C (10°F). In winter the ground is frozen, the permafrost reaching great depths, perhaps as much as 150 metres. In summer the permafrost melts to a depth of a metre or so. In the valleys the ground is saturated and the rivers are almost impassable so swollen are they with melt water. In a hut on the 'route' from Longyearbyen to Svea the visitor's book holds a wonderful drawing of a Japanese hiker in one melt-swollen river, desperately holding his precious bits above his head. The words I did not understand; the drawing was an obvious *cri de coeur*.

The difficulties of moving are compounded by the lack of a transport infrastructure. With virtually no roads, the only travel is by air or boat. The former, charter planes or helicopters, is horrendously expensive and it is in any case not easy to find places to land. Boats are better. Within reason you can land anywhere: you can be dropped off on the way out and collected on the way back; and you can be dropped off by one boat and picked up elsewhere by another. Boats are also a very fine way of seeing Svalbard. Many a visitor has spent a week waiting for his plane out and seeing little but Longyearbyen and Adventdalen, which is little in the way of a wilderness adventure.

Finally, and most importantly, those travelling to Svalbard must think about the polar bears. The polar bear is the world's only purely carnivorous bear. Please read our appendix on polar bears – it could be very important to you. A full-grown bear can haul a 95-kilogram seal out of its breathing hole. How heavy are you? Polar bears are also astonishingly quick for their size, with speeds on land of up to 30kph being claimed. How fast are you, bearing in mind that the bear may be doing that speed on ice on which you may have difficulty standing up?

In practice visitors are very unlikely to meet an adult bear on Spitsbergen in summer, particularly if they stay in the south-west. The bears retreat with the ice, following the seals who do the same. Occasionally a young adult, not yet in tune with his lifestyle and environment, will be left behind and will find himself – and it is usually a male, the female cubs being more worldy-wise – stranded on an island, like Amsterdamøya, or on the mainland. He may not be 500 kilograms, but he will certainly

Bearded seal.

be over 100 kilograms. By the time you arrive he may be very hungry and very miserable and this will make him aggressive. Polar bears are the masters of this area. They are at best unafraid of anything except a full-grown walrus which you do not in the least resemble. If a young male is hungry he will not be afraid of anything. Be in no doubt; if he can, he will eat you.

You will not talk a polar bear out of eating you. Not so many years ago a group of tourists from a civilized mid-European country camped out at Magdalenefjorden on Spitsbergen's north-west coast. In the quiet hours – in Svalbard in summer there is no 'night' – one visitor was woken by something messing about with his tent. He poked his head outside. A young male bear took him, his shouts waking his colleagues. The whole party – which included the man's wife and daughter – was unarmed. They threw stones and sticks at the bear, who ignored it all, hauling their hopefully

now dead companion off to an ice floe in the fjord. There, in front of the rest of the party, the bear ate him. All of him.

If you are travelling in Svalbard in summer you must be armed, with rifle and flare pistol. If you are sleeping out you must have trip wires and flashes around the tent. Better still, for your first visit go by boat, going ashore with a guide until you have gauged the country.

From the deck of the boat Tony and I watch Longyearbyen disappear. It seems the better for being a long way off. A Svalbard fulmar, thicker-set and greyer than the home variety, takes up a position a metre above the deck rail. It is dragged along in the boat's slipstream and looks like a kite. He allows us to get quite close, inclining his head to peer at us with unchanging eyes, deciding if we are harmless or malevolent. If we move too close he is gone, barely imperceptible flicks of wings and tail breaking him free of the towing air and hurling him down and out across the sea.

For the first few days of midnight sun it is impossible to sleep, then impossible to stay awake, and only after is the biological clock reprogrammed well enough to allow a normal cycle to re-establish itself. I am in the second phase and disappear towards a more sheltered piece of deck.

Magdalenefjorden, named for St Mary Magdalene, is by common consent the most beautiful fjord of Spitsbergen. Here there is hard, igneous rock intruded into the soft carboniferous strata. The mountains are angular, almost alpine, free of the rounded hummocks that frost shattering of the sedimentary rocks creates. At its back Waggonwaybreen (a *breen* is a glacier) falls into the fjord, a spur of the glacier reaching the sea on the southern side. Further back Gullybreen also reaches the sea here. Between Gullybreen and the arm of the bigger glacier a hook of land pokes out into the fjord. As we head for this in the early morning, a

mixture of snow and rain falling on our anorak hoods, the whole place seems unreal. Heavy clouds hang over the glaciers and wrap themselves around the peaks like ruffs. Just inland the quiet is broken by an angry chattering of birds. Arctic skuas, those pirates we grew to respect in Iceland, are furiously mobbing a *polarmåke*. The common English name for this gull is 'glaucous', but polar gull seems a much better description. The gull has decided to breakfast on the skua's chick, a case of the biter bit. We watch as it makes tentative forays, retreating in the face of a pair of sharp beaks, but it is persistent, and eventually succeeds, moving rapidly off with the chick helplessly dangling from its beak and the adult skuas frantically diving and chattering above it. It pays no attention now, and quietly dismembers and eats its catch.

Tony points out a hut that is well camouflaged and hidden among the rocks, and we amble over. It is occupied by Thorbjørn, a retired policeman from southern Norway. We ask why anyone

Walrus.

should want to spend time here alone – Thorbjørn has been here for several weeks and will stay several more. Sadly, even here, at the extremity of the earth, there is a need to police the area. Recently a large cruise ship – of one country but full of tourists from another – dropped anchor in Magdalenefjorden. The crew shuttled the tourists ashore, erected a series of tents, laid out a buffet and installed a bar. There was music, loud music, and soon there was dancing and a sing-song. The tourist with a mind to do it could ignore the fact that he was in Svalbard and that outside was some of the most breathtaking scenery in the world. He could eat, drink and be merry just as though he were in London or Paris, in New York or Sydney. The tourists did just that.

The hook-shaped land spit has a rise at its seaward end. The rise is topped by a memorial that records the existence of a cemetery of British and Dutch whalers, men who died in this beautiful but alien land. Little remains to indicate the position of the graves, and if you journey through the area the terns dive-bomb you because their chicks hatch among the old cairn headstones. The more drunken – it is to be hoped – of the tourists from the cruise ship came to the rise and, looking for souvenirs, set about digging up the graves (which were shallow because of the permafrost), anxious for a bone or shred of clothing to take home as a reminder of a great party. Because of this the *Sysselmann* has installed Thorbjørn to police the cruise ships, and there are others like him at other well-known spots. And to think there are those who would find the spectacle of a polar gull eating a skua chick distasteful.

I ask Thorbjørn what he is expected to do if a few hundred drunken tourists start rampaging through the area. I must, he says seriously, talk to the ship's captain and tell him he must take his cow home. Pardon? I *have* heard correctly. It transpires that this is the literal translation of a Norwegian phrase that is better translated as 'on yer bike'. Thorbjørn is in radio contact with the *Sysselmann*'s office for back-up – it is a long way to Longyearbyen, but I decide not to ask if he will suggest that he is going to set his dog on the captain; just hang on, he'll be here in two days – and can authorize the captain's licence to be revoked. The latter is a powerful threat. The captain will probably leave immediately and, says Thorbjørn with a smile, the sight of the ship leaving is likely to have a sobering effect on the tourists.

Near Thorbjørn's hut is a pool where moss and algae of such an intense green grow that you could forget for the moment that there is little vegetation here. On again, towards the edge of Gullybreen, the vegetation is more normal Svalbard, the occasional surprising pocket of colour among the rocks. Here there is a bedraggled clump of tufted saxifrage, there a more elegant dome of moss campion. Tony calls me over to show me a Svalbard poppy, a single and somewhat forlorn specimen. For the rest it is mostly lichen, an exquisite radiating orange type and a brown clumpy species.

We round a spur of the hill to our left and Gullybreen comes into view, vaguely through the low cloud. Up on the hill there is the noise of falling stones and when we look up to see what caused it, an Arctic fox, already out of its white winter jacket, stares back at us. It is nervous of us and runs away, its retreat accompanied by little rock falls. It runs a bit, then stops and turns to watch us, anxious that while it is running we might be doing something dangerous. I am reminded of an American president who also, it was claimed, could do only one thing at a time. Tony tells me the story of his father-in-law – or was it an earlier relative? – who bought a horse from a milkman and could never persuade it to go up the road without stopping at every house. Eventually the fox decides we are far enough away and legs it furiously, its long tail flung out behind.

The weather is really miserable by the time we reach Gullybreen and neither of us is keen to go too close. Through the cloud there are ominous cracks, some short like rifle shots, some long like trees falling, as the ice settles and snaps.

Back at the hut Thorbjørn comes out to ask if we want a ride in his inflatable. We can go in close to Waggonwaybreen if we wish. So, in gathering rain and cloud we speed in towards the glacier, the hull of *Isprinsen* incongruous among the ice floes and bergs. Waggonwaybreen is huge, its seaward tongue over two kilometres wide and ending in ice cliffs nearly a hundred metres high. The cliffs are cracked and pitted. As we approach there are roars like thunder as the glacier splits to relieve its stresses. At any time a section of the ice wall could crack free and fall. It is termed iceberg calving, although knowing the name would be scant use if you were underneath at the time. Even if we avoided the fall, the wash from the berg creation would swamp the boat. The sea is 2°C (37°F), the survival time perhaps four minutes (less if you are wearing Lundhags, Tony points out). We ask Thorbjørn to stay clear. Dead centre is a huge cavern in the glacier where the underlying stream has bored its way out of the ice, and in the cave gulls turn and twitter. On several other Svalbard glaciers we see the same caverns filled with birds, but can never convince ourselves we know why they are there. The cavern itself is blue-walled, that colour of hard ice which can only be described as 'ice-blue'.

Thorbjørn is a master of the rubber boat and has us crashing around at speed. He is concerned about whacking his propellor on a chunk of glacial ice, which, he assures us, is like steel. Fighting to change the lens on my camera I almost fall out of the boat, settling eventually for a side rope around one hand. In minutes Tony and I are soaked with saltwater and frozen. To our right a bearded seal breaks surface to observe. You want photo? shouts Thorbjørn, and not waiting for a reply he hurls the boat around towards the seal which promptly disappears. Braced across the boat by Lundhags and back and I am rapidly losing interest in the trip, the thudding and banging, the spray and the cold. OK? I ask Tony, but I can tell from his face that he too has had enough. Slower, yells Tony and Thorbjørn quietens down. We may get closer if we are slower. We don't, and Thorbjørn is off again, giving us a quick Cook's tour of the fjord before dropping us back at the ship.

Northward, Tony has camped out on the bridge, his camera tripoded and ready to catch the point at which we cross the 80° parallel as registered on the digitized output of the satellite navigation system. Jan Sorenson, our captain, a smiling, white-haired giant of a man, clearly thinks it is best to humour the idiots. He offers us coffee; we accept, drink and chat. And as we do the boat slides gently pass the mark, unseen by camera or camera crew.

Moffen is a curious annular island lying off the northern Spitsbergen coast, four or so kilometres north of the 80 degree parallel. In the early 1980s those on visiting ships could hope to see 200–300 walrus lying out on its shores. Walrus are wonderfully impressive; they are huge animals that are surprisingly elegant in the water but monstrous lumberers on land. Their turned-forward hind flippers are always referred to as the feature that distinguishes them from other seals. It is an absurdly technical point, for what chiefly distinguishes a walrus from a seal is that adult males of the former species are up to four metres long, weigh over 1,000 kilograms and have tusks up to one metre in length. Even the female, which is smaller and has smaller tusks, is huge by comparison. The tusks are used to drag the animal up on to its chosen ice floe – the scientific name for the walrus is '*tooth-walker*' – and also for collecting food. Despite its bulk, the walrus lives almost exclusively on shellfish, the tusks being used to prise the shells off the rock and to open them. There are persistent stories of walrus eating seals and it does seem likely that some animals or, perhaps, most animals at some time, are carnivorous.

On Moffen the walrus used to eat *haneskjell* and *kamskjell*, together with echinoderms. Then came the Norwegian shellfish trawlers. The trawlers used vacuum cleaners to strip the shells off the rock and, though there was a ten-centimetre size limit, they brought everything onboard, the smaller animals together with the shells of the bigger animals being ground up into a paste and discharged back into the sea. The EEC was a good export market for the flesh and up came the shellfish in buckets. The trawl not only savaged the stock, it also broke the rocks so that the walrus, hungrily searching the crevices, was cut about the head and body. In the cold waters of the Arctic the re-colonization time of the island is long, perhaps seven years, perhaps even longer since the discharged paste, a lime sludge, damages what it touches. There are no walrus on Moffen as we steam past.

Later we discussed the fishing with the *Sysselmann*. He was emphatic that the story was wrong, and that the walrus had moved for other reasons, although he did not deny that Moffen had been fished out as far as the trawlermen were concerned. We were left wondering how many fishermen were supported by the shellfish trade over that cruel five-year period; as many as would have been supported by the tourist trade of people wanting to see these magnificent animals?

I brood on these questions as we head north and east. Here and there a large bearded seal or smaller ringed seal lolls on its ice floe, but there are fewer animals than before. The food chain up here includes the *lodde*, a small salmon-like fish, perhaps thirteen centimetres at its longest. It is food for seals and also for the cod which, in turn, are preyed on by the seals. The Norwegians had fished *lodde* in a small way for many years, to make fish meal. Recently the Japanese 'discovered' that the roe was an aphrodisiac, and because they were willing to pay a high price for it, the number of trawlers increased. The male fish, killed by the trawl, were dumped immediately, the females cleaned of their eggs and dumped. By election year, in 1985, the estimated stock of *lodde* was 86,000 tonnes, the quota agreed being 75,000 tonnes. The *lodde* was fished to extinction, its absence causing the fishermen to grumble that the government was at fault, and that those scientists who had predicted the stock crash and had been ignored should have been more vociferous, more adamant. With the *lodde* gone, the cod declined, with the fishermen blaming not their own over-fishing but the activities of other nations' deep-sea trawlers. Either way the cod were gone. The seals starved, or their blubber thinned and they froze when the winter came. The polar bears moved north and away.

So there are fewer seals, or so it seems, as we make it into Hinlopenstretet this time. We are heading for Wahlenbergfjorden, as close as you can get to Nordaustland, where landings are forbidden as the island is a nature reserve. The fjord encapsulates the Svalbard problems that are milling around in my head.

We enter it towards midnight, with the sky clearing and the sun blinding. To the west a thick grey mass of cloud reminds us of the previous day's storm and makes an impressive backdrop for a huge iceberg that goes slowly past. The berg is picked out white by the sun. To the north, looking towards the sun, the light off the floe-ice is dazzling. Wahlenbergfjorden is full of ice – ice as huge bergs, ice as smaller lumps, but mostly ice as pack-ice, thin sheets of ice, their surface pitted by rain and sunshine. The ice is not continuous, but much of the open water between the sheets is not real sea. Rather, it is the five or eight centimetres of sea that lie over a submerged section of sheet. At one stage Tony proves this by cleverly dropping a lens filter over the side. Being mean, he clambers down a rope hanging over the side to retrieve it, watched by a dubious crew. The filter is on the ice, just below the water.

The sun makes patterns on the ice sheets, and turns the whole picture black and white, so stark is its light. Overhead, the sky turns that shade of blue that no artist, not even Van Gogh, has ever captured. To the south the peaks of Zeipelodden and Clarendonnaeringane are a pale brown that

could even be called pink, with clumps of snow and ice studding their flattened tops. With the low-angled sun that we have now at two in the morning giving the best shadow and side lighting it is a glorious scene. As I stare across the pack-ice, back along the sun line, a fulmar swings across the light puddle and is held, briefly, in silhouette.

Only to the north now is there any cloud, and that

Orographic cloud over Gustav V Land.

is the most perfect orographic cloud we have yet seen. Orographic clouds are an Arctic phenomenon, caused because the water vapour of the Arctic air is usually close to the saturation point. As a result, when the air is forced to rise over a mountain, the cooling as it rises causes a cloud of condensed water droplets to form. The cloud produced has remarkably clean-cut edges and is a shape replica of the underlying land. As wind moves the air across the mountain, the leading edge droplets revapourize as the air mass falls on the 'other' side of the hill. Since the vapour of the new air in the trailing edge is condensing, the cloud shape itself is absolutely stationary, irrespective of the wind speed. It is a beautiful sight.

Two hours later we are watching a seal lazily

149

Pack-ice, Wahlenbergfjorden.

150

basking in the sun on an ice floe at the mouth of Kløverbladbukta. Beyond, on the edge of Etonbreen, a large polar bear is ambling down towards the sea. Another, nearer the sea's edge, is shuffling nervously, dipping its head and circling in the way that suggests it is angry, probably at the other's intrusion rather than at us.

Polar bears are supposed to be white, but they are not. Against the dazzling blue-white of a glacier they are cream, even yellow-cream. Stories are told that they hide the black of their noses with a paw while hunting, but it is not conspicious at this range when compared to the massive cream body. The bear walks with the lazy but insistent walk of a policeman advancing on a group of kids caught stealing apples. The walk betrays both the owner's personal power and the species dominance. These animals survive outside from birth to death, in temperatures down to −40°C (−40°F) and below in winds that would knock over a man. They swim in water that is barely above freezing. Evidence of their presence has been discovered within yards of the North Pole itself.

The last few hours have made my head ache. We are in one of the most beautiful places on earth, and close to one of the earth's most fascinating and impressive animals; wanting to come here is understandable for those reasons. What separates man from other species is his desire for new experiences, his quest for knowledge and his recognition of aesthetic beauty. In search of these we have come here, but when we came we brought guns for our protection. By being here, when we are ashore and walking, we are endangering the bears, putting them at risk by being prepared to kill them in order to save ourselves. Saving yourself is a reasonable strategy, and I know that if the time comes I will shoot, but it concerns me greatly that these wonderful creatures, so much in command of this land, should be threatened by the presence of creatures who cannot survive, let alone prosper, alone among them.

The big bear turns northward off the end of the glacier. It seems uninterested in the seal, or in the other bear, who has temporarily vanished among the ice bluffs at the sea's edge. He swings his head in our direction, puffs out a cloud of condensing breath and plods on to be lost among the ice.

When I wake we are still among the pack-ice, although here in more open sea the sheets are broken and it is water, emerald-green water, between the floes. Occasionally a big berg glides by, its colour not the ice-blue of the Magdalenafjord glacier but a turquoise blue. By contrast, some smaller sheets are slushy grey. The huge size of the bergs can be gauged by the effect of the ship's wake on them. The small floes bob up and down, the larger ones rock restlessly, but the biggest do not move at all, the wake crashing on them as it would on to a breakwater. I imagine that if we were to hit one it would react the same way. Small wonder the *Titanic* fared so badly.

There are seals, both ringed and bearded, on the ice floes. On one, the huge sleeping presence is a male walrus, an enormous solitary male that is so sound asleep we get within a metre before he wakes. Half-asleep and fearful, he hurls himself off the floe, surfacing a few metres away to stare at us from over the top of his tusks. He is not pleased about the intrusion and snorts water at us before diving again.

Time has been misplaced, and I find myself watching for seal and walrus at two in the morning, still fascinated by the low-angled light on the pack ice. Tony arrives with two cups of coffee, pulls his hood up and sits beside me facing into the wind. An ivory gull, the first we have seen, floats overhead. No words are exchanged. It is a moment to savour.

Ashore at Mosselbukta, Mussel Bay, Tony and I go off in search of flowers. The beach is littered with timber, most of it pine poles washed ashore here after spending weeks in the Ocean drifting westward from Siberia. The timber was useful to the early whalers, offering them shelter and fuel. Nearby the remains of an old hut, probably used by sealers rather than whalers, is witness to this usefulness. Such ruins are strictly protected by Norway and it is forbidden to damage them or to rob them for souvenirs. The protection does not extend as far as restoration or even stabilization, however, and after a few more winters this precarious structure will have collapsed. As far as I can judge, there were two rooms, one a kitchen if the evidence of an old iron cooking and heating range is to be believed. The range is iron, not steel and has not rusted. I suggest to Tony that it would make a good photograph, even a good publicity shot – yer actual Aga, as found 975 kilometres from the North Pole. He is unimpressed and returns to the tripod erected over a clump of Mountain Aven. Later we walk along the beach to a tern colony where Tony positions himself on the ground a

Diving walrus.

metre away from a sitting female. The bird is wonderfully good, eyeing him nervously but remaining glued to her nest. Finally I tell him that he should let her be as she has been a good girl. He agrees and starts to move back. The bird lifts off her nest and flies at him, positioning herself like a humming-bird a metre from his head, calling loudly. Tony shoots off a couple of frames, turns to me, shouts, that's fantastic, and fails to avoid a stream of bird shit from above. It lands square on head and camera. Honours even, I think. Later Tony tells me that the sight of the tern landing and then slowly ruffling her feathers over her egg has made his microprisms shimmer with delight.

We trek off across the bay towards a smoke-shrouded tent that turns out to be occupied by three Russian geologists. One comes out to greet us, offering us his hand and a warm welcome.

Please to come into tent for tea. We please to.

The tent is vast, a canvas Hilton with chairs and a stove built to belch smoke out of a chimney through the canvas, but choosing to leave enough smoke inside to make your eyes smart. Please to sit down. You smoke cigarette? No, thank you.

A second, taller man arrives. Unlike the first, who could pass in any European street as a native of the country, being possessed of that size and shape, those features and tones, that say 'European' rather than anything more specific, this man is unmistakeably Russian. He shakes our hands, gravely and over a long time, during which he mentally strips us to our prejudices and inner desires. We say hello. He grunts. The first man suggests that this grunt is 'hello', explaining that his boss – this is the leader of the group – speaks no English. In truth the grunt is recognition that

Arctic tern.

Arctic tern.

these newcomers are not tourists off a boat, but people on the make. They have not come here for tea, comrade, they seek an angle. The boss sits down. Or, rather, he sits *up*, straight-backed and pensive, watching, analysing. The tent door flutters again and in comes a third Russian, a girl, tall and of such angular beauty that all either of us can do for a few seconds is follow her progress behind the stove. The boss says something in a whiplash voice. It is hastily translated. We are told that the girl sleeps in the same tent as the men because she is afraid of the ice bears. Tony gives me a look that suggests that this story is one of the finest he has ever heard. He seems on the point of saying as much, perhaps adding something about our willingness to cover for them if they wanted time off – the odd night, or month.

To avoid World War III being declared unilaterally, I ask about their work. Svalbard is the perfect place for the geology, the friendly Russian tells us; all of the rocks are here, from the pre-Cambrian to the Quaternary. There are, too, many fossils in the sedimentary layers. At this place there are some of the oldest rocks, pre-Cambrian and Ordovician. There are too some igneous intrusions. He continues with enthusiasm through two refills of Russian tea while his boss smokes an evil-smelling cigarette, and then another, and the girl sits very still and beautiful. As he nears the end of his second cigarette the boss becomes restless, and I suspect that Tony and I have become as intrusive to him as the local granite outcrops. We leave. All three shake our hands solemnly, the boss without feeling, his eyes still searching our faces, the girl awkwardly. They watch us as we walk away, continuing to stare until we are out of sight. Tony offers me his thoughts on the reception, relative to *glasnost*, and some suggestions about the girl. In most respects they agree with mine.

On Amsterdamøya two reindeer hurl themselves away from us towards the high ground as we approach. Their flight startles an Arctic fox

Old seal hunting or whaling hut, Mosselbukta.

which, in turn, startles them and they jump and turn in a frenzied fashion before hurling themselves off again. Svalbard reindeer are smaller than their Norwegian mainland cousins, and have heavier, shaggy coats. They herd less readily and are, if possible, even more timid. It's not surprising. Arne, a Norwegian with a tea-cosy hat and a camouflage suit, who carries our 762 protection rifle as though born to it and tells us at every opportunity that we are OK when he is there because he is a mean bastard, tells us that he has heard that until recently there were three reindeer here. And one hungry polar bear. Today, he says with obvious relish, there are two reindeer and a less hungry polar bear. Need any help with the gun, Arne?

Smeerenburg is a showpiece Svalbard heritage site. Here, once, there was a town of over 1,000 people and several whale blubber boilers. There was wood smoke and oil smoke thick enough to cut with a knife, and there was the stench of disembowelled whale and boiling fat. The town had raised wooden pavements to keep the inhabitants off the saturated ground when the permafrost melted. Today there is little to show for it all and it is a surprise that the site is viewed as significant in heritage terms. There is an old whale bone at the edge of a pond that appears now to occupy the space where the houses once stood. There are the remains of baked clay boilers, perhaps three are discernible. There is nothing else. Tony and I discuss the merits of living in Smeerenberg. The outlook here is spectacular, although hardly beautiful in the sense that Magdalenefjorden is beautiful. The fjord in front of the old town is hemmed in and dark, although it does end in a fine glacier. Both fjord and glacier are named for Smeerenburg, to make the folk feel at home. Overall, Blaenau Ffestiniog is much maligned.

Woodfjorden, to the west of Wijdefjorden, ends with steep striated cliffs falling directly into the sea. At a dog-leg a smaller, stumpy fjord, Bockfjorden, almost as wide as it is long, leads on along the line of the main waterway. On the shallow plateau that is the southern beach of Bockfjorden there are thermal springs. Single blow holes of sulphurous water bubble out from basaltic pavements. Those who have been to Krísuvík or Geysir in Iceland will be unimpressed, yet the background, the deep purple, pointed peaks above a spur arm of the Monacobreen, gives the place a certain charm. We learn that this is Volcano Bay, so named as much because of the volcano-like shape of a sugar loaf mountain as for the warm springs. Jan Christian tells us this. He is a tall, ear-ringed Norwegian with crew-cut hair squared off, it seems, with a spirit level. He has a wide mouth and a square jaw. A humorous, if sarcastic, man might suggest Mr Toad. He would be unwise to make this suggestion within Jan Christian's hearing range. His own hearing could become seriously impaired.

Jan Christian has long legs and they are striding out across the level plateau between sea and mountains here on the Andréeland peninsula that separates Wijdefjorden and Woodfjorden. Tony and (especially) I are having difficulty in keeping with him on the flat, if boggy, going. We get our own back on the uphill sections. The hills of Snougla and, later, Bråvatlafjella – only 500–600 metres or so high, but composed of a scree of frost-smashed rock – slow him down, allowing the lower centre of gravity and experience of uphill work to come into its own. But still it is exhausting work, both physically and mentally. With each step the scree slips and there is an agonizing moment while I wait to see how far it will take me. Occasionally it takes me back past where I was. Usually you have to wait for a restabilizing of the fist-sized scree; the delay before you can move up again gives you time to look at the work ahead and to be appalled at how much more of this God-awful rubbish there still is. Going straight up soon becomes too much of a misery to contemplate, compounded by the rucsac hauling me backwards. A rising traverse is easier on the spirit – the hill's flank offering a goal, however illusory – if not on the legs and ankles. We have long since given up walking together, each of us picking a way as best he can. Who has the air to talk? And what would we say?

Ahead there is something on the scree. It is worth heading towards – the first goal I have been able to set myself since we left level ground. When I reach it the object is the last thirty centimetres of a reindeer's leg.

Polar bear! In panic I search the slope and skyline for a bear, then search again for Jan Christian who was carrying the gun when last I saw it. Tony is a couple of hundred metres or so away, perhaps sixty-seven metres below. I holler at him to attract his attention. He pauses and looks up with a pained expression. Where is the gun? He looks around for Jan Christian, and points to a spot

Svalbard reindeer in summer coat.

Svalbard reindeer in winter coat.

A tongue of Monacobreen and mountains above Bockfjorden.

View to Andrée Land from Bråvatlafjella.

out of sight of me. It takes an age for Tony to arrive, time during which I do little except scan the slope and horizon. Tony pokes at the bone. How the hell did that get here, he wonders. Bear? I ask, nonchalantly. Idiot! Can you see a bear getting up here over that lot? No, when it comes to it I really can't imagine 500 kilograms of bear lugging a reindeer, or catching one either, on this pile of crockery. Jan Christian arrives. Convinced by now that the leg was brought here by an Arctic fox or even, since it is so light, by a polar gull, I offer to do a spell with the gun. He readily agrees; it is an old and heavy Mauser.

Check for shells. Yes, all there. Slip one into the chamber. Check safety for off, good. Put safety on. I return to the climb, feeling a little more composed.

Nearer the top of the ridge the hill steepens and the desperate nature of the scree becomes more of a danger than a nuisance. The old dilemma of Alpine climbing seems to have returned – go fast and risk a mistake or go slow and spend longer at risk. But a moment's thought shows that our problem is different. The objective dangers are limited as not once have we seen a spontaneous rock fall. I am sure they happen, but only when the frost that glazes the upper rocks together is softened by the sun. That happened some weeks ago. Our scree is dry and even the melt water has been burnt off, so we have to take our time, stay out of the fall line of the guy ahead, and concentrate. And, finally, hope that our agreed principle that polar bears do not climb scree is a principle shared by polar bears. If there is one just over the ridge he and I are in for a surprise.

There is only the blue-green ribbon of Woodfjorden and the pinkish flat land of Reinsdryflya beyond, a noted goose breeding area that Tony and I long to visit. Below a small boat – from a geological survey we later discover – is moving silently out of Mushama, a tiny bay. The walking effort eases and we are able to savour the view to the pointed peaks of Dachstein inland. Thin lengths of misty cloud, like half-seen snakes, wrap themselves around the peaks. The black morainic streaks and crevasse shadows look like veins in the glacial arm. And it is so quiet. What is wonderful about this country is that it is so quiet for so long. You can – we do – go for days without hearing anything. No cars, no factories, not even a voice.

Going down, the scree can be run, but it is exhausting work. I aim for a pool where two blobs are moving. As they come into focus I see they are

reindeer, one with a fine set of antlers. I wonder if they will notice that I am no longer carrying the gun. Of course they do not and are gone as soon as they sense my presence. The vegetation here is the usual Svalbard mix; moss mostly on the saturated ground, with the remains of this spring's flowers in isolated clumps on the higher sections. I notice as I walk across one particularly boggy section that the moss does not spring back into place as it would in the UK, but just collapses. My bootprint fills with water, but is still clearly visible. I recall the *Sysselmann* telling us that the tracks left by a tracked vehicle driven from Longyearbyen to Barentsburg were still there, with almost perfect clean-cut edges, half a century later. I edge cautiously to more stable-looking ground. Ahead is a hut and tent, together with other odds and ends. The hut is empty, but nearby are half a dozen sledge dogs on chains. Here too is a wooden structure with what look like old carpets suspended from it. I go over.

The hut belongs to a seal hunter. The structure is a drying frame from which skinned seal carcasses hang. To stop bears reaching the carcasses the frame is sitting on a raised platform that gives the whole thing the look of a gallows with the bodies of twenty condemned men hanging in unison. Nearby on a table are the last few centimetres of a seal, hind flippers and short stump of body, neatly cut through. The exposed end is ringed like a chopped carrot. The place is horrifyingly fascinating.

Ny Ålesund, new Ålesund, has the world's most northerly post office, and the world's most northerly public telephone. Here, too, are the most northerly shop, art gallery and so on. I visited what is probably the world's most northerly public 'urinal', just to the left of a mound that supported a wooden overhead sewer pipe; certainly public, but scarcely qualifying for the rest of the title. On a large, dirty warehouse near the harbour there is a huge white painted coffin. Look hard and you will see that beneath the white paint is a whiter painted cross and the figure '50', one above the other. It is not clear exactly why these were done, but it is known that King Olaf was coming to visit Ny Ålesund once, and the day before, or so it is said, an unknown man arrived on skis and painted the cross and the '50', in bold white, choosing the warehouse wall that would face the king as he arrived. The man left without a word. If this is true, it sheds a revealing light on Svalbardians. To arrive here on skis the man must have come a long way. He did this carrying a paint tin and brush. He would, too, have needed an abseil rope or, less likely, a long ladder. He gained entrance to private property, climbed to the roof and did his work. No one questioned him, no one challenged him. I am speechless.

The symbols were supposed to represent the number of men who died in an avoidable accident in the local mine, but most chronicles have that number much lower. The number of dead is disputed, it is true, but nobody claims as many as fifty. Others say that the sign was a comment on fifty years of Svalbard misrule. Either way, the local chiefs decided to obliterate the symbols, but, horrors, there is sufficient local paint only to poorly mask out the original with an overlay in the shape of a coffin. *Quel dommage!*

Elsewhere I am surprised to see a bust of Roald Amundsen, not realizing at the time the significance of this settlement in the story of his final journey. Near to it a wild blue fox is sniffing at a blue fox caged up behind a house. It gallops away when it sees me. Given the choice what would each of them choose — captivity and food, or freedom and hunger?

Tony has disappeared, intent on getting the ultimate photograph, a flock of barnacle geese against a background of the (restored) world's most northerly railway. Strange to think that these birds are probably the same ones that we could see again in Caerlaverock in Scotland this winter. Nearby, a hut has a large board outside inscribed, in English, 'Ny Ålesund Railway Preservation Society Headquarters. Volunteers welcome.' Volunteers welcome? Where you off to, love? Well, I thought I'd just nip out for an afternoon on the railway. OK, love, don't be too long. No, should be back in three months.

The railway hauled from, you've guessed it, the world's most northerly mine.

On the far side of Kongsfjorden from Ny Ålesund is a huge glacial tongue where the Kronebreen and Conwaybreen join and reach the sea. On to this glacial tongue we take Arne the Mean, a man who has shot elk — which he consistently refers to as moose — has been there and done that, but has never yet been on a glacier. We beach the inflatable on shingle close to the glacier's five-kilometre-wide front wall. Near our end rather than the centre is the now familiar blue cavern, again bird-filled. Our intention is to follow the glacier's left edge towards the top of Conwaytoppen, a peak of around 1,000 metres. Getting on is easy; the bergschrund — if I may be permitted to use so grand a name — is a thirty-centimetre channel a metre deep and filled with a fast-flowing stream. We step over. Arne is amazed by the glacier, by its texture — expecting smooth ice and finding a roughened sandy surface — by its colour — expecting blue-white and finding dirty grey with occasional black streaks — by the fact that there is water streaming down it, and by the crevasses in these lower regions, discernible only as thin cracks so intense has the side pressure been. He is anxious to go to the lip to peer over, a little less keen when we explain that the notice he may get of imminent berg creation could be measured in fractions of a second. What surprises him most of all is that he can walk comfortably without ice axe and crampons — although we have both — as the surface is not slippery. He is rapidly dissuaded from this view when we reach a steeper section. There Tony skitters a stone back down the glacier and Arne watches as it goes on and on and . . .

The climb is uneventful, although finding a crossing point back on to the scree mountain is trickier the higher we go, but the eventual return journey by inflatable, early in the morning with the sun well off the fjord and a strange twilight on the water, is far from straightforward. The wind has picked up and the sea is running, giving us waves that are short and tall. The inflatable can, and does, lift both nose and tail out together when it sits on a crest, the outboard racing, threatening to injure itself. When we launch the outboard is stowed. Arne lowers it and wraps up the starting cord. He pulls. Nothing. By the time he has pulled twice more I notice that the boat has drifted past the mouth of an incut into the beach. It is a long way to shore now, and the water might even be quite deep here. The wind and sea are pushing us straight at the cavern in the glacier which is a few hundred metres away and getting closer rapidly. Start the engine, Arne. Now.

He does, and we take off across the bay. It is a long way to go and soon the flying spray has cooled us all. The way ahead is barred by ice chunks from a section of pack ice broken by wind and wave. Fearful of hitting the chunks and puncturing, Arne slows, and the waves are now pushing us faster than the engine. To make headway we have to have Tony in the front of the boat with his head over the rubber side peering ahead

Barnacle geese and the world's most northerly railway at Ny Ålesund.

and pointing with his arms to give Arne instructions on left and right. I hold Tony's legs and offer the occasional shout as well. Slow down! *Slow*! Left; *left* for Christ's sake! We go up over a wave crest, the outboard accelerates to wrecking speed. Arne drops the throttle, and the boat lurches down off the wave, thwacking into the sea with a jarring thump that leaves half of Tony's jaw raw and numb from a collision with the edge. Right; *right*! he shouts and frantically points.

The journey takes an hour or so. However, it feels like several hours.

Tony's great idea for travelling southern Spitsbergen on a budget is to use the mountain bikes on hire from Longyearbyen. Given that he is one of the best cycle designer/builders in the UK, a man very familiar with the concept of sprocket and crank, this seems a reasonable venture. My own view of engineering is that it mostly involves big lumps of metal moving about in oil. I have little

160

Conwaybreen, Spitsbergen.

Glacial cavern, Conwaybreen.

understanding and even less empathy with things mechanical. The bikes are lightweight, the young lady tells us, which proves only that she is comparing their weight to that of a fully-ladened armoured personnel carrier. Do you need the key? Jesus, they have ignition. Heart leaps. Allen key, Tony says. He turns to the girl. Take no notice, he says, he is an idiot. No, we don't need a key, these are fine.

I wheel the monster outside. It has a bell, a tender thought. If there is a polar bear on the uplands above Adventdalen I can tinkle it and so warn the bear of my presence in time for it to move to one side. Morning Mr Bear. Morning Dick.

Tony is off down the road like a madman. I follow more cautiously. Not needing to pedal I idly rotate my feet backwards, just for something to do. The back wheel locks solid and the monster lurches over the road like a crazed rodeo horse. When I catch Tony at the café – 'catch' in the sense that he has stopped, dismounted and is already considering rucsac placement – I ask him about this. They've made the back brake operate by back pedalling, he says. This does, at least, save me the embarrassment of asking why I only have one brake lever.

We start up Adventdalen with rucsacs that weigh close on thirty-five kilograms strapped half on us and half on the bike's carry frame. Pedalling on the flat is agony. Our itinerary has us reaching Pyramiden. I rapidly scale this down to the idea of making a last bid to get the bike back to the office. We persevere. My rucsac falls off the carrier and I fall off the bike. Evening sees us still in Adventdalen – though it is a very long valley – with Tony admitting that one of the reasons we are having so much trouble is saddle height. Should have adjusted it. How? With the Allen key, he says, sheepishly. You pillock.

We spend happy hours photographing flowers in weather rarely less than glorious. We stalk reindeer, glimpse a blue fox, spot ptarmigan – the only birds to winter on Svalbard, although polar gulls do stay as near as the ice will allow. Finally, we are moving back along the road to the airport campsite. The rucsac feels heavier, which can't be true. It has been a long haul. I pause at the top of a rise and photograph Tony as he comes up it. Now it seems to be downhill all the way, but it isn't. By the time we are at the site I am bushed. Tony sees a glorious patch of Arctic cotton grass and disappears. When he returns an hour later I am still

putting up the tent, sitting down beside the peg I am pushing in. He puts the Trangia together while I use the bike to fetch water. He stands his cup on my Karrimat, as usual. I point this out. I always use that one. I know. But it's the one with all the cup rings on, he says, by way of explanation.

After tea we have cup-a-soup. I spill some of the powder trying to get it into Tony's cup. He says nothing, but later when I suggest he gets the next kettle of water he complains that I ought to. I am the stronger, and I've had more soup than him. I am so hungry that I could eat sledge dog. We prepare the most expensive packet meal we have brought; it promises energy without limit, flavour *à la haute cuisine*. It has a picture of a youth wreathed in smiles on the front. It tastes so foul I can't eat it, hungry as I am. Tony feels the same. The youth on the packet, we decide, is the company owner's son. I dump the lot away from the tent. In Svalbard whatever food you drop is gone at the end of the next quiet patch, so little natural food is there. Next morning the brown sludge is still there. Neither birds nor fox will touch it.

I am too tired to cook any more, so we have custard and then hot chocolate as easy substitutes. As I drink my chocolate I notice the custard ring emerge as the liquid level drops. On the next sip a pea rises to the surface, having freed itself from the soup sludge at the bottom. For seven days I have eaten out of a cup. My plate broke on the plane coming out and I have had everything, including breakfast muesli, from a cup, even, on one memorable occasion, beef stew.

Even here on Svalbard we are troubled – troubled rather than plagued – by mosquitos. Tony tells me that he has discovered that they don't like meths. How? I just hit this one with the Sigg bottle and he hasn't moved since.

We visit Barentsburg. It is an extraordinary place. Never have I been among so many shifty-looking people, although here and there a happier type is busily painting over the rust on the railings beside the steps leading from town to sea. Everywhere we are approached by groups of men trying to barter badges and beads for dollars and consumables. They are not interested in Norwegian kroner. Dollars are fine – which is fine by us as we don't have any – but a watch or camera would be better. You want *chapka*? Twenty dollar, or good watch. You have good camera. I give you doll, Russian doll. Come here, see. You give me video-recorder – well, of course, I have several in my rucsac – I give you this. What is it? You see. It turns out to be a Kalashnikov AK47. Never have I seen such rampant capitalism.

One comrade, a short, thick-set man with a steel look that unnerves us, is the KGB Tony decides, although in truth he is acting no differently from the rest. Tony suggests we try our newly-learnt Russian swearing on him. A cold war Norwegian, unimpressed by Russians irrespective of Gorbachev and *glasnost*, has taught us a couple of phrases guaranteed to have the mob escorting us to an alley between warehouses and helping us suddenly to the ground. Make a fist, then ease your thumb up between your fingers so that the top of it pokes out, with two fingers on each side. Put your arm straight, thumb poking upwards to the sky. Point straight arm and fist at offending Russian and say *'bletch'* in a loud and deep voice. It means 'assholes' said our Norwegian linguist, and the thumb and fingers are imaginatively representative. It is very good, very rude, he said, but better is to say *'yop tea mock'* (that is a phonetic rendering). He told us what this meant too. Few Russians would appreciate being told to indulge in such an activity with their mothers. They do not like that, he said. We could imagine and, given the choice, would rather imagine than find out.

You give him *bletch*, Tony suggested, casually indicating the man from the KGB. *Yop tea mock*, I tell him, but quietly. We move on. The steel-eyed man does not follow. Within 100 metres we have decided that he was a bit of a joke. It is a measure of the unnerving qualities of his sinister gaze.

Barentsburg is dour, grey and drab. A sign informs us that 'Communism is Our Goal'. Photographs show us the smiling faces of the worker-heroes of the month. A list on the wall gives particulars of something we can't fathom; it could be the Top Ten – I see that Datsanastikov has ousted the Proletariat Trio from Number One. Near the town's flats some old women and other old-before-their-time women look nervously at us, hide their heads in shawls and hurry away. Apart from those trying to sell us Mother Russia for ten dollars or a Casio digital, no one speaks a word to us.

Back at the tent Tony is trying to persuade the Trangia into a usable pile. Some gunge on it keeps trying to grab his finger, he maintains. I am writing notes. What are you writing? he asks. The good bits about Barentsburg, I say. He pauses for about ten seconds. What are you writing now then? he asks.

Next day, appalled by what dehydrated food is doing to his insides, Tony insists we go into Longyearbyen to see if they have anything worth eating. There is a restaurant we are told; it serves polar bear in season and charges an arm and a leg. We go in the self-service kaff and try to explain to the girl behind the counter that there would be good mileage in changing the name of the place to 'Restaurant at the End of the Universe'. She has clearly not heard of the *Hitchhiker's Guide*. We give up trying to explain when she gets a look on her face that implies that any minute now she is going to call the manager, or the police.

The food is solid, the first thing I have needed to use a knife on, or to use a plate to hold, for over a week. Tony savours each mouthful. If it wasn't for the ride back to the site, life would be really good.

Svalbard museum turns out to be the best part of Longyearbyen; its sections on polar exploration and the area's wildlife are excellent. Tony reads and re-reads the part on the discovery and processing of the photographic plates from the tragic 1897 Andree expedition. Thirty-three years after the expedition was lost the last bodies were found, and the negative plates, preserved by the cold. Development allowed some idea of the last moments of the members to be discovered. I am more taken by the Spanish North-Pole-on-motorbike expedition that intended to use bikes with studded tyres to haul sledges all the way to the Pole. They arrived at the airport, set up camp at the official site, looked at the task ahead and caught the next plane out, leaving their kit behind. Hey, Tone, we got closer to the Pole than an official Pole expedition. And we were on push-bikes too.

Next morning, our last, I make two mugfuls of tea and offer one to his lordship. I suggest he might try a short address, along the lines of, 'Thank you seems wholly inappropriate as a means of expressing the gratitude I feel for your having made me a cup of tea, Dick, but perhaps it will suffice until I am able to offer a more tangible expression.' He opens an eye and peers at me. Piss off, he says.

Later I make two mugfuls of muesli. I poke about in the bag – we have all of it in two-man-day plastic bags. What's up? asks Tony. There seems to be a bit of grass in here. Well stick it in my mug then, he says. You have been all week.

Moss campion.

A rare white Svalbard poppy.

Snow buttercup.

Arctic cotton grass.

We pack. It is all over for another trip. It looks as though it might be going to end in anti-climax, the way all trips seem to, but Tony has spellbinding news. He has apparently enjoyed a 'good clean break'. A sign of healthy living, he chortles. Knew we should have had the meal in town yesterday.

I recall the Canadians who shared time with us once on Svalbard. At the end of the trip, as the bus was preparing to return them to civilization, but to leave us behind in our wilderness, one of the girls in their party came over and seized our hands emphatically. Bye guys, she said, it's been a slice.

I thought of this as we waited for our call to board. This was another fine day Svalbard had gotten us into – though it is prone to what Yorkshiremen would call a 'fret', Svalbard is very dry. Blue sky was piled up on top of the brown hills. The Ocean was green and still.

'Would all passengers . . . '

Bye Svalbard; it's been a slice.

Winter

Gavin Dunlop runs a ski equipment agency, which partially explains why he, Tony and I were wearing identical jackets as we swallowed our way through yet another pot of tea in Gatwick's departure lounge. The idiot who booked the tickets had not thought to ask about a change from winter to summer schedules and so had not noticed the change in departure time. The five-hour change in departure time. I was not flavour of the day. That, most definitely, was Earl Grey. Tony, a coffee drinker, maintained a shocked silence. He had red, bleary eyes from a cold and loss of sleep, had worked too long, too hard when unwell, had driven from North Wales and then worked too long and too hard again, slept too little and been woken too early in order to arrive in time to catch a non-existent plane. It was altogether too many toos.

The flight was called and in our anxiety to get moving at last we left without the brown paper parcel with the Easter eggs that Tony was delivering to a Welshman now resident in Oslo. At the gate a frantic man arrived as the tannoy announced the discovery of the package. My stock was low, so I was deputed to return to the canteen where staff had evacuated part of the eating area and were standing guard over the sinister pile of brown paper and string. I had a vision of the result of a controlled explosion, with chocolate streamers hanging in festoons from the light fittings.

In Oslo Tony was asleep before he reached the cheap city hotel, waking only to transfer from bus to bed. Gavin drank Norwegian beer and talked quietly of his excitement and anxiety. This was his first major trip for years and the heady mixture was giving him a thirst.

Back at Fornebu we repossessed our rucsacs and skis from the pawn shop, well, the left luggage office. Repossession took a whole heap of gronks (cash), a heap big enough to take our breath and hopes for a quick bite away. We had told Gavin all about Scandinavian air hostesses, so he was bound to be disappointed by the one who served him his apology for a real breakfast. He was grateful to

reach Tromsø where we joined the flight to Longyearbyen.

Longyearbyen was a culture shock. Dressed for a spring Oslo morning, we were deposited into an icy waste at −18°C (0°F). We changed behind the Svalbard equivalent of bike sheds, and within two hours of arriving the three of us, together with our three travelling companions, were pulling the start cords of Polaris snow scooters. Ulf, a true Viking with his blonde hair, blonde beard, lean good looks (and glasses) heads a company that specializes in offering tours to Svalbard. He was coming with us to prospect new places for his tours to visit. With him came Lars, one of his team leaders, another true Viking with a haircut I promised never to comment on, and Mats, a Swede with designer stubble and a long record of work on Antarctic birds.

The snow scooter is a curious invention, at once great transport and great fun, and yet a bloody nuisance. If you have worked hard to ski-haul your kit to some remote valley where you have pitched your tent and started to commune with nature, a squadron of two-stroke snow scooters sounding like a swarm of hornets is as welcome as a hot-water enema. Yet to reach further out into the wilderness than you could otherwise go, to travel more safely, and to thoroughly enjoy it all, there is no better machine. Being mechanically inept I was likely to lean heavily on Tony's experience with motorbikes, although as it happened the machines were well behaved. There is no clutch, the brake succeeds only in producing a back-end slide, particularly if you are sledge-towing, the steering is normally not good and downright appalling on ice, and the machine frightens the daylights out of you going across any slope that is respectably non-flat. We learned early that in any situation that looked difficult the best technique was to wind open the throttle; round corners, uphill, downhill, whatever, the machine was under better control at speed, with the traction increasing noticeably.

We wound open our throttles – in practice pushed a lever forward, as the machines have a deadman's handle brake-lever type throttle – and moved out of Longyearbyen into Adventdalen. We turned right and took the second valley on the right, heading south towards Svea. The trip up Adventdalen was up memory lane, although it was difficult now to recognize the valley that Tony and I had cycled up, except for the distinctive range of hills to the north.

The light was starting to fail as we headed up Todalen and then down Gangdalen to the Sørhytta at the edge of Reindalen. We turned east and burnt snow – as Tony so ineloquently put it – to and on to Slakbreen. On the glacier we paused to check the sledge loads, the banging and bumping occasionally disturbing the packed order, and to find the Snickers bars. Tony shot off a few 'snaps' and checked the temperature. It was −29°C (−20°F) and falling by 1°C (1.8°F) even during our short stop. On the glacier we drove in a line abreast at 100kph; this would have induced a wind chill temperature of around −70°C (−94°F) on any flesh laid bare, but with anorak hoods pulled up to the level of our goggles there was nothing bare. We crossed twelve kilometres of the glacier, then dropped steeply down a glacial tongue to emerge near the old mining town of Sveagruva. On this last section, a too-casually constructed face-masking system meant that I breathed out over my glasses and goggles. Each was immediately covered by a thin layer of ice which combined with the dying light to make me blind. I drove the last hundred metres down off the glacier too close to Gavin to have been able to stop if he had. It was either that or maybe go over the edge.

Svea is an ugly town in summer, but winter's snow had covered many of the horrors, softening it into, if not beauty, then acceptability. Ulf talked us into the miner's lodge for which we were grateful – one last night of warmth and comfort, a chance to find all the bits mislaid in the airport's rush. Next morning we fed and watered the scooters. We chortled at the road sign in the 'main' street that warned of polar bears, re-packed the scooters, bought petrol, initiated Sale into the mysteries of two-stroke engines. And got bored waiting and re-doing. Why does everything take so long in the cold? Talking of which, why is it so cold? True, if we had been given the choice we would have taken the sun, blue skies and −30°C (−36°F), but we had actually hoped for something a little warmer, perhaps around −20°C (−4°F).

Our first sea-ice drive was over the Bragan-zavågen bay next to Svea, an exhilarating drive with one pause while Tony filmed a lone reindeer that mooched lazily across the ice to our left. Conscious of the need not to startle it, we stayed well clear, but it seemed oblivious to our presence, wrapped up in white hair and the needs of survival.

Then it was on again up Kjellströmdalen, in summer a sandy delta of melt-water rivers, now frozen into the perfect driving surface. We paused near a hut below Passnuten, Ulf explaining that these were emergency shelters only, forbidden to the casual visitor. Despite that, Tony and I had already, previously, noted that visitor's books inside them contain notes that read 'stayed for two days in glorious weather'. The only way to stop shoplifting it would seem is to pull down all the shops. I hope that if the day ever comes – and God forbid that it ever should – when we need a hut in earnest, the one we find will have not been de-fuelled and eaten bare by an idle idiot with no sense of perspective.

Beyond the hut the machines chugged in the shadows of Passnuten to the summit of the pass on to the glacier of Passbreen. There, as the east coast came into view, with Aghardh Bay below us and sea-ice to the horizon, a lump came into my throat. The beauty, the majesty of the view, the purity of the moment held me still and quiet. I pushed up my goggles to see better. There were acres of white – humped peaks, glacial smooth-ness, a morainic jumble. I turned to Tony, who had stopped a little back. His mouth was half-open, he looked at me, and without smiling he shook his head slowly. He too could not fully register the incomparable loveliness of Svalbard's east coast.

My repositioned goggles fogged and froze and I swapped seats with Mats and let Lars drive me the last few kilometres down off Passbreen and across Aghardhdalen. Being a passenger is horrendous. Unable to see clearly the ground ahead, you cannot anticipate the bumps, and each one throws you up so that you are jarred appallingly and spine-crunchingly by the landing.

We mount a rise by the two emergency huts near the bay's eastern tip. Mats scans the flat sea-ice of the bay and announces calmly, matter-of-factly, that there are three bears about two kilometres away. A mother and two cubs, he says, probably second-year cubs. Tony, his eyes redder and more watery, his feet cold, his self miserable, is all for

Snow scooters, Agardh Bay, Spitsbergen.

Sea-ice, Dunér Bay, Spitsbergen.

leaving them. He wants rest, food and drink. But we need the photos, I say. I cajole. I call upon his professionalism (a call to his better nature is doomed to failure). Wearily he unpacks his cameras as we unclip the sledges.

We dump a scooter in favour of both Tony and I having drivers for our cameras and speed off across the ice. I know bears are dangerous but there is no fear, only excitement, an excitement that rapidly falls away as my scanning of the ice reveals nothing but icebergs frozen into immobility by the pack-ice. We stop. Let's forget it, Tony suggests, no longer convinced that Mats saw anything at all. Mats stands on the scooter seat and scans the ice with his binoculars. He points and we strain our eyes to see . . . nothing at all. On again.

Then, suddenly, I see three dots ahead that are getting rapidly closer and are clearly moving. At 400 metres it is just three dots. At 300 metres I can see three bears, one large, two smaller. At 200 metres they are big enough to discern colour, head and legs. The excitement returns with a rush, a

Glacial cliff, Hayesbreen.

Campsite above the east coast of Spitsbergen.

tingling rush that dispels all thoughts of cold. At 150 metres we stop. The family group stops too, the female paying us no attention but settling gently on to the ice. One cub joins her, but the other turns to us and stares.

Female bears are mated in July or August and enter cubbing dens in October or November. On Svalbard the dens are concentrated on Edgeøya and Kong Karls Land, where the den density has increased significantly since total protection was afforded in 1976. The cubs are born around Christmas time after a relatively short gestation period for so large an animal. The cubs – there are usually two, although triplets and, of course, single cubs are possible – leave the den with the female around March, and the female by then has lost as much as half her body weight as she has both nurtured and fasted in the den for as many as five months. The cubs stay with their mother for two years, the female mating again three years after her previous mate. The cubs before us now are too big to be new-born and are, therefore, likely to be around sixteen months old. It is just possible they are two years old.

One cub starts coming towards us. Tony has a 560mm lens on, I have a 400mm. We shoot as it approaches. It changes in size from half the microprism to all of it, to half-frame. It closes still further and I have to drop down to a 200mm lens. Tony calls to me that the cub is so close that he cannot focus the big lens. He quickly changes to a more usable 35mm lens!

By now the bear is only thirty or forty metres away and is still closing. It is now so close that very small details are apparent. Its mouth forms a 'miserable' line, straight, with drooped-down ends, rather than the more normal 'smiling' line. Its eye is black and glinting. It is now close enough to see that it is whiter than adult bears are, its hair shaggier than I have seen. As it comes closer still I can see the dark brown claws of its paws, heavy and mean-looking against its fur. At twenty metres I suddenly lose interest in the bear as animal and switch to seeing it as a threat. I whisper to Lars, my driver, that it is time to go, but he ignores me. Ahead of us are Tony and Ulf and now there is only ten metres between them and the bear.

It stops. It eyes them curiously. It sniffs the air with uplifted nose on craned neck. It edges sideways. It advances, stops, sniffs, advances again. It is now clear to me and to the rest that the cub is intrigued by us, but also that it is more nervous of us than we are of it. Ulf edges away from his scooter towards it, and it turns away from him nervously. Watch the mother, Ulf calls, softly and without looking back. No need to remind me – I am. She is still lying on the ice apparently disinterested. The other cub is watching, but not following.

Over the next few minutes we experience one of the great moments of our lives. Eventually, its curiosity overcoming its nervousness, the cub comes so close that we can see individual hairs in its fur. At one point only the width of a snow scooter separates me from it as it quietly chews the handlebar. I am not more than half a metre from one of Nature's greatest achievements. I recall the line of an American Arctic poet who, when travelling north to see bears, wrote, 'we had come to behold the white lord.'

This bear could live for more than fifty years, surviving that number of Arctic winters with nothing between it and the cold but a layer of blubber and a fur coat. Each of us, one at a time, leaves the security of the scooters to stand close to cub. The braver approach to within two metres, the less brave to perhaps half as much again. I rest on haunches in front of it, my head at its head height and stare into its eyes. A voice from behind tells me the mother has decided to take an interest, has stood up and is ambling towards us. It is time to take our leave while we can do so gracefully.

So go, white lord. And though you will doubtless forget me, I will never forget you.

From a distance we watch as the mother and the more timid cub cross the sun splash on the ice. Behind them the mountains of Heer Land are grey against the light. The Arctic is vast, and all of it is home to these creatures. The same Arctic poet also wrote for the bear as well as of it:

Without me you walk in deserts
Imprison me, you cage yourself

The lines return to me that night as I lie caged in my sleeping bag. Outside the tent the temperature is around −40°C (−40°F). And down on the frozen sea the bears sleep soundly on the ice.

Our camp is in Væringsdalen, high enough above the sea to make it unlikely we will have troublesome night visitors. To make our sleep even easier we drive the scooters and sledges into a circle around the tents, playing wagon-train cowboys to the bears' Indians. Within the circle we dig in the tent, then choose, wrongly, to sit outside the tent on a Karrimat to cook our evening meal. We are tired, exhausted by the drive, the visual experiences, the encounter with the bear, the cold. Tony is further exhausted by his cold which is making his head ache and his feet cold. The corned beef we choose is frozen solid and Gavin has a happy few minutes breaking it into spoon-sized lumps with hunting knife and ice axe. Tony and I, anxious to refill ourselves, pour pasta, instant potato, anything that is powdered and savoury, into a pan. Gavin hacks and thwacks. Look at that daft bastard, Tony says, as Gavin thrashes away again. Hold on, I say. He's a company director. It's *Mr* Bastard to you. The meal is a gastronomic orgasm. Not until we reach Tromsø and go in the sea-kayaker's 'pub' where the blackboard menu – written by a humorist – offers Rudolf reindyrsuppe as a prelude to seal curry, do we experience anything so cultured.

We load water bottles, clothes and boot liners into our sleeping bags, layer on balaclavas and haul the bags over our heads. I wonder if the apprehension about bears will disturb my sleep, but my next thought is a waking one, hours later with light turning everything in the tent orange. The opening of the bag is solid with breath-ice, the tent above me glistening with more of the same. Tony snorts through a blocked nose to my left, Gavin breathes luxuriously in his Tangerine Dream to my right. Outside I find, when I have won the struggle with cold and tent-ice, that the sky is blue and Væringsdalen is beautiful. I step over the carefully erected trip wires and scrunch off for the first pee of the day. A solitary reindeer trudges the valley floor below.

Tony greets me as I return, complaining that he forgot to put his toothbrush in his bag last night and has just half knocked out his teeth plunging it into his mouth and expecting bristles but finding concrete. Ulf is moaning that his toothpaste has frozen solid. Tony offers him his toothpowder – we seasoned Arctic performers have worked that one out, Ulf!

The breakfast muesli tastes divine, despite my forgetting to pre-warm my spoon so it sticks to the skin of my lower lip and has to be warmed off. We talk of yesterday's bear. I recall seeing the sun glinting off its teeth. Ulf recalls how it sat up on its hind legs, lovable yet dangerous. Gavin suggests that the reason it didn't attack us was that its mother had told it not to eat between seals.

Preparing the scooters is a burden, breaking camp more so, but we get away. We travel north along the line where the sea-ice joins the land-ice, under the bulk of Agardhfjellet. To our right, but far out and unreachable among the crumpled hummock ice, a huge male bear pads gently and purposefully northwards. Further we pause at a spot where the sea-ice is visually interesting, with grease ice, a slushy dull surface ice, as well as the harder, older grey-blue ice, and hummocks of blue-green ice like mushrooms created by pressure. We play like kids, then move on.

Ahead, tracks tell us that a bear has passed this way, their freshness suggesting he is but a little way ahead. We pass recently-frozen bear shit, and similar signs and the tracks of an Arctic fox that has decided to attach itself to the trail. In winter the Svalbard foxes have no prey, all birds except the wily ptarmigan have left for the warmer south, and some head for the coast and track bears, feeding on the left-over offal of seals they have killed. It is a dangerous game. The bear provides food, but if the fox gets too close and drops his guard, the bear will feed on him.

Beyond an ice hummock we realize we have startled a male bear into a trot and stop immediately so that he can slow to a walk again. We decide to eat while he retreats. Mats scans the horizon and finds a mother and cub on a jutting section of hummock ice. Nearby an iceberg rather than hummock rises clear of the sea-ice. It is about fifteen metres high and offers Ulf, Gavin and I an exciting short climb to a knife-edge summit. Tony, exhausted again by his cold which is developing ominous flu signs, declines to follow us, but shoots pictures with the full moon behind us. From the iceberg we scan south and see that the huge male we saw earlier is still padding our way, and is now less than 600 metres away. We rapidly climb down and prepare for his arrival, but the wait is in vain as a sniff of our presence or some other call turns him east towards the sea and he disappears out among the hummocks.

We visit Mohnbukta – Mohn Bay – where the edge of Hayesbreen, its calving activities frozen into submission, can be touched. The blue-green ice walls, capped by squat cornices, are steel-hard and cold. In winter there are no groans from the settling glacier. Even sound has been frozen in. Far out across the sea-ice the peaks of Barentsøya and Edgeøya stand out, sharply focused, despite their distances.

Mother and cub, Agardh Bay, Spitsbergen.

Polar bear cub, Agardh Bay, Spitsbergen.

It would be good to be able to write that it was the possibility of a change in the weather that might maroon us on the east coast, together with the increasing difficulty that Tony was having in staying warm and sociable, that drove us back westward. It would be good, but it would be wrong. Both Tony and I were finding the trip anti-climactic after the bear. We had spent so long trying to get that one bear shot, that elusive, unique bear shot, that once we had it the trip seemed to lose focus. For all the world, feeling the way he felt, Tony would have gone home. But that would have been to deny the beauty around us. So we headed back to Agardh Bay for our final night on the east coast.

We cross Elfenbeinbreen, a steeply-angled glacial tongue surrounded by crazed moraine, and drop down Fulmardalen to reach Sassandalen, where we find that all the wonders are not on the east coast. Sassendalen is four kilometres wide, framed by crested peaks. It is nearly twenty kilometres long in an unbroken section that follows its first, bent section. Imagine eighty square kilometres of perfectly flat, perfectly white snow. In the light of the unobscured sun the snow sparkles. When we stop the scooters and walk, our feet throw up snow powder like flour that sparkles in the sun and rasps on our throats. We decide to eat right in the middle of the valley, to take advantage of its space, its stillness and its beauty.

Tony and I concoct a meal of soup, pasta and tuna, dried apricots and custard. Gavin, his feet nearly frozen, trudges out across the ice to try to induce warmth. We can tell from his position when the Trangia will boil – it will be when he is just out of earshot. Over the last few days we have grown used to Gavin's retreats at meal-times. It is not, we know, a retreat from the work – not at all, he does at least his share – rather, it seems that the enforced inactivity of waiting for water to boil bores him so much that he must move about to relieve the boredom. We start a scooter to attract his attention and wave wildly when he turns. I ask Tony if there is anything left of the orange juice that we made up from powder that morning. He checks, but the Sigg has frozen solid. Amazed, he checks the temperature. The noon in-sun temperature is −28°C (−18°F). How many days is it now since we were last as warm as −20°C (−4°F)? I ask. He shrugs and coughs.

Later, as we reach the end of Sassendale, Tony's flu symptons erupt with savagery. His insides rebel against the meal. This drains his strength so much that he has to be coaxed back into his jackets, and his hands warmed. He needs rest and warmth, and in a tight wound ball of feathers he sweats and cooks for thirty hours, until the fever leaves him. We ease him back to Longyearbyen, and Gavin and I leave him there while we explore the local area. Gavin considers the town or, to be more precise, the coal mining waste, to be a slap in the face to nature. We go fox-searching in Bjørndalen, but give up in disgust when we see the state of the snow, grimy with coal dust in one of the world's most beautiful places.

Tony recovers enough to come with us on the easy trip to Barentsburg. He is along for the ride feeling, like me, that one trip to the town is rather more than enough. But Gavin wants to see it, and to get a Russian doll for his daughter. The journey out is superb, quite the most exciting snow scootering we have had with long flat, fast sections interspersed with climbs and drops. There is a river section which we ride like a wall of death on the banked snow of summer's riverbanks. There is a steep drop that brings a gasp of surprise and a fast run in to the town past a decrepit Russian scooter broken down in the fast lane.

The rules have altered since Tony and I were here last, the covert capitalism having been made legal so that everyone we pass in the street stops us to offer souvenirs. You want *balalaika*, you want *madrushka*. You want *samovar*, you want *chapka*. Gavin and I visit a seedy flat, its walls lined with pornographic pictures, where a drunken miner feeds us rot-gut vodka and tells us he is a karate champion. We give him a pair of ski glasses and he weeps tears of joy. He gives me a French kiss in my right ear and tells me I am *tovarich*, no, no I am better, I am his brother. Gavin gets his *madrushka* and a fine *chapka* which he wears for the rest of the trip, looking like a Cossack warrior riding an iron horse over the frozen steppes. My new brother gives me his watch. Outside a man in a Lada – the official black market? – asks in poor Italian if we wish to stay the night in the town. We think not. What we wish to do is gun the scooters out of town, to be away from the swarming hordes who bar our way and menace us with hats and dolls. But the limit sign says 20kph and we feel that to disobey it will plunge us into even hotter water. At last we are free. We wind open the machines and head for Colesbukta.

There we spend time walking the sea-ice in

Snow scooter.

search of seal, a nerve-wracking time as every hummock could hide a bear on the same search. Gavin rides shotgun with the Mauser, Tony has his camera and I hold a flare pistol. Tony, his humour taken away by the bugs, is irritated by what he sees as my Clint Eastwood approach to holding the pistol, but the conversation ends rapidly when his gut erupts again, leaving Gavin and I to stand guard over his hunched, embarrassed form.

It is late, but it seems a good idea to get Tony back to town. The dying sun is not providing enough light, particularly in the shadowed areas, to allow us to see the snow. In full daylight riding the machines is easy, the shadows on the snow allowing you to read where the ice hummocks, dips and slopes lie, but what we have now is a broad, blurred grey blanket and even at reduced speed we clank over ridges and troughs that we cannot see, shaking backs, legs and arms unmercifully. The final drop into Longyearbyen is a real test of skill, the scooters sliding and tilting every time we slow to peer ahead. Three days ago on a steep traverse slope I throttled back and braked while coming to terms with the line – a fatal mistake. My sledge slid sideways, hauling the back end of the scooter with it. The pair tumbled on the slope throwing me off and then threatening to catch me. I relive this moment several times before the flat ground beyond Longyearbyen is reached.

In the Arctic twilight Gavin and I take the Upski parachutes to Adventfjorden where in a difficult, gusting wind we use them to tow us across sea-ice. Is this a first? Residents of the town arrive on scooters to watch, and clearly it is a novelty to

Lunch-time, Sassendalen, Spitsbergen.

Approach to Colesbukta.

them. A small group of reindeer eye me as I cross the border between sea- and land-ice. The wind is not as strong or as dependable as it was in Iceland, but there is something special about the cold, the view, the light. With just the swish of the skis on the ice, if I close my eyes I could almost be sledging.

Our final day dawns the way all final days should, with thick snow falling silently. At the airport it is so thick we can barely see the plane and the walk to it is through a new snow mantle, centimetres thick. I peer for a last look, but there is nothing beyond the wing tip. I had hoped for one more view of the east coast of southern Spitsbergen, but sadly I am denied this. Goodbye, white lord.

Appendices

I KIT

It is said that when two economists talk you are guaranteed three good economic policies. It is a moot point how many ideas you will get if two Arctic travellers fall into conversation. Tony and I now largely agree about kit – with certain personal variations – and below are present thoughts distilled from a large number of trips in both summer and winter. But these are only thoughts, intended for guidance and to draw attention to what we think are critical areas for consideration. They are not gospel: if you choices differ from ours that does not make them (or ours) less valid.

In summer – apart from certain areas of Svalbard and Greenland and the interior of Iceland – the Arctic is just a wild version of elsewhere, perhaps a little cooler, but not necessarily and not as much as you might think. The experienced camper/trekker will have few problems.

It is presumptious of us to tell anyone who has experience of a wilderness area how to behave in winter, but the Arctic winter is a little different and a few minor details are worth remembering. If your boots are not in your sleeping bag, fold the laces inside or they will freeze to the ground. Take time over dressing and undressing, cooking and packing – you will have plenty of it, and it will save aggravation later. Store water in your sleeping bag overnight for that first cup of tea. Keep matches in several different places so as to be sure not only of finding dry ones, but of finding some at all. Stay dry. If you get wet, stop, get under cover and change into dry clothes. And on the move be cautious; the Arctic rarely takes prisoners and a moment's consideration of consequences could stop a disaster. Finally, do check the compass variation of your chosen area. Remember that Svalbard is further north than the Magnetic Pole, *but* the deviation is usually near zero as the flux lines go over the true pole to reach it. There are places where local magnetic geological disturbances cause substantial deviations. By contrast in west Greenland the macro deviation can be as much as 40 degrees, *but* only in places.

The majority of what follows covers the period from September to May, the Arctic autumn, winter and spring. Clearly, the more exposed and northerly your area, the longer the time extremes will hold sway.

Tents

Having slept in tents and snow holes we believe the former are preferable unless it is imperative that carried weight is reduced. In summer there is no worthwhile snow to cave, except in Svalbard and Greenland, and even there it can be difficult to work. In winter you spend a long time indoors. The Arctic night is excellent for travelling if the sky is clear or nearly so. If not, you may find the time spent in a snow hole to be composed of hours with, apparently, more than the usual quota of minutes in them. There is also the lack of light – and batteries are heavy – and the problems with drips and lying water. It is not a good idea to get wet in the Arctic.

We use a Phoenix Phreespirit, a standard model but with snow valances added by the company. It is superb: lightweight, small packing – for its volume and surface area – and easy to erect. Having tried other tents the specifics that mark it out as a good Arctic tent are the (relatively) limited number of guys – especially worthwhile when snow camping: you will only have skis, ski poles and ice axes – and the double opening which allows access downwind and cooking away from the entrance, avoiding chaos and damage to your breakfast. The tent is fly-pitched first. This has the disadvantage that the inner hangs like a bag which gives the appearance of there being less room and also allows the restless sleeper to kick the inner on to the outer, but has significant advantages. On wet days, in summer and warm winters, the inner is erected with both you and it in the dry, and the fly can be put up on its own as a midday shelter. The tent is a dome. Early on our travels we used a hooped tent, a semi-geodesic version of the old-fashioned '6×4'. The advantages of a dome, where you can sit up to cook, eat and dress, are overwhelming. Neither of us can understand how we ever survived without one.

Finally, the tent has a mosquito net. This is an essential for Arctic summers, and is useful to vent the tent in winter. Being nylon-nylon the tent suffers from condensation, but with full venting of the inner this is minimized. It is never eliminated, and you must resign yourself to a morning session of drying. In winter this is easy as the condensation will be ice, which will shake free. Leave any water for a few moments to freeze and then shake it off. As an aside, this is also a useful way of drying washing or a wet jacket – hang it up to freeze, shake the surface free of ice, turn it inside out and repeat.

On the Lappland bike trip Peter and Tony used a Phoenix Phor 3, a larger version of the same dome, taken to accommodate the three of us, but used by just those two. The tent was, Tony says, equally good.

Survival

Tony and I do not carry a radio so if things go badly wrong we have problems. We do leave details of our intended route so a rescue is possible, although, given the remoteness of some of the areas we travel, not likely. We carry a strobe light from Medik CI, which has a visual range of about five kilometres. It is only fractionally heavier than the U2 battery that powers it, a battery which is very temperature-sensitive, and flashes about once every second for up to seventy-two hours. A strong safety pin attaches it to a rucsac.

From the same company we carry emergency space blankets. These have come in for some criticism of late, but still seem reasonable value for weight. In an emergency Tony and I would combine them with an emergency insulator raft, also available from the company. These two essentials, plus map and compass, are in a map case (we use plastic because there is no realistic alternative, but they do not like the cold and one journey usually sees them off) around our necks at all times. If you get separated from your rucsac you are in deep trouble, but the small package, which also contains a few first aid items, could give you an extra day before the elements take over. When we were sledging in Norway and on the scooters in Svalbard we also carried mini-flares, fired from a pen-sized gun. On the mainland this is fine as the chances of someone seeing it are good. The flare

may even be seen in certain areas in Svalbard, but in general if you are three days out from Longyearbyen or Ammassilak you can forget it.

Our main first aid kit is a Gregson Pack, an absolutely essential piece of kit which all mountaineers should carry. When weight was not a problem (on sledging and scooter trips) we also carried a Medik pneumatic splint, as a significant risk was a high speed fall with potential for a broken bone. We should also have carried one on the mountain bike tour in Svalbard, but didn't.

We carry Lappish hunting knives which have long, heavy blades. These will open a tin, cut wood for fires or tent pegs, turn fish into lunch and most other things too. It replaced the Swiss Army knife when we realized that we rarely used them because they were rarely man enough for the job in hand. We never wanted to get a Boy Scout out of a horse's hoof either, so half the gadgets were a waste of space.

In winter we always carry an aluminium shovel head that fits our ice axe shafts. Usually these are sold with Allen key fixers which is ridiculous as the key head fills with ice and requires thawing and clearing. Tony, in his role of Super Bicycle Repairman, fixed this for us.

We carry head lamps for winter use. The head (as opposed to the hand) lamp is good for freeing the hands, but many carry their batteries at the back of the head as a counterweight to the lamp. This exposes the batteries to the cold and rapidly reduces their power. Petzl have now produced a lamp with the battery in a pouch that hangs round the shoulder and fits under the arm. Go for that version.

As a back-up I carry a small Tekna Splashlite. It's about five centimetres long, one centimetre in diameter, weighs nothing and runs off a cold-resistant lithium battery. On one memorable occasion Tony brought along a hurricane lamp. It was awkward, smelly, dirty and romantically wonderful.

Finally, I carry a small Survival Aids pouch with spare silk socks and gloves, soap/shampoo and toothbrush/paste. The first items are insurance, the soap is laughable in winter – not least because it is liquid and freezes – the third helps Tony and I cope more easily with the world. In addition the pouch contains a few 'Baby Wipes', and you should always pinch the sachets out of your meal box on the plane. Face and hands get dirty, dry and rough in winter, and washing can chap the skin if you are mad enough to try it. The sachets are very good for cleaning and moistening. I also take a glacier stick to avoid chapped lips in the wind.

Cooking

Long ago we were Primus men, accepting the inconvenience of lighting, the smell and the soot, in exchange for the speed of service. Now we've got rid of all that paraffin-alia. Look no further than the Trangia. Meths (*raud* – red – *spirit* in all Scandinavian countries) is high in calories per gram, easy to burn and clean. In addition, a pair of mugs and the Trangia system offers everything you need for two people for a whole trip. We have tried gas cookers, but you have to keep the gas in your sleeping bag overnight, and if there is water and your boots in there too it becomes a pain. In addition most gas cookers are tall and narrow and much less stable than the Trangia, which is short and wide. Meths is a vapour not liquid burner and so can be awkward to light in the very cold. If it declines to burn use a paper or match wick. A by-product of this reluctance to vapourize is that in real cold the burner can be refilled while it is alight. *Do not* try this trick when the temperatue is above the vapour temperature or your Sigg bottle will become a bomb.

As a rule we take an extra plate so we can eat and cook at the same time. I use a metal knife, fork and spoon – not always wonderful if I need to pre-warm them before handling in winter, but saving all the hassle of plastic breaking.

Clothing

Even if you are a layer-clothing person, and do not use insulated jackets, everything starts with a thermal layer. Having tried many we have come down to a basic two – those in Modal and those in Tactel. Of the former we prefer Ami Chaud, with the distinct advantage of tops in presentable colours for the flight out or back. Be sure to get the roll-neck version as cold wind down the neck is a nightmare and is easily stopped by layering your balaclava and neck roll. I prefer a zipped neck to allow a little ventilation; Tony prefers the comforting feel of a plain, no-zip roll. The best Tactel is from Sub-Zero Technology who make it in several weights. That company's clothing can be used as a complete layered system of its own, although we did not use it, finding the Tactel fleece tops too short. This deficiency has now been overcome.

Over the thermal layer we wear fleece. Head and shoulders above the competition at present is Lowe Alpine Lite, a four-way stretch fleece with reinforced knees and seat in Spandura, a stretch cordura. This hugs the body, giving a comforting, secure feeling which is psychologically important as well as reducing the dead air space and so being good in terms of heat retention. On the Russian border we skied for days in only thermals and Alpine Lite – occasionally with a pile jacket – in temperatures down around −15°C (5°F). We had calm days, however. Had the wind blown we would have needed a shell.

Over this tightly-fitting second layer we wear, if needed, a pile or fleece top. The Sub-Zero Technology Tactel jackets are really good and significantly more windproof than a standard pile fibre like Polar-Plus. I have a personal horror of my kidney area being exposed and that jacket exposed it. For the rest of the pile range you pay your money and take your colour choice. We find we rarely need a third layer of legwear, although I did constantly when scootering below −30°C (−22°F). In general, if you protect your head, hands, feet and torso, your legs will survive. As a rule they are working hardest anyway. Pile trousers do exist for those wanting another layer. The disadvantage of those and the Alpine Lites is that you look like an idiot at the airport. Pile jackets are no longer noticed, unless you specifically choose a dubious colour match, but if you stand around in woolly pyjama bottoms you do get odd looks. On one trip Tony wore Alpine Lite trousers and Lundhags to Heathrow. He looked like he was auditioning for a Max Wall part (and was likely to get it). I wore Rohan Bags and pretended I wasn't with him.

As a shell, it is important to wear salopettes as the wind can go up under a jacket and over the top of overtrousers. The braces of salopettes also secure the leg shells in place better, which adds psychological benefits if you are just ambling about at camp. I have a full-length zip pair from Latok which also have a built-in gaiter – of sorts. They are good, although a little heavy, and a bit 'suit-of-armourish', but the zip is covered by a full-length velcro-fastened flap. It is a good idea but, God, the epics I have had trying to make sense of metre-long two-way zips and metre-long pieces of velcro. All in all, Tony's Phoenix pair are to be preferred. Even these have problems, though. They have a standard leg-bottom gusset that is not wide enough to go over a Lundhag and is threatened with shredding if it goes over a crampon. As a rule he starts the day in them.

That said, it is also worth noting that Tony did not, except in the blizzards, wear salopettes on our big sledge trip. In fact he did not even wear proper shell gear, preferring to go about in a Karrimor Climaguard suit which was lighter, and so more comfortable, and astonishingly windproof. So impressed were we that we wore it almost exclusively on ski trips, taking heavier weight shells only when the weather threatened or when we were going to be out so long that anything might happen.

Shell jackets are now widely available. A few years ago I used a Sprayway insulated jacket for downhill skiing in the Alps and was well pleased. It offered freedom from cold on the slopes and ease of removing a lot of insulation at the mid-point café. In the Arctic I was less happy with it, although Nathan, who wore it sledging, thought the sun shone out of its pocket.

Tony and I use a standard shell, usually three layers for hardiness as they take a tanking, being used as seats as well as jackets and being scuffed and battered regularly. The choice is personal. I go for big pockets to take maps and Snickers bars, a security pocket for money and passport and a wired hood because I wear glasses and need to keep rain/snow off them or I go blind. I also prefer pop-fastened zip flaps to velcro, although Tony disagrees with me on this.

And the material? Gore-tex is now so much a part of the outdoor landscape that it is deemed heresy to question its usefulness. But let me pose a question – how well does a micro-porous work when there is ice on the material surface? Tony and I have had ice on the inside of our shells as well as the outside. Mind you, given those conditions, no other breathables would work either – in fact, you might as well be in standard nylon. For summer wear Gore-tex works as well in the Arctic as it does elsewhere. Tony wears a Karrimor Sympatex jacket and is pleased. I still wear Gore-tex.

On our scooter trip to Svalbard we wore a co-ordinated system from Bailo, an Italian maker for which Gavin is agent. The kit comprised Gore-tex drop-lined shell with zip-in pile jacket and a mildly insulated sleeved waistcoat, if that is not a contradiction. There were matched salopettes. Overall, the system was the best that Tony and I had used.

On our feet we wear silk inner socks and loop-stitch wool socks. Ancient wisdom has two socks necessary for doing the Snowdon Horseshoe in June, but if your boots are that bad you should not be going to the Arctic in them. The silk inners give added warmth, but are really there to minimize the number of pairs of socks we have to take. After a couple of hard days socks can be stiff and horrid, and need changing (providing you can catch and tame them). If you wear silk inners they will suffer. Take them off each night, swill them out, dry them off and wear them again. This has advantages for your feet, and for your companion's olfactory equipment.

Boots have come on in leaps and bounds, in a manner of speaking, of late. It is now rare to hear of serious frostbite problems, except in the very unfortunate who have been trapped for a long time. We use Lundhags, a Swedish boot, most of the time. They are old-fashioned in many ways, but amazingly tough, high-calfed to give good protection in the Arctic summer when the ground can be saturated, and with a fibre liner that is beautifully warm. At first we were dubious about whether they would be comfortable enough for prolonged walking, but they are. A minor grouse is their comparative lack of ankle support, but that may not be so much of a problem for those who, unlike the pair of us, are not carrying dodgy ankles. The Lundhags do fit a cross-country ski, but not wonderfully well. As a rule we change into a standard, fleece-lined Nordic shoe.

Where we know we are going to be cramponing we leave the Lundhags behind. They are square-toed and broad-soled and fitting crampons to them is a pain. We now use plastic-shelled boots, the Raichle Futura Expedition to be exact, but made a mistake when we took them scootering. They are not made for, nor are they very good at, that job. For ski mountaineering we hear good things about the Asolo range and the Raichle Nanga Parbat, but have no direct evidence as our mountain ski trips involved parachutes and so necessitated the use of alpine skis.

On all our winter trips where we are not taking skis we include a lightweight pair of snow shoes made of aluminium and heavy-duty plastic. Arctic snow is soft, deep and absolutely exhausting. The shoes are essential for conserving energy.

As we take a lot of photographs we take special note of our gloves. Each of us wears Survival Aids silk inner gloves which we rarely remove. Over these we used to wear Dachsteins and, if need be, an over-mitt. However Tony came on one trip with

Wild Country pile-lined Gore-tex mitts and these had obvious and significant advantages in terms of being fast and easy to put on – the problem with three layers is getting the third on while wearing the other two – and in retaining a lot of heat while off so that your hands went into something that was warm and snug. I now have a Mountain Equipment version of the same thing. Same thing, did I say? Tony and I have yet to discern any difference between his and mine other than the company label. Who does make them?

It is a well-known adage that if you have cold feet you should put a hat on, and this is based on sound scientific sense, the body pumping a lot of heat to the brain which is poorly insulated by fatty tissue. Significant body heat losses are therefore made through the head. I tend to grow my hair long but, as I am now going bald, as well as having (Tony says) most of the other attributes of being past it – Sale Over The Hill, official – I need to supplement Nature's quilting. We use any combination of silk, pile and wool. As a rule the silk is on more or less constantly, the others being added or subtracted as and when. If the wind picks up, pull over your shell hood immediately. The Arctic is no place for heroes – if you are going to be out for many days in winter there you must start to conserve heat from day one.

I wear glasses constantly and these are photochromic to overcome a personal photo-sensitivity. This means that as a rule I am OK even on bright days. Tony wears snow glasses – last time out sporting a snazzy pair of Christian Dallioz that he claimed were excellent. On sledge or scooter, especially into wind, we wear standard ski goggles, as much to protect our eyes from the chill as for the vision.

Sleeping

No matter how good your sleeping bag is you will need to insulate yourself from the ground in winter, and a Karrimat, or equivalent, is essential. It will also be useful for sitting on midday and evenings, so have it within easy reach.

Sleeping bags are a matter of personal choice, but some general comments may be worthwhile. Ignore the manufacturer's recommended lowest temperature, except as a guide to which bag has more insulation than another. The price will do the same job. The reasons are several. First the tent or snow hole has an effect on local temperature,

raising it by perhaps 5°C (44°F) so that the bag will not be working against outside temperature. More importantly, everyone has his or her own specific metabolic rate and generates internal warmth accordingly, the rate varying for any of a number of reasons. This may well mean that in a bag that one man finds cosy at −20°C (−4°F) another may be experiencing alloy simian lost property syndrome.

The effectiveness of a bag depends upon many variables. Between you and it there is dead air, and if you have to warm this up it will cost you calories. Some evidence suggests that the piston effect – warm air pushed out of the neck of the bag by the body as it turns during sleep – can be significant. Cold air replaces the warm and you lose more calories heating the new, cold, dead air. If you are, like me, gnome-like, don't get a bag big enough to accommodate another person, even if you were hoping to get lucky.

When you get in the bag your metabolic rate will be high and may even, initially, go higher especially if you are anxious for any reason. This is temporary, and the rate falls when you are asleep. You will therefore find out if your bag works at about 2am, not an ideal time. The best method is to take time over the last meal, drink hot chocolate as a last drink rather than coffee which is a stimulant, and relax. Don't worry about the weather; you won't change it if you do. If you've done everything to stop the tent falling down in the blizzard, then forget it. Everything looks better after a few hours' furious zzzzzzing.

Because we travel in both summer and winter we need two bags. I, as a rule, use a Caravan Carricombi which gives me three, a lightweight down, a lightweight fibre-fill – better if it is likely to be wet – and the two together. It performs well, but I have a Karrimor Lhotse as a one-bag spring and autumn standby. Tony uses a light weight down in summer, putting it inside a medium weight down in winter. We each wear something if it gets really cold.

The new Mountain Equipment bags which are gently elasticated on the inside look to be the best idea in years, the elastication reducing the dead air space and increasing loft and, therefore, insulation for the same weight. The problem with tulip-shaped bags that also reduce dead air is that they feel constricting and dreadful. The new ME gets over that problem as the inner gives as you move. This is probably the bag for the future.

Also worth considering is the Buffalo system. This uses pile bags to overcome the problem of your escaping sweat freezing half-way through a down bag, which can reduce the effectiveness of the down by creating hard balls of frozen feathers. We have not tried the system, but have great respect for the opinions of some who have and are enthused.

Food

This is so personal that to offer any ideas seems impertinent, but we are going to anyway. But briefly.

Dehydrated food is fine, but try it before you go. Tony and I have had to tolerate some real rubbish because we believed the packaging. The problem with the dehydrated stuff is that after a prolonged period your body starts to notice the absence of all the extras that have been removed with the water. Consequently, we delay the onset of the packet stuff by taking a day or so's worth of good food. Sod the weight; you won't carry or enjoy *anything* if you are skeletal in a fortnight. Obviously for a short trip this does not apply. For the same reasons I am prone to taking real milk and to husbanding it out over the first couple of days – anything to put off having to suffer a cup of Earl Grey with that sand they call powdered 'milk'. Since the stuff is necessary, buy the best, which have anti-caking agents so that you at least don't have to dispose of the dregs with a knife and fork. Do remember though that both tinned food and liquid milk will freeze solid in your rucsac in winter.

Tony and I start with a good breakfast – muesli made with warm milk or milk powder or custard. It helps your insides. It also has the advantage of increasing the time you spend each morning in getting ready for the day. When buying your custard be careful. In general, supermarkets now cater for the weight-watcher and it is difficult to find the high-calorie food that you will be wanting. At the same time be careful not to buy food that requires a great deal of simmering as this is very fuel-intensive.

We fear dehydration which is prevalent in the cold because of the intense dryness of the atmosphere. We drink a lot, chiefly packet cup-a-soup and Birds Apeel powders which come in several flavours. In addition we chew dried apricots. Salted peanuts are heavy but do add salt to the system. We have tried salt tablets but have still to be convinced.

For the rest, suck it (or chew it or whatever), and see.

II CAMERAS IN THE COLD

The Arctic areas are special. The light is unique and the atmospheric clarity quite daunting. Because of the low light, rainbows are more frequent and you should never be caught without a loaded camera. The cold creates some problems although the summer traveller need take no special precautions; except to take lots of film. Once below freezing point a little planning may be required. For the day traveller, hotelling it, a thermos box is ideal for keeping equipment warm. This is the advice most camera manufacturers and film distributors give, however, beware of thermal cycling and the limitations of their usefulness.

Outdoors in the winter, I believe in keeping everything cold, at outside temperature. Overnight I will leave all my films and camera gear outside in their camera bags and just dig them out of the snow in the morning. This seems strange behaviour but it does minimize thermal cycling – it is sudden changes in conditions that ruin emulsions. The worst change is going from below −5°C (23°F) to the inside of someone's home. The cold camera will cool the warm air surrounding it in the house. Warm air contains moisture and as it cools it becomes saturated, depositing water all over the camera, both outside and inside, and including the emulsion. If you go out again these water drops will freeze and create havoc. To avoid condensation put all your gear in a plastic bag whilst outside, tie it tight and only then take it in. The condensation will only form on the outside of the plastic bag, the air inside the bag being free from water vapour. Once the whole affair has warmed, then, and only then, it is safe to take out your cameras.

Other advice you will frequently be given is to keep your camera warm inside your clothing. My advice is don't if you are going to do anything that can create even a slight sweat. If you do, water vapour will swamp the camera and its inner will instantly freeze on exposure to the outside. For a ten-minute stroll from your hotel this is OK, but for dogging, skiing and so on, forget it.

Unfortunately, allowing your cameras to get cold

183

and remain cold is not without problems. Batteries will cease to work with alarming regularity and many spares, kept warm inside your clothing, should be carried. Several camera manufacturers offer remote battery packs so you can, via a lead, keep your batteries inside your thermal underwear. Both Dick and I do this. Luckily both my Canons and Bronicas work off 6 volts, so I can use a common remote battery pack. Dick's Pentaxes work off 3 volts so he has to have a separate system. The manufactured leads all come as a unit; you must either take the battery pack out of your thermals when packing your camera away, or you must remove the dummy battery from the camera when you want to release the camera from your person. Either is a pain, as we will both testify. I have taken my leads, cut them in their middles and installed, careful to make sure positive wires are not crossed, stereo jack plugs and sockets to allow quick power attachment. I leave the remote battery pack, undisturbed, in my thermal underwear and a jack socket sticks out of my outer shell clothing. To stop snow or ice filling the socket I have a dummy jack plug fitted to the cable end with string. Lithium batteries can work quite well in some cameras down to −25°C (−13°F) but not all cameras can take lithiums. Silver oxides give up at about −5°C (23°F) so remote battery packs are essential.

Batteries are not the whole story as some cameras do not themselves work below about −10°C (14°F). My Canon F1n and my Bronica ETRSi both work at −45°C (−49°F) as does Dick's Pentax LX and his old and trusted standby MX. I have used my F1n without remote battery pack for long durations at −25°C (−13°F) but I usually attach the remote pack in order to prolong battery life.

Camera electronics can be suspect at low temperatures as below −25°C (−13°F) is beyond the specification range of accuracy of nearly all camera light meters. I carry a Gossen selenium cell meter inside my clothes, a battery-free device that can be kept warm and give incident reading in any conditions. It has saved many a situation.

Camera choice is personal, there being no *best* camera, only the one most suited to your individual needs. For the cold, and I mean below −10°C (14°F), simple non-electronic-fired, non-autofocus, non-dependent on batteries and non-autowind are all essential. Dick had a near nightmare with a Pentax Super A in Svalbard that resulted in a very expensive repair job on the delicate electronics, and with no mechanical shutter option left him with only his MX for a while.

The problem is that a simple camera is getting hard to find, especially in the sensible price range. I have had problems with focus and aperture rings freezing but luckily no problems with iris sticking or shutters stopping. As a precaution I leave my lenses on a nominal aperture setting, and the corresponding hyperfocal focus point just in case the temperature falls to the point that makes movement impossible. Excess pressure, forcing a frozen ring, can easily cause the lens housing to crack, as the plastics used today are also brittle when cold.

Motor and auto winders should be taken off. They use up huge quantities of battery power and batteries will only emit a small percentage of their output at normal temperature. More importantly, they will tear your film to shreds as film gets extremely brittle at low temperatures. Another likely problem with power winding is lightning streaks caused by discharging static as the film hurries through the back. In these incredibly dry conditions you must wind on and rewind *very* slowly or your slides may be ruined.

With an ever-low sun I have thrown my wide-angle zooms away. The sun is either in picture or just out of shot, causing degradation in quality. I put up with carrying small, more simply designed standard optics, as flare is less and efficient lens hoods exist. No lens hood can successfully protect, with total efficiency, a zoom lens. I also choose simple standard lenses; a 24mm f2.8 has fewer elements and gives less flare than a 24mm f2 lens. It is also lighter. Simplicity is the key to all Arctic photography.

Touching a cold camera can also cause problems. Eyelashes can freeze to viewfinders and cheeks to film backs. Use a rubber viewfinder shield and put sticking plaster on the camera back, just in case. Hands will get cold holding the camera so wear silk thermogloves and/or thin thermal gloves. Changing 35mm film gets quite easy after a few rolls, but 120 and 220 films need considerable patience in a blizzard and getting the tab to stick can be tricky in very low temperatures as your spit may well freeze before it moistens the gum. You will find that 5×4 film is a pain.

In theory, leaf shutters are better than focal plane shutters as the latter can travel at non-linear rates across the film, giving uneven exposure. This is why high-quality cameras, usually the most expensive, give better results – their internals are made within tighter tolerance limits and made bearing in mind the differential expansion properties of the make-up of the machine. Cameras I know will work cold include the Canon F1n, Nikon FM2, Pentax LX and Leica R5/R6. Forget Nikon F3s and F4s (and that's official Nikon advice) and Canon EOSs. I have rarely seen anything other than 35mm on my travels but I lug my Bronica system around and it is highly recommended.

Film will lose its speed rating in the cold, although by how much is difficult to determine as the apparent speed loss could be due to light meter inaccuracies or the slowing in reaction rates of light with emulsion. Whichever it is, I reckon a half stop is lost with my F1n and Kodachrome 25 at −35°C (−31°F), with similar on the Bronica with Fujichrome 100. As I check reading with my warm Gossen, I suspect the film and allow a ½ stop at −35°C (−31°F) and one stop below −55°C (−67°F).

For the record, the pictures you have hopefully enjoyed in this book were taken on Kodachrome 25, 64 and 200, Ektachrome 100, 200 and 400, Fujichrome 50 and 100, Agfachrome RS200 and RS1000, as thought appropriate at the time.

I carry two Canon F1ns with 20mm f2.8, 24mm f2.8, 28mm f2.8, 35mm f2.8, 50mm f1.8, 80–200mm f4L and a 2× converter. For wildlife I use a Canon 400 f4.5 or a Tamron SP400 f4 lens with matching 1.4× converters; the latter is one of my favourite wildlife lenses, with close focusing and easy handling. Dick uses Pentax exclusively, with standard 28mm f2.8, 50mm f1.7 lens, a 35–70mm f3.5, a 70–210mm f4 zoom and a 2× converter. Whichever you choose, quality of optics has to be high to capture the delicate subtleties and hues. For the more static shots I use a Bronica ETRSi with 40mm, 75mm, 150mm and 500mm lenses. I take 220 films as it gives twice the number of frames for the same weight and bulk. This limits choice of emulsion so a 120 back is taken for unusuals. I have tried Canon AE1s and AT1s only to return pictureless when at below −8°C (18°F), but, surprisingly, my T70 works well at −30°C (−22°F).

Do not be put off if you own other than my suggestions. We go into the extremes and ask a lot of our gear. The average Arctic traveller can easily capture the rareties on offer using any modern camera, but should you be encouraged to rough it I hope the advice is of use.

Finally, a word on carrying. I use Karrimor bags to transport my cameras with several bodies and lens in each, whereas Dick uses CCS bags, one per body/lens unit. The former are marginally easier on the journey, the latter very worthwhile in the field.

III   TRAVEL REGULATIONS

There are no travel regulations – other than those standard for foreign travel, in other words, passport, medical insurance, and so on or required by common sense – to Iceland or the Arctic regions of the Scandinavian mainland except to the area of the Russian/Norwegian/Finnish border. The regulations covering travel to that area, and to Greenland and Svalbard, are given below.

Russian Border

At the border it is prohibited to:

● Cross the border, on land or water, or in the air without specific permission
● To talk or otherwise make contact across the border with Soviet border personnel or citizens
● To act in any insulting manner to any Soviet border personnel or citizens, or to the Soviet flag or border installations, or to Soviet territory
● To damage border markers
● To fire weapons into Soviet territory
● To fish in any river which forms part of the border (this regulation applies to aliens only!)
● To use a boat on any river which forms part of the border unless the boat is registered with the border commissioner and carries a registration board and number
● In addition there is a restriction on photography. Until September 1986 no photographs were permitted which included any part of Soviet territory. Now it is permitted, provided the photographs are for private use only, provided no lens greater than 200mm is used and provided no tripod is used to stabilize the camera. It is still forbidden to take any photographs of, or including, Soviet border personnel or installations.

The border authorities and police are entitled to stop and search any person they suspect of violating the regulations or whom they suspect may be setting out to violate the regulations. They are permitted to confiscate weapons, cameras and film.

Any violation of the regulations, whether intentional or inadvertent, or any attempted violation will be punished. The punishment will be a heavy fine and/or imprisonment for up to one year.

Greenland

The visitor to either the east or west coasts can travel freely, and small treks from and between towns are allowed. However, longer treks, especially those that are covering part of the Greenlandic ice cap, are subject to very special regulations. Such trips are classified as expeditions, and all expeditions are required to file forms with the Ministry for Greenland in Copenhagen. One of the particular reasons for this is that there are few rescue services in Greenland, and an expedition must be insured so as to be able to pay for any rescue attempt. It should be noted that the Danish authorities reserve the right to refuse approval for any expedition they believe to be at risk for any reason, so careful planning should be made *before* the application. Also, the fact that an expedition has asked for help does not mean that it will be forthcoming. If the authorities decide that the services are required elsewhere or that the attempt is hazardous then they reserve the right not to render assistance. Your rescue may be of the highest priority to you, but it may not be to the authorities. Since their word is final it is probably best not to need rescuing in the first place – another advantage of strenuous pre-planning.

Once in Greenland, especially in the National Park, the party must not harm animals or flowers, or disturb any archaeological site. All waste must be burnt or brought out, no permanent structures can be constructed and no campsites are allowed near nesting birds, particularly, sensitive birds of prey, the sea eagle, gyrfalcon and peregrine falcon.

Application forms for expeditions are available from The Ministry for Greenland, 3 Hausergade, DK–1128 Copenhagen, Denmark tel: IAC 45.1.13.68.25 (IAC is the International Access Code, 010 in Great Britain).

Svalbard

There are no rules governing access to Spitsbergen, but access to Nordaustland, Prince Karls Forland, Barentsøya, Edgeøya and Bjørnøya is controlled and permission must be sought. It is forbidden to land on Moffen, Kong Karls Land and Hoppen. Indeed, it is forbidden to approach within 500 metres of these islands.

In all areas of Svalbard the use of vehicles in summer is restricted to certain routes to prevent damage to the extremely fragile eco-system. In winter you must be careful not to use snow scooters where the snow cover is thin as the scooter track plays havoc with the ground.

Care must be taken near bird nesting sites. In particular it is not permitted to land from boats near to duck or geese colonies or to make unnecessary noise near seabird cliffs. Svalbard is a hunting area and certain specimens may be taken at certain times in certain areas. However, visiting the area purely to hunt is to be deplored, – take a camera for your shots and leave the hunting to the (thankfully small) band of professionals. Travellers to the area should respect the wildlife, taking care not to harm it. This is especially important in winter. Svalbard is a harsh area and many of the resident animals merely survive rather than live through the winter. If an animal is chased by, for instance, a snow sooter, the chase will burn up potentially irreplaceable energy reserves. You may enjoy it all hugely, but for the animal it could make all the difference between surviving the winter and being one of its victims. On a similar note, please remember that chasing polar bears on snow scooters is illegal and will result in a ferocious fine if you are observed. It may also lead to the bear overheating and being harmed internally. And if all that were not enough, there are several recorded incidents of desperate males turning and running at their tormentor.

All waste must be burned or brought back. Do not bury waste – except sewage – as the permafrost will bring it to the surface. If you discover someone else's rubbish, deal with it as you would your own. Yes, they are dirty idiots, but that is not the fault of the landscape, so help it out by cleaning up.

And finally, remember that the use of vehicles is banned in all National Parks.

SPECIAL NOTE

GREENLAND AND SVALBARD ARE RABIES AREAS

In addition, rabies is endemic in southern Finland, so caution should be exercised in the north of that country.

IV TEMPERATURE

Do not be put off by the cold. Many who have not experienced it assume that it will take away all pleasure and leave you fighting to stay warm and wishing to be out of it. Neither is true. With modern equipment staying warm is no great problem even down around −40°C (−40°F), although by then you may well be wishing you were somewhere else. Remember that the Inuit, the Lapps and many in Siberia live half their lives in 'extreme' cold and still manage to do rather more than just exist, so to go into their areas for a few weeks should not be a ridiculous venture. As a rule of thumb, dry air temperatures to −20°C (−4°F) are no problem. When we returned to Tromsø from a sledging trip once, both Tony and I, having just spent a fortnight in temperatures between −15°C (5°F) and −30°C (−22°F), were absolutely schrammed (frozen) by the seaside damp air temperatures of −6°C (21°F). Between −20°C (−4°F) and −30°C (−22°F) life becomes more difficult as every move has to be planned in advance. Below −30°C you will be overdressed for easy movement and lethargy sets in, the more so as the temperature drops still further. We have worked – as opposed to existed – in −40 to −45°C (−40 to −49°F) and it was precious little fun.

At −40 the Centigrade and Fahrenheit scales equate; this fact gave rise to one of the funnier incidents I have seen including a reporter. In a previous incarnation, when Tony and I were glaciologists, I was with a member of the British Antarctic Survey in Cambridge. A local reporter arrived to 'do a piece'. How cold was it? he asked at one point. About −40, said the team man. Is that C or F? asked the hack, a benign smile of knowledgeable intelligence. At that temperature it doesn't matter, said the scientist. I have rarely seen a look of such puzzlement on a face.

The numbers stated above are ambient. In still air these are the experienced temperatures, but in the wind there will be a further cooling effect, now referred to as 'wind chill'. Talking about wind chill has become popular of late, but most of what has been said or written is nonsense. Recently an American garage-owning 'entrepreneur' was advising people to put extra anti-freeze in their cars in order to cope with the wind-chill effect!

No object can be colder than the ambient air temperature unless it has been pre-cooled. Thus, the water in your car radiator can never go lower than −10 (12), say, if the air temperature is −10 (12). Wind increases the rate of cooling of warm objects by adding forced convectional losses to normal convective and conductive losses. In a wind any object will cool more rapidly to ambient temperature than it will in still air, but the cooling will cease when that ambient temperature is reached. People – indeed all warm-blooded creatures – are different from inanimate objects in that they generate internal heat. Only when dead do body temperatures fall to ambient. While you are alive your body will work frantically to keep your body temperatures at their optimal level. As you cool, or lose energy, the body will preferentially close down blood – and, therefore, heat – supply to extremities in favour of maintaining brain and core temperatures.

In trying to maintain skin and finger temperatures the body has to replace the heat lost by convection and conduction, and also by radiation, although this is very small for the (relatively) cool human body, and by evaporation if you are unfortunate enough to be wet. If there is a wind blowing the heat loss will increase and the internal heat replacement rate will have to increase. It is possible to equate the heat loss in the wind to that of a lower still-air temperature, and doing that produces the wind-chill temperature. This wind-chill, or apparent, temperature is, therefore, the still-air temperature that would 'feel as cold' as the current combination of air temperature and wind.

Since the metabolic rate of people varies, as does their ability to withstand the cold, wind chill is actually very difficult to measure. Only two calculations of the effect exist. The first, referred to as the Siple-Passel formula, is based on experiments carried out by Americans in Antarctica in 1941. In the experiments the rate of cooling of a given quantity of water was measured at different temperatures and wind speeds. The second work, by Steadman, is theoretical and deals with thermal equilibrium for a body with a certain internal heat generation and thickness of insulating clothing. The two derived formulae calculate quite different apparent temperatures, with the Siple-Passel work giving the lower temperatures. In general it is believed that the Steadman work offers the most appropriate formula for calculation, although the calculated temperatures should be seen as indicative rather than authoritative. Overleaf, wind-chill temperatures (rounded to the nearest degree) using the Steadman formula are given. The last

Wind speed		Air temperature (°C)												
kph	mph	10	5	0	−5	−10	−15	−20	−25	−30	−35	−40	−45	−50
Still air		10	5	0	−5	−10	−15	−20	−25	−30	−35	−40	−45	−50
10	6	8	2	−2	−7	−12	−17	−23	−28	−33	−38	−43	−48	−54
20	12½	5	0	−6	−11	−17	−23	−28	−34	−40	−45	−51	−55	−60
30	19	3	−2	−8	−14	−20	−26	−32	−38	−43	−49	−55	−59	−65
40	25	2	−4	−10	−17	−21	−29	−35	−41	−47	−53	−59	−65	−69
50	31	1	−6	−12	−19	−25	−32	−37	−44	−51	−56	−62	−69	−76
60	37½	0	−7	−14	−20	−26	−33	−39	−46	−53	−58	−64	−74	−81
70	44	−1	−9	−16	−22	−29	−36	−43	−50	−56	−62	−69	−76	−84
80	50	−2	−10	−17	−24	−31	−38	−45	−52	−59	−65	−72	−78	−86
90	56	−4	−12	−19	−26	−33	−40	−47	−54	−62	−68	−75	−81	−88
100	62½	−5	−13	−20	−27	−34	−43	−50	−57	−64	−70	−77	−84	−92

Please Note:

1. Wind-chill temperatures apply *only* to bare flesh. The apparent temperature for the body clad in windproof clothing will be a little lower as no clothing – and particuarly not working breathables – can totally elminate heat losses, but will be *much* higher than the bare flesh temperature. In a tent at night there will be no wind-chill effect, even with single-skin tents.

2. Full sunshine increases apparent temperature. This effect is due to radiative heat gain. In the Arctic the sun, even in winter, is worth as much as 7°C (if the still air temperature is −30°C the sun will make the body 'feel as warm' as −23°C). This effect exists even if there is a wind, although clearly it is then less pronounced. With a 40kph (25mph) wind the apparent 'increase' in temperature is about 3°C. These temperatures are, as you would expect, largely independent of ambient temperature.

three temperatures have been extrapolated – these lie outside the range of Steadman's work, and should be treated with caution.

V POLAR BEARS

The Polar bear – in Norwegian, Isbjørn or 'ice bear' – is the world's only wholly carnivorous bear. Males can grown to three and a half metres in length and weigh up to 750 kilograms, although statistics of two and a half metres and 500 kilograms are more normal. A large male could be one and a half metres high at the shoulder and when standing on its hind legs – as they frequently do – would be taller than an elephant. Females are smaller, perhaps two metres long and about 350 kilograms. An adult bear can take a 100-kilogram seal out of a breath hole with one paw, crushing its skull with the blow and frequently splintering the pelvis and backbone at the same time.

Polar bears are pack-ice dwellers, living off a diet of seals supplemented by anything else they can get their paws on. In winter pack-ice surrounds Svalbard, reaching as far south as Bjørnøya (Bear Island) so the bears you encounter will be on their normal hunting ground and will probably not be aggressive. In summer, when the pack-ice has retreated, only Nordaustland (as a rule) offers a normal hunting ground. Elsewhere, any bears you encounter will be those that have been left behind by the retreat of the ice. They will be hungry and very aggressive. In their natural habitat only a full-grown bull walrus will offer any threat to a bear. The bear you meet may never have seen a man before: even if it has, since Svalbard is a total protection zone it will not have learned to fear men. It may well decide to eat you.

Bears are very inquisitive animals and may well approach you with the simple intention of satisfying their curiosity. That will allow you a close-up view, which is wonderful but not without its dangers. Bears are very unpredictable and curiosity may change to aggression in a short space of time for no reason apparent to you. A strange or sudden movement could make the bear feel threatened and it will then attack, very quickly and without warning. In Svalbard you must be armed, but in addition to the last-resort rifle, carry mini-flares, buying those that go bang as well as flash. These can be used in conjunction with trip wires to protect your camp and are very good against a bear as they startle it without harming it permanently, and have the distinct advantage of not requiring the shooting ability of a marksman. Even in a panic you will probably get one into the area between you and it.

As a rule a curious bear will approach slowly, stopping often to sniff and stare. It may walk or move its head from side to side. An aggressive bear may blow hard from its nose; it may open and snap its mouth; it may lower its head. But it may do none of these things. If an attack comes it will be rapid and direct. The bear will head straight at you, at a run or in large bounds. If you have sufficient warning, withdraw slowly and calmly. Do not do anything rapidly as the sudden movement will alarm the bear. If you are pursued, drop a hat or glove. Usually the bear will stop at the article, sniff it and even knock it around a little. Two or three dropped bits may allow you the time to reach safety – your snow scooter or higher ground. If not, fire a flare at the bear or in front of it. Reload immediately. If the bear retreats do not follow it in order to fire again, it may just turn. If it retreats you should do the same, with thanks. As a last resort you will need to shoot. Do not aim at the head: it is a small target and it has been known for bullets to glance off the hard cranial bone. Aim at the body, reload and fire again. Once you have hit the bear you will have to kill it to prevent its suffering, so there is no virtue in waiting. Once you are certain the bear is dead you must immediately protect the carcass and inform the *Sysselmann* (the Governor). He owns the carcass, including the skull and skin. He will need a statement from you on the circumstances of the killing.

In the field choose a campsite above the sea-ice; bears rarely travel inland and then usually along valley floors. Even so, protect your camp with trip wires and be cautious at meal-times – the smell of your cooking may not be appetising to you alone. If you have to camp at sea level, keep your food well away from your tent – several tens of metres, and preferably a hundred metres – and in line of sight from the doorway so you can observe a foraging bear from relative safety.

Finally, never feed a bear to encourage it closer; not only may you create a situation that gets out of hand for yourself, but you may create one that endangers a poor unsuspecting individual a few days later.

Index